Tao of Healing

Rayne
&
Light

Chok

Tao of Healing

The Incredible Golden Light Energy

Chok C. Hiew

Writer's Showcase
presented by *Writer's Digest*
San Jose New York Lincoln Shanghai

Tao of Healing
The Incredible Golden Light Energy

Writer's Showcase
presented by *Writer's Digest*
an imprint of iUniverse.com, Inc.

For information address:
iUniverse.com, Inc.
5220 S 16th, Ste. 200
Lincoln, NE 68512
www.iuniverse.com

ISBN: 0-595-15753-X

Printed in the United States of America

In gratitude for the Amazing Light of
Mother Meera

On the spiritual odyssey
to the boundless Radiance of Golden Light:
To play is human and to replay divine
Rebirth with Energy pure
Radiates the Sublime.

Contents

Foreword

by

Mu Soeng

Director, Barre Center for Buddhist Studies, Barre, MA

Chok Hiew's personal journey parallels America's own journey into the pathways of holistic healing and alternate ways of thinking and being. He arrived in the United States from his hometown in Malaysia at a time (in 1968) when the interests of a whole generation were engaged in looking away from a Euro-centered perception of the world and searching for relief from the collective madness of involvement in war in Vietnam.

Although his professional career has taken him from earning his doctorate in psychology from the University of Colorado to teaching psychology at the University of New Brunswick in Canada for the last twenty-five years, his personal interests have always ranged far and wide from the academic settings. His Chinese heritage cannot be discounted in the perspectives he has brought to the issues of mental health, healing arts, and psychological states of consciousness. As someone with citizenship in both cultures, he is uniquely qualified to make meaningful excursions into these pathways.

Tao of Healing is largely autobiographical but it is also a journey of self-discovery which resonates for each one of us. He speaks persuasively of his laboratory research in sleep and dream states using electrode technology but his heritage allows him to keep an open mind about claims of energy healers in his native Malaysia.

One of these healers, Yap Soon-Yeong, is central to most recent aspects of Chok's journeying into both the Eastern healing and wisdom traditions. Chok's book is an invitation to step into what Carlos Castaneda's teacher Don Juan Matus called 'a crack between two worlds.' To enter into that crack is to open up to an altogether different dimension of reality. This dimension challenges all our preconceived notions of reality but it is also a transforming process. Only when this new dimension of reality has been authentically embraced does one 'let go,' a central theme in both the Buddhist wisdom tradition and Master Yap's system of energy healing. It is a reminder of where we have been, and also a potent hope that as we learn more about energy healing the more we are forced to look at what we hold on to, and what we need to let go.

This book is a valuable addition to the relatively new energy field between meditation and healing through contemporary understanding. The perspectives here are cutting edge and the insights timeless. Chok closes his narrative by quoting the Buddha's famous phrase, '*Ehi passiko*,' or, 'Come see for yourself.' Unless we see for ourselves, deeply and authentically, we are not allowing ourselves to be open to healing. When we do open up, we find that each one of us is a container of healing energy. I have no doubt that Chok's book will provide such an opening for both professionals and seekers. May all beings be happy and free.

Preface

Tao of Healing is largely an autobiographical journey of self-discovery and provides a unique approach to health and energy healing. It is grounded in today's Western scientific ethos while being firmly rooted in the ancient Taoist medical arts and Buddhist insight-meditative traditions. The book is about how to create transforming changes in self and society in pursuit of the highest human ideals. A new perspective of who we are is rediscovered based on the truth that all reality is energy and all matter is connected by energy. The hope is that for the reader who understands the Tao of radiant Heart energy, the winds of change in the new millennium, while inevitable, will be golden. Three strands are woven together to form the fabric that merges into a Heart Energy path of purifying one's vital energy to unfold the perfect nature of who we are, i.e., the *Gold-Body Energy State*.

The first strand is the story of the author's search for the roots of the earthly self. This journey led to revisiting South-East Asia, and an experiential rediscovery of traditional energy-healing practices and their historical evolution, and to the transplanting of these practices to North America.

The book traces the evolution of the Tao to *I Ching*, the earliest of comprehensive philosophies, to its integration in contemporary energy healing. From ancient times, this has been an oral, esoteric tradition to condition the body, relax the mind, and free the spirit. Its meditative Buddhist roots and practical significance are explored in first-hand visits to the opium killing fields, refugee camps, and AIDS clinics of the Golden Triangle, to the horrors of the pandemic sexual exploitation of and violence against children, and in the enduring cultures, sacred sites, and golden temples in Burma, Thailand, and the Yucatan.

The trail which crisscrossed between returning to birthplace and roots in the East to the West in search of the Golden Light, drew me to the seven sacred and historic ancient cities and kingdoms of the legendary Golden Peninsula. This was the golden land recorded as *Suvannabhumi* where Asoka the Great, the first Emperor of Buddhist India, had, in 250 B.C., dispatched his *arhants* or enlightened, liberated monks. From that time, the *Dharma*, or the teachings of the Buddha, were propagated northwards to China and southwards to Indochina.

My journey also extended to New World cultures and centers of learning and spirituality in New Brunswick, New England, the American Southwest, and Mexico. Central to this journey is encountering in Malaysia an Eastern Master healer, whom I witnessed performing near-miraculous cures–the remarkable spiritual teacher and mystic, Sifu Yap Soon-Yeong. The life and work of Master Yap is the second strand recounted in this book. Sifu revealed to me the dynamics of his revolutionary interpretations of the Taoist and Heart energy healing system, that he calls *CFQ Meditation*–liberation from disease, distress, and depression.

Sifu's own healing and spiritual development began during initiations into the hexagram forces of the *I Ching* and the Golden Light. The insights of a purified energy consciousness led to revelations about the inner wisdom or 'instinctual knowledge' of the supra-mental Tao energy.

I have analyzed to academic standards Sifu's approach to radiant energy healing and transcendence referenced to the experiences and benefits gained by his patients, students, and practitioners. The evaluation of their experiences is the third strand of the book delineating the Tao energy principles of CFQ Meditation and its challenge to current scientific theories and practices in relation to health, disease, aging, and life-span extension.

In a state of ultimate relaxation, the practitioner of the Gold-Body energy liberates a golden radiant energy from the eternal Pure Heart to transform him or her to optimal health, and to a life of serenity.

The Golden Light also liberates the Bodhisattva vow, a special life-goal based on a new ethic of human relatedness which radiates energy to cure individual illnesses, heal communities, and advance contemporary civilization.

Acknowledgments

I am grateful to the many friends whom I encountered, in journeying, on the roads, cities, and sacred energy places in the Golden Peninsula as well as in my home in the West. Thanks also especially to my spiritual and temporal family, my energy teacher Sifu, and my grandchildren Kalian Logan, Kaliong Patrick, Mariah Jiawei, and Kaiden Kachung who gave me the meaning of living with unconditional love. From the innermost core of Heart energy, my appreciation to all met and in memory of Mother.

Introducing
The Search of Healing

Prologue

Enter the Golden Triangle

THERE was a time when meadow, grove, and stream
The earth, and every common sight,
To me did seem
Apparelled in Celestial light,
The glory and the freshness of a dream.
It is not now as it had been of yore.

Wordsworth

After a graceful departure from Bangkok an hour earlier, the plane began its turbulent descent into the borders of Thailand's 'Golden Triangle', crossing the lush, green mountain range that separates the former Siam from Burma. The morning sun blazed beyond the valley casting a golden hue across a patchwork of rice fields encircling the town below. The familiar, yet never-really-at-ease feeling took over, as the jet dropped altitude and settled safely on the runway.

I had arrived in Chiengrai, a minor town in Northern Thailand. It has a slow centuries-old, rustic pace of life, but with one claim to infamy. A few miles away lies the famous Golden Triangle on a remote section of the famed 2,500 miles long Mekong River, where Burma, Laos, and Thailand intersect.

Opium is grown in this isolated, 75,000-mile triangular pocket, the world's richest source of black gold. Here, an estimated 2,000 tons of dark sticky goo is produced annually. Nature has provided a plant with great medicinal value, but greed for gold has debased the raw product into its narcotic street derivatives. A single kilo of raw opium can sell for US$200 in Burma but its value goes up a thousand-fold in the West.

The area is bereft of high technology, except for state-of-the-art methods used to process the poppy ooze into morphine and heroin. This situation led to the establishment of the world's biggest trafficker of synthetic methamphetamines that are sold as cheaply as candy. The drugs instantly become available around the world to feed the addicted brains, minds, lungs, muscles, and blood of lost youth and humanity.

In this new voyage of discovery, I was making a stopover in the same enchanting and bedeviling area in Northern Thailand. My final destination was in Malaysia to revisit a master healer and meditation teacher whom I had met seven years earlier and whose methods intrigued me. I had now studied and cultivated his unique, revolutionary energy healing method called the Gold-Body Energy State, or CFQ and achieved some measure of proficiency, but there was further work to be done.

My goal was to learn a meditation system of regenerative pure cleansing 'Golden Light' that could not only heal the body and transform the self, but ultimately touch the transcendent state of the *Pure Heart*. This was a quest for awakening to Perfection, the Tao, the Way of cultivation to return to cosmic consciousness. On this quest, I had taken a hiatus in northern Thailand to fulfill a teaching assignment.

At the airport, waiting for the baggage, a flood of memories triggered a feeling that this was a time of endings oddly juxtaposed with beginnings.

The thought crossed my mind, "The journey and the work ahead in Malaysia, symbolically and literally, begin and end here."

This time around, however, I was not alone. With me was Acharn Tiplada, a university psychologist who had invited me. She was to accompany me to Payao Town in the next province where I was to present a seminar to Public Health departmental staff that afternoon. A van, courtesy of the Center for Disease Control, was waiting after we had wheeled our luggage out of Chiengrai airport.

"When," I wondered, "would medicine embrace a paradigm shift toward holistic health rather than only treating disease and body parts?"

This was a recurring theme that I had contemplated often in the past. As in the case with many great inventions, this simple thought started me on my quest for the Gold-Body Energy State. However, unlike the legendary knights of King Arthur's court, I had not known what this golden grail was or even that I was searching for it. Suddenly, I became fully conscious that something new had bloomed within me and my old identity had been shed.

We immediately set out on our two-hour serpentine drive across the Payao Hills. The peaceful mountain scenery bedecked with gilded pagodas, or '*wats*', belied a terrifying fact of life. Thailand had acknowledged that it was in the midst of an unprecedented AIDS epidemic, the highest rate in East Asia. Epidemiological surveillance reported that over forty per cent of the disease was located here in the sparsely populated northern region, south of the Golden Triangle.

Our first stop-over was the village of Dokam Tai, famous in Thailand for its fair-skinned, beautiful, graceful women. Traditionally, this is the source of Thailand's vicious entertainment or prostitution industry. Parents, willingly or unknowingly, send their daughters off to distant urban cities into the sex and flesh entertainment trades. Again, those greedy for gold had latched on to the lucrative billion-dollar sex and drug trade ready to exploit and enslave, dehumanize, and infect defenseless young children and girls for profit. AIDS is ubiquitous in this region. In the hospital I visited in Dokam Tai, a village and community of nearly seventy thousand, AIDS victims take up 35 per cent of all the hospital beds. One heart-wrenching example was a once-beautiful female infected victim in her late twenties, haggard, skeletal, alone and dying, a year after her husband had died from AIDS. Here, with expensive medication out of the reach of people with HIV infections, patients tend to advance to full-blown AIDS within an average of two-and-half years, much faster than in North America.

Leaving the sad, tragic scene behind us, we finally arrived in Payao greeting Dr. Petsri, the Chief Medical Officer who had invited us to give the workshop. The seminar site was unusual for such a purpose. We had to climb up to the summit of a mountain to *Wat Analayo*, a large temple and retreat complex.

The conference room was an imposing, ornate shrine hall in the expansive main *Wat* nesting within a verdant forest. Attending were seventy government workers, most in somber, monochrome Thai uniforms, while a few women were dressed in traditional, colorful silk blouses and sarongs. They were all seated cross-legged on the dark, gleaming teak floor. Others were leaning against regal, red pillars and gilded, decorative walls that adorned the elegant structure.

Chairs and tables were absent at the podium, so Tiplada and I sat on the hard floor facing our audience. There was a shortage of cushions, but generously our hosts had provided two for us. Behind us was a life-size radiant Buddha, covered with gold-leaf, seated on a platform in a deeply relaxed lotus repose emitting an inspiring glow.

To succeed, these professionals would have to take on the role of understanding and interact with community people and develop programs to eliminate the risk factors that infected their communities with AIDS, drug addiction, and sexual exploitation. But, I did not say or mention any of this, at least not until the next day of formal presentation.

That first day, I wanted the participants simply to experience radiant energy, the kind that was pure enough to have helped them live their own lives, unadulterated in times of crisis and hardship. I wanted them to recall the times when this energy had given them the resilience to withstand and rebound from all adversities.

To do so, I used an effective sound-induced deep relaxation process with special tones and music, rapidly shifted minds and bodies into deep meditative states. Soon remembrance of their childhood resilience was vividly recalled. I ended the seminar by imparting to them some of my research for a United Nations-affiliated NGO (non-government organizations working in the front-line) on sexually abused children and their resilience. I showed them how to recognize resilient traits and how family, friends, and faith can promote community resilience to face and overcome problems.

That night, we were housed in a elegant hillside villa just below the *Wat*. As we looked at the large Payao Lake shimmering with the reflected light of the town below, and I remembered the Golden Light of the Buddha, we chatted over the day's events.

"Even if we succeed in confronting the devastating problems of AIDS, drug addiction, and sexual exploitation of children," I sighed, "we are merely scratching the surface of the many evils of present society."

Earlier, Tiplada and I had strolled over the extensive temple grounds on the mountain summit. The main, open square had a 60-foot-high standing Golden Buddha, with an enigmatic half-smile, and one hand raised to dispel fear and bestow blessings. Spreading from this center were a dozen exquisite temples, housing all kinds of sacred marble and jade images and objects. In one secluded area on the western side, was a newly constructed but incomplete set of apparently Greek-influenced ancient replicas of the sublime Indian-born Buddha with the countenance of Apollo.

This is the historic Sakyamuni Buddha of Indo-European origins, who was born as Prince Siddhartha Gautama, over 2,500 years ago. Siddhartha was the son of a king of the Sakya Clan who ruled over a region in Northern India in the heart of the Ganges valley in what is present-day Nepal. He renounced his life of princely luxury, and endeavored to unravel the secret of existence. Spending years of study with renowned holy men, he lived as a mendicant ascetic, practicing penance, self-mortification, and continuous fasting.

There is a celebrated statue of the Fasting Buddha of Peshawar showing, in excruciating detail, the starving body of the skeletal Siddhartha after six years of fasting. Yet the physical agony and suffering cannot mask the light that lifted the human spirit to triumphant serenity.

Even near death, his goal eluded him. But one day, at the age of 35, sitting comfortably in meditation under a Bodhi-tree in Bodhgaya, the 'Eternal Truth' came to him. The Golden Sage attained Nirvana, a blissful, radiant state of Non-existence, where Self becomes extinct to be reabsorbed into the Absolute. He was awakened into the enlightenment of Buddhahood, demonstrating Man's triumph toward the accomplishment of immortal perfection.

This single sublime, golden state, exemplified in the countenance of incalculable Buddha images, has inspired countless numbers of humans in the past 2,500 years to try to emulate the Tao or way to *'Prajna-paramita'*, or perfect wisdom of the Pure Heart.

Dotting the hillside, were small villas, tastefully garnished with traditional Thai and Chinese decor. These are the retreat homes of affluent families living in Bangkok. Every temple, building, and Buddha image was a creative marvel, architecturally designed by the resident abbot, who apparently envisioned them during his meditations. The whole was certainly a lofty, secluded corner, where the cares of the world could be readily dropped and replaced by peace and serenity.

I said it was paradoxical that here in *Wat Analayo*, a mountain retreat created for the contemplation of inner peace, we had spent the day trying to solve the heinous problems of society.

Tiplada shared with me how she felt. *"That golden hue, Chok—did you see the radiance flooding behind you?"*

She noticed that during the seminar, the hall was often flooded with sunshine and a glowing yellowish tinge, reflected from the Buddha image behind us. I smiled in recognition and said I had felt the light shining behind me and illuminating the space, which had made me feel warm, relaxed, happy, and satisfied with all that had transpired, including the recollection of Wordsworth's Celestial Light.

Tiplada was breath-taking sitting erect on a teak chair with such graceful poise and serene demeanor. She told me about her next assignment in Bangkok, conducting a program to teach the traditional Vipassana, or insight meditation, to counselors. She had been a Vipassana meditator for many years, learning it from Thai and Burmese meditation monks. She felt that meditators not only learned to de-stress, and get rid of 'defilements', but through mindful meditation, also cultivated and developed 'karuna' and 'metta', which meant empathy or compassion and loving-kindness respectively, for people they were helping.

I replied that these were energy concepts and that, for me, the purpose of meditation was to cleanse the body and mind to allow for the free flow of serene energy into the purified heart.

But recalling the teaching of a famous Thai forest monk, Acharn Chah, whose Vipassana teachings had already spread to America, learning meditation to get something defeated its very purpose. Meditation was an approach to let go of everything that the ordinary self desired. Pure energy could not possibly flow in if we remained attached, I argued. At the same time, I could not put much faith in any method of cultivation unless it could sustain and extend human existence toward health and freedom from disease.

I suggested to Tiplada that it bodes well, when thinking of moving forward, to also recollect past traditions and weigh events in world history to discern and deal with what lies ahead.

Somehow, the golden mantle cast on that sacred spot on Wat Analayo had affirmed the arrival of some process of great import. The treasures of the past are never really lost, provided that we are prepared to look for them.

I recalled the visit to an old temple called *Wat Trimitr* in Bangkok, believed to be a 13th-century temple, and the story of the fabulous Golden Buddha. In 1952, a three-meter high, and an old, but apparently plain, plaster-covered Buddha was unearthed by accident. On the night before it was scheduled to be moved by crane, torrential rains soaked the stucco exterior. When workers attempted to move the now much heavier statue, the crane cable snapped and crashed onto the soft mud. The plaster cracked to reveal the golden icon underneath.

When fully investigated, the wondrous, solid gold Buddha was shown to weigh 5.5 metric tonnes. It apparently had been hidden from the invading Burmese 200 years ago, when they sacked and ended the Thai Ayuthaya Kingdom. This Buddha image, a most beautiful and ageless masterpiece, showed the characteristic refined facial features, sinuous lineal fluidity, and harmony of form of the preeminent 13th century Sukothai period.

When I stood at the foot of the solid-Gold Buddha, it gleamed like no other earthly object I have ever seen. This event is symbolic of my ultimate journey to reach the Gold-Body Energy state, a path of healing and luminous Heart perfection.

The journey in the current spiral of re-discovery began to unfold seven years ago, when I returned to my birthplace in the East, whose historical roots and traditions needed to be examined to start my quest.

1

Investigating Ancient and Contemporary Methods

To unravel the mysteries of my quest I knew the way was to retrace my own personal history, first from my Eastern roots to my lasting sojourn in the West. The journey of rediscovery awakened the spirit upon my return to my roots, heritage, and birthplace in Southeast Asia. This region is geographically hemmed in and historically dominated by two monolithic, ancient civilizations with India to the west and China to the north.

Yet for over two millennia kingdoms and high civilizations in Indochina, like celestial stars, had sprung up, flourished, and declined. These magnificent cultures, emulating the flight of a mythical Garuda dragon, have stretched out from present-day Burma, Thailand, Laos, Cambodia, and Vietnam to the South China Sea extending to the far-flung 'ten-million' islands of the Indonesian archipelago.

The Malay Peninsula, which ancient Greeks identified as the fabled 'Golden Chersonese', begins with a slender bottle-neck south of Thailand. My native island of Penang is located at the northern border of Malaysia whose southern tip is within sight of the island nation of Singapore.

Two hundred years ago, in 1786, Penang island, a jungle off the northern coast of Malaya, was bought by Sir Francis Light for the

British East India Company to protect Britain's lucrative tea, spice, and opium trade. Governor Light in Penang turned the island into the area's only free-trade port with Georgetown, named after George III, as the central city. Its regional monopoly lasted until 1819, when Sir Stamford Raffles established Singapore, then a tiger-infested island, which he purchased from a Malay sultan. This began Britain's colonial empire in South-East Asia. By the 1920s, without firing a shot, all of Peninsular Malaya fell under British control.

Near the end of the reign of Queen Victoria, and at the height of the Western Industrial Revolution, great changes engulfed Asia. To keep the British Empire's economic juggernaut humming, new rubber plantations, tin mines, and timberlands in Malaya were exploited. British colonialists recruited a cheap and eager labor force by enticing tens of thousands of immigrants from southern China desperate for work.

From the 1890s, and for the next 30 years, some six million people fled an exhausted China scourged by conflict, war and famine, hopeful of a better life elsewhere. My parents, like many of their clan members, left their home village in the interior of south China for Canton, and sailed to the two largest overseas Chinese communities in British Malaya, staying first in Singapore, and finally settling in Georgetown city on the island of Penang. The immigrants who settled in South-East Asia left behind the feudal yoke in their home country only to face, as in British Malaya, the unfathomable ways of the red-haired 'kwei-lo '(names for foreigners), the colonial masters of their new homes. But the dream of a new beginning, and the hope and courage to endure against all odds, kept the new arrivals on an inexorable track of economic success.

The 1960's was a time of endings and a new beginning that culminated in my going to university in the U.S., eventually ending up, working and taking up residence in Canada. By the mid-1980's, I had established myself in North America, but soon the longing came to get back in touch with the heritage I had put behind me.

Back to the Future:
Consciousness, Disease, and Aging

Seven years ago, on a return visit to Penang, a harbinger came to my psychology workshop to hear what Western techniques and research on states of consciousness could offer to his interests in ancient Chinese healing. He was S. Y. Yap, and he turned out to be a healer by profession. He used energy transmission techniques originating from indigenous medical arts. However, even though I expressed interest in indigenous healing practices, I had long since questioned their validity and reliability to meet the needs of modern day ills. On issues relating to health psychology such as disease causation, aging and longevity, I accepted only what scientific evidence provided.

It had taken years for me to develop sophisticated high-tech gadgetry in the scientific study of human behavior and consciousness. I had publicly lectured, in a seminar held in Penang, that contemporary methods, using scientific methodology and technological hardware, were needed. I claimed that they were more efficient in inducing desirable psychological mind-brain states of consciousness to optimize creativity and performance as well as inner meditative states.

My interest in the study of consciousness began in 1970, not long after I arrived in Boulder, Colorado, during a short stint as a sleep laboratory and biofeedback assistant at the University of Colorado. Later, after finishing graduate school, and as a new psychology professor in Canada, I pursued research on sleep and dream states using electrode technology. Electrodes record electrical activity of the brain as it responds to internal as well as environmental stimulation.

The discovery of the electroencephalogram or EEG goes back to the turn of the century to Austrian scientist, Hans Berger. He fell off a horse, narrowly escaped serious injury and soon thereafter, coincidentally, received a telegram from his sister who felt that he was in grave danger.

That incident inspired Berger to investigate mental telepathy, or direct mind communication, by monitoring the electrical activity of the brain.

Berger failed to find physiological evidence of mental telepathy but his research identified two distinct rhythms of electrical frequencies. He called the relatively slow rhythm, alpha, a state associated with a relaxed but alert mental state. The faster rhythm, he called, beta, which is associated with an active, alert mental state.

EEG brain frequencies of interest measure variations in levels of cortical arousal. As cortical arousal slows down, so do the brain frequencies. Although a crude and simple measure, the EEG can reliably estimate states of consciousness based on the relative proportion of five types of frequencies. The faster beta frequencies are confined between 13 to 30 cycles per second and are associated with conscious awareness, concentration, and alert wakefulness. Alpha frequencies are generally produced with eyes closed and the mind at rest or at a relaxed state.

Theta frequencies are slower than alpha, as theta is bounded from four to eight cycles per second and relate to creative and meditative states, and to sleep. Delta is the slowest frequency, between zero to four cycles per second, and is associated with an advanced meditative state and deep, non-dreaming sleep.

The EEG is used to study the brain during states of arousal, processes involving sleeping and dreaming, and to diagnose abnormalities in the brain such as epilepsy and sleep disorders. Altered states of consciousness have also been investigated such as meditation, hypnosis, and chemical induction. With the advent of computer technology, high frequency gamma frequencies could readily be recorded, ranging from 30 cycles to over 50 cycles per second. The unique features associated with gamma have begun to be investigated suggesting a relationship to mystical and transcendent experiences during meditation.

Using computer-assisted techniques, EEG readings can be converted from brain wave patterns to a color code, to generate different-colored brain maps. In this new procedure, it is possible to compare the total brain-wave maps of normal individuals with patients who are suffering from depression, alcoholism, sociopathy, schizophrenia, and other abnormalities. However, the research to apply high-tech and high-speed means of developing desirable states of consciousness that lead to disease, aging, and health is still in its infancy.

"What," I queried, "have senescent scientists discovered about the age-old pursuit of longevity?"

A simple rule of life is being currently challenged by researchers studying aging in laboratories around the world–that organisms are born, live out their lives in a prescribed number of years, grow old, deteriorate, and then die. A new wave of researchers studying life extension are looking for not merely incremental but exponential gains that pursue doubling of the normal human lifespan. A child born today in the U.S., for example, can expect a life span of 76 years (and still rising), which is a 60+ per cent increase from a life expectancy of 47 years in 1900.

Scientists at the Max Planck Institute in Germany, however, claim that there is no evidence that human life-expectancy is anywhere close to its ultimate limit. I suspected they might have a point here, since there is an apparently authenticated and factual case of an oriental Taoist master and herbalist who was born in Szechuan province in 1678, lived his life in mountain ranges, outlived 14 wives, and died in 1928, at the age of 250 years!

The search for answers to human aging is uncovering some exciting clues. One clue is the concept of cellular aging first discovered in the early 1920s by Leonard Hayflick, an anatomist. He found that cells from human fetal tissue could be kept alive in a Petri dish and double themselves repeatedly for up to 100 times. Then replication stopped.

From that point on, the cells appeared to age and the culture as a whole deteriorated. But when the dish culture was redone with cells taken from an elderly person, cell replication ended and aging began much earlier. This was evident in Dolly, the cloned wonder sheep, who, despite being a mere couple of years old, was fast aging because the original cloning cell was taken from an adult sheep. Cell replication was apparently greatly limited by the age of the original cell.

Recently, it was discovered that each time a human cell divides, the DNA in the chromosomes of the daughter cells, called telomeres, shrunk a little in size. After about 100 replications, with the genes practically used up, they can no longer reproduce healthy cells. More recently, this gene of 'eternal youth' has been isolated.

The notion is that some mechanism in the cell acts as a cellular time-keeper that gives it only so much time to live and no more. One idea proposed to explain this was the cellular damage, or waste by-product, model of aging. Cells, as well as the tissues and organs they formed, when carrying out their work to sustain life, produced waste products that contaminated the entire living system. Over time, this decay process led to the biological breakdowns associated with aging. The anti-aging solution appears equally simple–clean up the cells some-how–and research on ways of doing this is being pursued vigorously.

One cell function that wears out cells the most is processing food to metabolize energy. The waste by-product which, for some time, has been considered as the most troublesome residue of cell metabolism is free radical molecules. These have lost an electron which produces an electrical imbalance that the molecule seeks to correct by bonding with other molecules.

Typically, the weak link of easiest resolution is the sugar phosphite-bonds of the DNA. The process leads to damaged cells. This in turn causes physical disorders such as cancer, aging, and arthritis. Foods containing carotenoid and other substances are believed to act as antioxidants to absorb the free radicals and expel them from the body. However, research has not provided conclusive evidence of this.

More promising was new research into another by-product of the natural process of cell metabolism called glycosylation. When sugars and proteins bonded together in the course of metabolism, they attracted other proteins thus forming a sticky, web-like coating. This was similar to heating fresh maple sap and turning it into a caramel-like, dark brown gooey syrup.

Biochemists theorized that glycosylation could account for diabetes, as excess sugars when metabolized gradually produced the build-up of this residue. The gluey residue could stiffen joints, block arteries, induce blotchy pigmentation, and cloud clear tissue like the clear lens of the eye leading to cataracts.

Appropriately, the acronym given for this residue is 'A.G.E.S.', for advanced glycosylation end products. The AGES residue gummed up the cells preventing healthy body functioning. Medication that could act as AGES solvent has been tested but is still at an early stage of development.

The evidence is that the same biochemistry of glycosylation occurred in many other medical conditions. In addition, clearly, these symptoms of joint pain, blood circulatory disease, and poor vision are ailments of the aged and elderly. Longevity specialists believe that perhaps the disease process is no different from the aging process. Albeit much slower, both are the product of glycosylation. The waste products of living eventually terminate the cell's ability to rejuvenate, and as cell division deteriorates aging sets in.

Apparently, the killer diseases that afflict the majority of human-ity–heart disease, strokes, and cancers as well as other debilitating diseases–are merely by-products of normal aging. Only when aging is understood, can all diseases be vanquished.

But I could not feel enthusiasm for the orthodox medical approach based solely on discovering some wonder drug or chemical, or tinkering with genetic material to stimulate cell growth, to treat diseases or extend life. Nor are radiation, organ removal, and transplants palatable alternatives to me.

One thing was clear, the research on aging and the inevitable decline of once healthy cells did not provide any action that I could do or culti-vate at the personal level to promote health and longevity.

But my voyages returning to the East caused me to ask, "Is there an available alternative approach to understand how to stop this decline, that could develop self-regulation in disease prevention, and the pursuit of healthy, youthful longevity?"

These are issues that have long been the pursuit of Eastern civilizations, recorded in ancient traditional medicine, as well as passed down orally by legendary sages and masters. But these sources are either obscure or inaccessible in the West, while those who proclaim themselves knowledgeable, on deeper scrutiny, usually turn out to be long on promises, and short on effectiveness.

Yet, I felt it important to renew the pursuit of ancient wisdom paths and oral traditions. I had to keep in touch with my new workshop acquaintance, Yap, who professed to be an indigenous healer. His healing flowed from traditional meditation and Taoist health practices such as 'Chi-kung', or the art of cultivating 'chi' energy. Since the introduction of the official Chinese phonetic system a few decades earlier, chi is spelled as 'qi' and 'chi-kung' is now 'Qigong'.

Despite my Western skepticism, I had not given up the Eastern hope of rediscovering truths and lost healing knowledge. Besides, Yap was open enough to attend my workshop on Western techniques. I could do no less than to investigate his methods. There was also something refreshing about the youthful Eastern energy therapist, that I trusted.

Lost and Found:
An Ancient Wisdom Path

It was not until a year later that what Master Yap had said about the nature of energy, and its place in human evolution reduced my reluctance, and captured my attention to investigate further. Master Yap's healing system claimed to lead to dramatic outcomes that were like no other form of Taoism that I knew, and I was already quite familiar with the various traditional Taoist methods. Over the past 20 years I had cultivated the practice of Tai-chi, studied Taoism as well as numerous meditation techniques. While they all seemed worthwhile, I remained unconvinced that there was anything extraordinary about their impact on me.

As I got to know more of him, my appreciation grew to a deep respect for what he had accomplished and mastered. I began to accept that he was, 'Master Yap' or *Sifu* (Master in Chinese), as he was often called by his students. I will call him Sifu from here on.

My evaluation first changed when he described a new form of Tao or energy healing and meditation technique abbreviated as 'CFQ' meditation. He did not explain what the initials stood for until later.

"In the past," Sifu asserted, "cultivators of Taoist healing arts have gone through masters who claimed much but in practice, found that the benefits were short-lived. They came to see me, and I taught them CFQ meditation rather than conventional Taoist healing. Soon, after studying my method, they feel and see continual changes that they have only dreamed about but were never able to accomplish previously and are now manifested physically. Meditation to them once meant something that is dream-like, the energy to be experienced is abstract, and rarely captured concretely. For a start, they have been told that they must learn to relax in practicing."

"But what is relaxation?" he asked.

"It seems as if they are falling into sleep for maybe one hour while in meditation and then they wake up and they say they are relaxed and have attained rare and wonderful states. However, when they follow the conventional Taoist or Qigong master's prescribed way of doing things in meditation or breathing, that method can in fact cause a lot of disappointments and heartaches. They are misled into a state of disease and misfortune and yet they are still happily following it. So much good should be their reward but they have received little."

Sifu pointed out that for thousands of years, the Ancients had been researching the use of herbs in traditional Eastern medicine. Yet they discovered only limited usage and so there continued to be a search for better ways.

"Most traditional practices have outlived their usefulness," he emphasized.

"Another limiting factor of traditional ways is that conditions in today's society have changed. People increasingly are using grey brain matter rather than muscle. Today's situation is totally different from how people lived even a hundred years ago."

Sifu insisted that even though circumstances had changed drastically, and spiritual truth was a constant, the spiritual path should not be a deviation from real physical life.

"They must work together. Worldly problems must be solved from the spiritual plane as well," he said.

A lot of past wisdom was still relevant.

"We must have the wisdom to choose and select," he asserted, "between the relevant and the obsolete, and what has to be clarified in today's context. This is what CFQ meditation is all about."

Thus begun my growing acquaintance with Sifu and my interest in his method of meditative healing. Yet in essence, CFQ is no new creation at all. It is about the cultivation of 'qi' in Taoism (remember, it is pronounced as 'chi'), and everything about Sifu's approach was age-old, drawn from knowledge understood thousands of years ago.

CFQ meditation is a healing approach better described as a re-emphasis or highlighting of some ancient Tao energy and Eastern meditation principles that had been conveniently discarded or distorted and finally lost over time.

"For example, when we say, 'Relax' in meditation, we are emphasizing the principle of letting go," Sifu explained. "The Chinese character for relaxation means to 'let go, loosen, and relax'. If one does not let go during meditation, there is no relaxation."

In most conventional Taoist and meditation practices today, relaxation or natural stillness, is still emphasized.

"But somehow in the practice," Sifu said, "relaxation had been forgotten, replaced by acquiring 'qi' energy, with the belief that more was better. But that itself contradicts what relaxation means. Never in the long history of Tao has the practice meant acquiring power and strength. It is only letting go."

I began to realize as he was describing CFQ, that it seemed to be a radical form of traditional Tao. Sifu asserted that contemporary Qigong methods had deviated from their original Taoist conception and purpose. Qigong had many roots, blending Buddhist, Taoism, Eastern healing, and martial arts. Popular conception is that in Buddhism, the goal is ending birth and death, while Taoist practice is more concerned with health and longevity.

However, in ancient days, Buddhist monks and priests were also practitioners of Tao. So there was no difference between spiritual and health practices. Taoism, as taught by the sage Lao-Tze, also had a non-acquiring philosophy with emphasis on relaxation. But over the ages, Taoist practitioners had distorted it into the art of enjoying life, magical practices, and gaining good fortune and wealth. Present day Taoism has become distorted from the original teachings.

Sifu stated, "The antidote is not to concentrate on endlessly learning, absorbing, and accumulating from the external environment, all that is conventionally considered as valuable. We do not counteract any perceived weakness in the body by strengthening the person in the normal sense.

"For example, people may think that by taking food supplements such as vitamins or herbal medication, they feel strengthened. But the way we look at this is comparative. We believe people will feel weak because there is that kind of energy present in the body, and that it contradicts the weakened body, making you feel weak. So what we do is just release the energy that caused the weakness and then you are healthy. You don't have to put anything in."

I mentally attempted to recast his notions of a dependence on food consumption and the deleterious effects of cell metabolism. That led to unnecessary accumulation of cellular waste products such as 'AGES' from glycosylation, as well as formation of free radical molecules that remained in the tissues and eventually to cellular damage.

Sifu continued to stress this most important principle of non-acquisition.

"In the same way, positive lifestyle actions as a way of enhancing productive living, can be beneficial. But there comes a time when what is boosting you becomes a problem as well. After the booster effect vanishes you are now weakened. Our approach in CFQ is, if you feel weak you just subtract the weakness, and you are well."

He repeated, "Our true nature is not supposed to be weak. A dependence on the external, no matter how positive, produces only superficial changes."

Sifu emphatically pointed out, "There is something in you that is perfect, and this pure energy shines out from within. It is difficult to define what this pure energy is by conceiving it as having positive and negative attributes. For example, definitions of love range from the very self-centered narrow kind of love to a universal energy of loving-kindness or Buddhist 'Metta' (in Sanskrit)."

I reflected on ancient paintings of the Buddha immersed in a halo or nimbus of Golden Light and thought, "Ah, that's the gold-body radiance illuminating and liberating all beings."

"People are constantly exploring all kinds of methods and techniques to learn to cope better and adjust to living," said Sifu. "Here in CFQ, there's really no method involved. But in order to have a way of dealing with life situations, we have to use some minimal way of knowing what needs to be done. At the same time, when we say relaxation is important in CFQ, that doesn't mean it's just doing nothing."

"People normally get carried away by all kinds of stray thoughts. They do a lot of things that are harmful to themselves. Maybe they are sleeping, but too much sleeping is also an accumulation of dense energy. What we do in CFQ is minimal. You see practitioners moving, they look very busy, but in fact there is no effort involved."

Again Sifu stressed, "The meditator does not participate in the activity. Remember that this is the method of no method, a way of cultivation whereby brain activity is curtailed and things are allowed to happen as they occur. When you participate it is already tension. It's non-participation that matters."

Sifu, in the short time that I had met him, had become a mystic. After twenty years studying and practicing numerous methods of healing, he had made the Zen-like discovery of this 'method of no-method'. His departure from contemporary Qigong sounded revolutionary yet seemed true to what I expect of ancient Tao. The approach promised to make a significant contribution to all aspects in the life of the practitioner. But not through strengthening the person in the usual sense. It was more from emptying oneself of dense energies, so that purified energy could sustain resilience and health in the midst of unhealthy life situations.

One thing was clear from the cutting edge discoveries of what causes human aging–as chromosomes deplete, mortal cells decay and age. If we can find out what is attacking cellular DNA, we can figure out what is causing aging and disease.

"Could it be," I thought, "similar to what Sifu was saying, if we remove the negative agent, in the form of decaying, noxious energies, we survive and prosper?"

I asked for evidence that the CFQ meditation was a powerful technique that could heal medically incurable diseases. He reviewed two cases for me.

The first case was a woman from Kuala Lumpur, the modern Malaysian capital. She had cervical cancer. Originally, the diagnosis was that cancer had spread everywhere in the genital and reproductive organs, so that the standard treatment of surgery, radiotherapy, and chemotherapy was recommended. Her friends convinced her to seek treatment with Sifu which she did for two weeks before the surgery. She was then scheduled for a radical hysterectomy. So insistent was she with her doctors on undergoing partial surgery, however, that the surgeons only performed a scraping.

After two weeks of Sifu's extraordinary CFQ healing treatment, and minor surgery, the hospital found that the cells had reverted to so-called pre-cancer cells. Her doctors still insisted she have another operation to remove all of her internal female organs, and undergo a full course of radiation treatment which she adamantly refused.

She continued her treatment with Sifu and drove north to the Healing Center every weekend for another two months for a total of ten sessions of treatment. On her next scheduled return to hospital, no biological signs of cancer were found and her doctor told her she would need no further surgery.

A year later, she went back for a checkup and again there was no evidence of cancer. The last time Sifu saw her, she had been free of cancer for one-and-a-half years and practiced CFQ meditation on her own. I thought that if this were true, the energy of CFQ is more potent than any ordinary healing form I knew about.

He went on to describe a diabetic patient who lived in Alor Star on the rich, rice-growing province on the mainland. His diabetes required insulin shots daily, and his sugar level sometimes almost went out of control. He had endured the childhood disease for twenty years. After practicing CFQ for six months, he found that on his business travel, he could cope without insulin shots. His health condition was excellent provided that he maintained his CFQ practice at home and on the road.

Previously, he could never go without daily insulin and he constantly felt worn out. Now, although the blood glucose was still higher than normal, it had stabilized. He was able to manage the diabetes and felt that the insulin shots were not necessary. I asked Sifu to explain this contradiction, as from the orthodox viewpoint he should not be feeling well without his medication.

"Measurement of blood sugar levels, and its relation to insulin functioning is one thing," he replied.

"To me, what medical science is doing is measuring the effects of a problem, often mistaking effects with the cause of the problem.. All physiological risk factors and signs in the body, such as levels of hormone, blood sugar or enzyme level, protein, immune cells, etc., are just consequences or simply the effect of the accumulation of tension forces or dense energies," Sifu said.

"Medical science looked at these biological changes in the blood and hypothesized a theory of disease pathology to explain and substantiate what was happening. The consequence of body deterioration giving rise to certain elements in the body is mistaken as the cause of the problem. Medicine treats the consequences of the problem, not the cause."

He elaborated further. "I am saying that insulin shots treat a malfunctioning of the pancreas, not what is causing the pancreas to malfunction. The pancreas has no reason to malfunction if the body and circulation are healthy, and free from previous abuse or damage."

I responded, "So you mean that the solution is not to treat the pancreas but instead deal with the cause of the pancreas malfunctioning?"

"If we treat the effect instead of the cause, very likely, the problem will become aggravated," Sifu replied. "In the short run, there is a suppression effect and patients feel that they can manage the disease. That's what medication is all about. After a while into the problem, the dosage has to be increased.

"Medicine today does not believe in cures," he added.

"Right, a disease like cancer after successful treatment, is said to be in remission only," I interjected.

"We say a lasting cure is possible if you can identify the right cause. To be cured by us, the patient has to bear with the inconvenience and allow time for the body to change back to normal functioning," Sifu concluded.

My initial interaction with Sifu had been brief, sparse, and anecdotal. He felt that transforming energy healing was his calling, and set up a

Healing Center. I had to find out more about his Tao energy healing approach on a first-hand basis. What heightened my curiosity was his reference to an extraordinary and personal mystical experience he had, from which all information about CFQ meditation came about. It was a state of consciousness infused and illuminated with the descent of the energy of 'radiant Golden Light.' My inquisitiveness was stirred. I made preparations to leave Canada for some extensive academic traveling in South-East Asia.

Part One

Golden Light Healer

2

Interview with a Remarkable Healer

The 747 Malaysian Airlines System plane with the acronym, 'MAS', meaning 'gold' in the Malaysian national language, did not escape my attention as I mused over what lay ahead in my island destination. The coastline came into view, flashing pearl-like through the window. I could see a distinct structure below that outlined the longest fixed link in Asia, bridging Penang Island with the peninsular mainland.

I recalled in my distant past growing up in Penang, being taken to the famed Eastern and Oriental Hotel by a newly met friend, a mustachioed, expatriate British army major turned local entrepreneur. What was more awesome than the hotel, to me as a budding youth was being driven there in his brand-new ultimate marvel, a 1957 olive green, Jaguar Mark VII M hard-top, then an impossible dream to ever possess.

But in this journey, at the present time, everything has become convertible, and what seems unattainable in one era has become an eminently possible mission. At Sifu's clinic, I glanced over the class of about 25 people practicing CFQ meditation outdoors in the front area of his Center. The Center, an ordinary bungalow house, was located outside the city in *Tanjong Bungah* (or Cape of Flowers), formerly a quiet beach area, which had become extensively developed and crowded.

I had arrived a few minutes earlier warmly greeting Sifu, who was in the midst of directing the meditation practice. But the behavior of the group did not conform to what would be expected in such practices. No one was sitting still nor seemed to be following any prescribed stylized Tai-chi or standard martial arts movements.

Each person's movements were different from everybody else's and the motions seemed chaotic, jarring, and far from graceful. Nor was the environment peaceful and quiet as one would expect in meditation centers. The Center was located at the edge of a busy, noisy outdoor market. Yet no one seemed disturbed by the constant whine of motor cycles, sporadic screaming sirens, and perpetual rumbling traffic.

Each practitioner was doing what Sifu called, 'sitting meditation'. As I focused on each meditator, a purposeful and recognizable pattern emerged. Each person would spontaneously initiate some self-directed body movements, which soon changed to a specific and constant wave-like motion. That continued until it appeared to be spent, before being replaced by a new pattern.

It was getting dark in the twilight and the sound of insects added to the traffic din. After about twenty minutes into the meditation, despite the vigorous physical movements and the eerie shadows, everyone seemed totally absorbed in their own actions.

Sifu beckoned to me, and commented that after the students had completed their meditation in the sitting position, they would just get up from their chairs, and continue with the meditation standing. Sitting and standing would help them to explore and activate the body more completely.

"Moving meditation," he assured me, "is necessary at the beginning stage for the body to relax and loosen itself in the fastest possible way. As the physical dense forces are allowed to move out, eventually the energy could settle downward. This results in a more thorough repair of the physical body."

The experience itself would often not be enjoyable because the movements were unpredictable, and the internal repairing process could be rather drastic.

"The physical and moving meditation actually changes one's entire energy system altogether," Sifu affirmed.

Each practitioner was absorbed doing what appeared to be a private dance that was tuned into some invisible tempo of his/her own. I observed that again, each practitioner initiated a repetitious series of strengthless, loosening movements that soon took on a rhythmic pattern. The duration of these movements may have lasted for a few minutes or was repeated, without a pause, for the entire meditation.

As the practice session continued, Sifu would periodically communicate with the group loudly exhorting them, "Be aware of abdomen, repeat your Mantra silently."

I heard him repeat, "Feel loose, let loose, and be carefree like a child."

Eventually, the entire group's movements seemed to slow down. One student started stamping his feet, alternating from left to right. Another was swinging her limp arms around and around. Someone moved erratically staggering like a drunk. Most of the practice was done with eyes either lowered or shut completely. Even though the movements were often done in this manner, no one collided into another or with the chairs and objects lying around.

Sifu said the students simply sensed the vibrations from the external surroundings and used the feedback to stay clear of each other's paths.

"The static energy environment can be sensed," he observed, "and remarkably, they are able to see this way."

I asked him to explain the significance of the movements, and how they released and unwound the dense energies stored.

"All energies drawn into the body become personalized. That is, they form some aspect of one's individual identity and eventually become impure. Of course, the lower quality energies tended to be more dense and easier to push out first," Sifu said.

"One's self-concept is a holding factor that connects and coalesces all the different aspects of one's personality or identities together. They accumulate as very dense energies and are very negative by nature. To begin with, if committed practitioners are not prepared to let go of their identities, they will not be starting on the right foot."

But eventually, through persistence, the identities that constitute the self, would all be removed.

"What is left," he asserted, "is truly the finer vibrations which were all positive by definition."

Concluding, he said, "The one identity that remains is created or defined by the 'Mantra' that brings in cosmic energy to become one's own vibration and true identity."

More students were standing up doing their meditations. One woman walked back and forth, with a smiling, happy face.

Sifu turned to the group and repeated, "Soft and loose, open and relax, repeat the Mantra."

He did not explain what 'mantra' was and where it came from until the following days. A few seconds later, he walked back to me and revealed that as they practiced, some became more sensitive to extrasensory events. He pointed at a woman doing vigorous hand movements despite a bandaged arm, inflicted in an accident some weeks back. Interestingly, a few days before the accident, during her practice, she had an image of something unpleasant happening that frightened her. It was a scene of a vehicle slamming into her.

"Of course," continued Sifu, "seeing an event of the future is never too precise because the event has yet to happen. One can know what will actually happen only when it actually takes place."

What she saw and felt earlier was only the suggestive trend of some possible event which remained uncertain until the end. Nevertheless, for this woman, three days later the accident occurred. But now after less than two months since the injury which fractured her arm, she was healing well, strength had returned to her, and she felt no pain at all.

"You can see her swinging her bandaged arm and moving around as if nothing is wrong with it," remarked Sifu.

Pointing out a middle-aged woman to me, he described someone who was shaking her body rhythmically.

"That's Meilee. Before she came to me, she had plenty of problems being hypertensive and diabetic. She has also been a serious Vipassana meditator. The particular incident I wish to mention is a motorbike accident that resulted in ripping out her toe-nail. You can see that it's bandaged. Within one week of the incident, the bleeding stopped, and the skin dried. This is very exceptional for people with chronic diabetes. She doesn't feel much pain now."

Sifu stated that, as a result of CFQ practice, her blood circulation had improved tremendously as the healing ability had sped up. But he explained that regaining health could be quite rapid as well.

"The healing process varies for different people. Some patients had complaints of problems going back for years. But it would take only several treatment sessions for them to feel very much improved."

"Once they continued with their own CFQ practice and got mobile themselves, they were even better off. New changes and developments continued to take place."

However, as they had to push out their problem from within, an outbreak of the old problem could develop as well. Sifu regarded this healing crisis as normative to complete the process of full recovery.

"But with CFQ, you have to bear with us, perhaps for as long as one or two years. It doesn't matter really since the person is improving along the way. The blood pressure goes down more and more, but in order to clear the negative off for complete health, the process does take time. It does not simply disappear into thin air. We deal with them as we go along clearing it out naturally."

I commented that the CFQ system of healing could be tested medically since the physical consequences of the energy manifestation were readily observable.

He flashed a broad smile, responded, "I will say that the way we deal with energy is not conventional where energy is viewed as something intangible, accessible only in imagination or in a dreamy state.

"But here," he persisted, "the way we deal with energy is very physical and concrete. You have seen how practitioners jerked and twitched with involuntary movements because as energy unwinds, this becomes manifested as jerks and movements. This is true even for a person or new patient who knows nothing and hasn't been taught about energy."

"However," Sifu added, "some take a longer time to move, for example, a person down with stroke, or a very old person with limited mobility. Whereas, for the young, they move straightaway. Moving is a good indication that energy is being activated and the body is undergoing repair."

The movements themselves, as I observed, never remained the same, changing on their own impetus, apparently in accord with the kind of energy released.

Sifu stressed that these movements were far from imaginary, random, or purposeless.

"You've got to let it go out. But you are not in a trance, as eventually you are in full control and become more vibrant. The mind is alert and not dreamy."

As they advanced, the automatic movements became more graceful. The pattern kept changing as they went along, creating new physical releasing patterns. That basically meant that some specific channel of tension had been primarily cleared.

"The cultivator continues to be open, that's all."

I described to him the movements that I had seen earlier. A couple of students, who were rotating their bodies, spun around effortlessly for one hour without apparent discomfort. I asked how this was related to the non-physical dense energies.

Sifu said, "These energies, once accumulated in the body, begin to form in force centers. Each type of energy has force, direction, and strength. As in physical energy, there is an equal and opposite reaction.

As the tension force is released, it goes out of the body in the manner that it was created."

I commented, "So the unwinding effects I saw as they moved are actually energy formations going out."

The release went beyond physical tension and included emotional memories, and trauma as well. A person who had been through tremendous shock and frightening experiences could release past fearful memories and images through physical and emotional unwinding. In the beginning, the movements could be very panicky with a lot of jumping around. Then the person would get emotional, expressed as crying, vocalizations, and laughing, but all these have been and must be released.

Once the negative energies were released and reduced, the practitioners would no longer be shielded or blocked off by such negative forces. The students would experience more positive emotions and this happened naturally. As I looked at the meditation group, I could see the faces of smiling people, apparently having fun and jumping around. Sometimes the cultivators seemed to be amused by their own childlike playful movements. When I spoke later to the CFQ practitioners, their feedback was that after a while they were more cheerful, their bodies felt lighter, they felt happier, and were less self-centered.

Sifu was saying to them, "Fresh and alert—Wake up, and open your eyes!"

Then it ended with each person slapping the whole body, stretching, and slowing down to a standstill. Sifu then walked me back to his room.

"One of the distinctive features is that we are detached from the movements. That means you do not participate in the movements. You are not part of the movements but just moving along with the movements without involvement. In practice, we know things are leaving and feel happy that unhealthy things are leaving us.

"The most important aspect of CFQ practice is to cultivate the detached or 'Still Heart', whereby one is not involved in the movement. This allows it to unwind on its own."

Pointing to his students, he continued to elaborate on the significance of energy detachment.

"We say that movement is necessary first to activate accumulated negative energy that has made the body heavy and dense, and has glued the tissues together. If you have not activated yourself internally, there will not be the possibility of such external movements. Once you activate it, movement happens naturally and is just an expression of it. And by moving out the negative energies, your outlook becomes more positive.

"We effortlessly remove what is blocking the golden or pure energy flowing in which will manifest itself potently."

Master Yap concluded with the purpose of CFQ meditation.

"In the advanced stage of cultivation, we come to know that beyond the physical body and identity, we are all connected. A person in that Gold-Body luminous energy stage won't do any harm to others, instead wants to help others to move along. In that manner, one is dealing with more positive, high-quality energies. Our intrinsic nature is to be pure, helpful, and positive. But we all acquire negative energies, first from birth that we inherit, and throughout our entire life."

"In CFQ, we are not trying to input positive energies into the body. Rather, just by removing the dense forces itself, the natural high quality golden energy will shine out on its own."

That night, I was happily left to myself to digest what I had heard and seen thus far. The system he had revealed to me went far beyond mending physical bodies to some ultimate mystical state of transcendence. It was clearly no ordinary Qigong, based on the subtle energy that flows in the body's meridians as ascribed in traditional Chinese medicine such as acupuncture.

Over the next few days I held back any sign of enthusiasm, and continued to play an objective, skeptical role. It was far from adequate to rely only on his words that physical healing occurred by means of some powerful transmission of purified 'Gold-Body energy'. I needed to see for myself how he personally carried out CFQ treatment. The opportunity came the next day with the patients scheduled to see Sifu for the morning.

The Dance of Tao:
Healing the Suffering

The approach to energy healing used by Sifu to cure disease worked apparently on the basis of clearing out accumulated energy waste products or tension forces amassing in the diseased body. Perhaps this could be a practical way of ridding the body of the physically toxic waste products that scientists believed caused aging. If diseases were curable in this manner, then a quantum leap would have been made to find practical remedies that have, thus far, eluded senescence scientists to prevent aging, as well as to have a healthy and extended lifespan.

At the least, it would be fascinating to have the opportunity to witness first hand, a reputed master healer performing a potent energy method of treating incurable diseases.

I was back at the Center, for the second day, determined to scrutinize everything I observed with detachment, and to watch out for any deception that might be employed. This was to be my first as well as the first time anyone was permitted a complete observation of the entire CFQ treatment process by Sifu. He was giving treatment to a 15-year-old patient with intense chronic pain.

"This is Liam, my son." The boy's mother explained to me that the problem began five years back. For the past six months, Liam endured the agony of intense, nightly pain, and he was unable to sleep. He had been in and out of hospital and medical tests including X-rays had not revealed any slipped discs or pinched nerves. The doctors could not find the cause of his problems except that he had a very low hemoglobin count. The boy was put on a dietary course of iron and vitamin supplements which did not work. Even the strongest prescribed pain-killers did not relieve him of his pain.

Liam's condition had been rapidly deteriorating. He had missed school often, for as long as six months at a time and presently had not been in school for over one month. The boy was underweight and his legs were emaciated and wobbly. He hardly spoke and his face looked ill and sad.

Sifu gave me a clearer physical description of the boy as well. Liam had come in for treatment with his mother ten days earlier supported by a walking stick. He struggled into the clinic with her help. His knees were bent at 60 degrees, and he could not straighten them. The body was very crooked and he was virtually dragging himself into the Center. He had complained of severe pain in his hips and an unbearably painful left leg.

Sifu felt Liam's inner thigh, which was hardened and swollen. There was a whole stretch of muscle that seemed lumpy and too rigid. The tension that accumulated there had to be released. His diagnosis included perceiving energy accumulation in the chest area forming a round ball-like structure in the upper thorax, even though the chest itself was emaciated.

He then asked me to watch the treatment process. The treatment room was plain, and without any decorative features. Standing motion-less over Liam, he raised his hands, holding them above the supine body of the boy lying on his back on a narrow couch. The boy's eyes were closed as he lay there quietly.

After a few seconds, the Master, standing a foot away, began to move his fingers, slowly opening and spreading them apart. Simultaneously, the boy's hands started twitching slightly. This was supposedly the Gold-Body energy transmission process that Sifu spoke about earlier, directed by his hands.

He stood two feet near Liam, then stepped back with his hands pointed at the boy's torso. One arm was fully extended while the other was bent at the elbow. He remained motionless for a couple of minutes. Then with both his arms bent, he stood back about three feet from the boy. Just as the fingers of his right hand began rotating, the boy's rib cage and abdomen began to heave. Sifu focused on this area with fingers pointed. He spoke to Liam softly to ask him to relax as much as possible.

The air in the treatment room seemed to have taken on a quality of stillness and denseness. The soft light filtering through the glass shutters somehow felt electrically charged. As I watched the 'remote control' effect the Master's actions had on his patient, I could not help feeling amazed.

He extended two fingers pointed at the boy, while rocking his body. Pulling motions appeared again on the boy. The boy's rib cage started quivering in tandem to the energy transmitted by the Master. He continued to rock on his feet, heel to toe, with fingers on his right hand revolving. The boy suddenly jerked three times, repeatedly in strong response. As Sifu's hands moved downward, the boy's body quivered again, moving to the right.

I watched his fingers pointed at the boy. Liam again twitched involuntarily, as his chest jerked, stopping and starting in spasms. Then his right shoulder suddenly moved, followed by the arms as well. As Sifu rotated his hips, beads of sweat dripped down his face. Extending the fingers of his right hand, he moved to curl his fingers slowly. The boy's right hand and fingers began to quiver and twitch in response.

He moved in even closer, fingers wriggling. The boy's wrists began rotating, followed by his diaphragm and rib-cage vibrating. Sifu then rotated his fingers faster, and again simultaneously the upper body of the boy arched up a few inches from the bed, beginning at the chest, and then followed by his shoulders.

At that moment, the boy stretched his whole body, muscles quivering rhythmically, beginning from the neck downward to the chest. The chest then heaved up making rapid, rolling, and rippling movements that seemed to have the effect of an electrical jolt convulsing his shoulders up and down, off the bed. The whole upper body jerked repeatedly, working its way down to the hips. Then his legs also began moving in rapid thrusting motions ending with the right leg jerking.

I had witnessed a potent demonstration of the power of Gold-Body energy transmission willed by Sifu. Through his dance-like fluid movements, the boy seemed to be connected by some invisible force to Sifu who could make him respond by remote control. It was as if he had locked into the boy's energy field cleansing it by ejecting the dense energies from him.

The process at this point had taken twenty minutes. Sifu then seemed to make clearing movements around the boy, with his arms sweeping above the boy from head to toe, pulling and plucking at the air. Slight jerks occurred down the side of the boy, with muscle twitches on the hips. The treatment appeared to wind down, and had taken some thirty minutes. Sifu stopped moving and for the first time since treatment began, he made direct physical contact. He grasped the patient's ankles momentarily, massaged his limbs from legs up to his arms and back to his feet. He pressed hard on the patient's inner thighs down to calves, and ankles on both legs. He spoke softly to arouse the drowsy boy, continuing slapping and massaging the boy's legs and fingers, and then shaking his shoulders.

I examined the gait and appearance of the boy as he slowly sat up, then got off the couch and walked away unaided. The pained expression on his face had gone and his posture and footsteps were almost normal, a far cry from what he was like a short, half hour earlier. Sifu prodded the boy's inner thigh, and found that the lump on the left side had gone completely. The muscles there looked good and the fascia felt good.

I turned to the beaming mother who expressed that she was extremely pleased with the improvement in the past two sessions. She affirmed that her son had felt less pain, was able to sleep, and to stand up a bit and walk slowly. The boy had been very passive previously, withdrawn, depressed, suicidal, and looked weak and lifeless but now he had shown dramatic improvement. From the mother's comments, it looked like he was on the way to recovery.

Sifu asked for my impressions of the treatment. All that I could see were his external movements as he danced around his patient. On the surface, what I saw of the treatment procedure seemed incomprehensible. But I could somehow sense the radiant energy behind his movements, perceiving how it activated and triggered movements in the boy. I wanted Sifu to explain what was happening at the energy level, what was going on as he was working on the boy, what his own movements were all about, and what the boy's movements meant.

Could he explain what he was doing?

"Actually," Sifu began, "I wasn't doing anything or following any prescribed method. I began the way I did because I had tuned in. 'There's the boy, something needs to be done for him'. That's it."

I suspected that he did not have to follow some planned procedure.

"It didn't exist and neither did I," he nodded.

"Whatever needed to be done, it happened that way. I had to get rid of his suffering fast because of his urgent need. I just worked along the energy flow. I discovered certain patterns, a certain energy force field that I needed to work on."

"I sensed it, or it was just there–the many-layered structure of all human energy patterns. I work according to the changes required in these tension structures."

Before he could complete his explanation, sounds of a car parking in the front of the Center signaled the arrival of the next client. This was a woman, past middle age, who was ushered into the treatment room. Sifu briefly mentioned that she first came to him after surgery to remove a malignant uterine tumor. Initially, she had plenty of body pain in her shoulders and upper and lower back. Her hands felt weak, and one side of her body felt numb and heavy. After a few treatments with the Master, her pain had disappeared but she continued treatment to be assured that she would remain healthy.

I followed him into the treatment room and again observed the treatment procedure over the next thirty minutes. The client was seated on a chair waiting for him. He sat motionless behind the patient for some time extending energy over her shoulders.

Then Sifu stood up in front of her with his hands pointed at her for a few minutes. He appeared to be directing energy to different parts of her body by repositioning himself every few minutes around her. He finally ended standing behind her again. Then he placed his hands on her shoulders for about thirty seconds before finishing. As she walked out, I could see her smiling and nodding warmly to me.

I asked him to describe his energy activation procedure with the woman client.

"To start off, I tuned in by focusing on the intention to heal and then I let go of that. My task is to try to loosen her energy system. So you saw me switching to the front, side, and back directing the energy with my hands here and there. This helped to loosen out the dense energy, or at least the surface tension.

"Then I sat behind and pointed my fingers downward as I wanted the patient's energy to settle down. That itself is sufficient since a downward movement also creates an outward releasing or radiation effect.

"The hands are merely a guide, or a tool like a steering wheel. The radiating energy to heal comes from all over my body. But I feel more comfortable with the hands moving in different positions. This helps me feel in full rapport with the patient. At the same time, the energy of the patient is being caught, and is not allowed to flow indiscriminately outward."

They were two sides of the same coin. The downward movement would naturally dissolve whatever stale energy was in the patient.

"The tension forces just slouch off; it will dissolve in chunks. The patient can be seen swaying slightly forward and backward," he concluded.

Sometimes, as in the case of the young patient, he told me that the large jerking action meant that a large chunk of stale energy had been released and was leaving the body.

I commented that with the woman client, I did not see any movements.

"I will say that in almost all cases there are minor swaying or quivering pulsations and movements. They may be less visibly obvious and, to the observer, they appear to be just random inconsequential movements. The uninformed observer will not recognize these movements as specific responses of the patient to the treatment."

Very often, Sifu recognized the movements before the patient's body moved. He knew that it should move a particular way and he knew what was happening.

"Something is leaving the body. If the energy blockage is from the upper body, on the left side, probably the body will sway toward the left. It will also be tilted toward the left. As the tension energy leaves, the body will sway again. This allows me to continue to work inward more thoroughly to take out the denser energies."

Sifu added, "Healing is a dissolving process."

But it was not necessary for him to bother with what was dissolving.

"You're just there. You just let it settle."

Settling meant that a lot of things would have to peel off from the patient. At the end of treatment, he would make sure that there were no specific spots where the energy remained trapped in the body.

"When there is tension, there is some energy causing difficulties that have to be loosened out. After that, I put my fingers on the patient's shoulders for a short while. I stand up and close my eyes to a deeper meditative state. This enables my energy to tune in further.

"I tune totally into the patient to check within, to check what else should be moved, and what needs to be done," Sifu said.

"What happened during the boy's treatment in the last five minutes? Could you see energy manifested at that point?" I asked.

"Oh yes. That is the point when I see more things. Earlier on, I would be alert so that the visual aspect is less. I see, at most, the external body energy or outer aura. It is only toward the end of treatment, when I tune deeper into the forces that I can see more."

"I see things moving and dissolving. As I said, disease-causing energies are visible as they are denser and appear greyish dark in color. They are also heavier, sticky and have a numb feeling. Good energies are not so visible."

At the end of the treatment, Sifu gives a pat followed by slapping downward along the body and the arms. This launches a vibratory effect to further loosen any energies that had been trapped in the body. Overall, this is a wake-up call so that the patient no longer feels dreamy.

A standard treatment session is about 20 to 30 minutes. In most cases, treatment is carried on for six months, once a week. During the process, the layered formation of related illness symptoms become evident. If obvious removal of problems by layers is called for, it is usually sufficient to remove several layers of dense forces to clear the problem. A patient may literally have hundreds of layers of impurities accumulated over a lifetime.

I responded that this objective reminded me of a therapist who described how she worked on clients with 'MPD', or multiple personality disorders. An MPD client had a dominant personality, who is normally unaware of literally hundreds of other co-existing, distinct, parasitic personalities or identities present. These often self-destructive personalities are inherently layered and each layer had a distinct set of separate identities.

If therapy were successful, several layers could be released, integrated, and rendered harmless. The treatment is continued to uncover even deeper layers of unresolved forces linked to a troubled or traumatic past. Presumably, trauma could be thought of as tension forces existing in the body as dense energy entities.

It was obvious that Sifu could harness, control, predict its effects, and transmit his healing energy for the benefit of his patients. It was certainly enigmatic and almost beyond comprehension. I wanted to interview people who had been treated, hear what they felt, and how they benefitted from CFQ treatment. The occasion would come the following day.

3

Golden Light Healing

Witnessing the 'Gold-Body energy' healing process was entrancing. I started out as a spectator but very quickly, I felt various sensations that seemed to emanate from the energy field originating from Sifu, and sensed how the patients were activated for healing. The energy he harnessed became tangible as he directed it at them. Energy meditation healing obviously did not resemble the familiar Western medical model of pathology and disease causation.

The medical model was a perfect derivative of a Newtonian physical world reality, while the Tao energy disease causation model was akin to the sub-atomic world of quantum physics where the laws of energy ruled. While the medical model pointed to microbes, aberrant biochemistry, or deviant cells as the causal agents of disease, the CFQ energy causation model maintained that these physical disease agents are themselves the residual effects of once vibrant cosmic energy absorbed in the human body.

In the ancient Eastern medical system, now scientifically validated, energy is the basic force that makes up all matter in the universe, including the space between all stellar material. Energy is believed to be the origin of the universe, and energy creates matter and gives rise to all physical existence. All organisms, to sustain life, must draw energy from the environment such as air, food, sunlight, and water and convert it to nutrients to nourish and develop cells and for organs to function.

Sifu elaborated on his Tao theory of how such stellar energy sustains life. Simply put, in humans, to interpret the environment and external conditions, the five senses become stimulated and the stimulants are drawn in as energy. The absorbed energy from external perceptions induces thoughts and emotions that are laid down as memories. When they activate the body to respond and adapt to the environment, mental activity further absorbs more energy into the body.

CFQ theory maintains that all these functional processes in the body normally leave behind large amounts of residual stale energy. The contention is that, over time, the continual build-up of such negative energy leads to the formation of energy blockages creating tension forces that harden, thicken, and shorten muscle cells resulting in tissue compression, deformation, and defects and wrinkles forming.

"All diseases," Sifu asserted, "by whatever specific name they are called, actually have one commonality, that is, they develop from tissues that have literally 'glued' together and that type of energy blockage prevents the normal circulation of blood, prevents the normal nervous system activity, etc."

My hunch was that disease causation goes well beyond brain or tissue malfunctioning.

"When the tension forces are removed, and the body is deeply relaxed and purified, the body reverts to being the perfect system that all humans are," Sifu said.

"Stress reactions in the long term also have pathological consequences," I pointed out.

"Stress and trauma also lead to dense energies that are stored in various parts of the body causing a lot of mental and physical disturbances," he explained.

"I believe," I replied, "there is no possibility of getting rid of psychosocial trauma without dealing with the energy causation factor."

Sifu acknowledged that as a matter of fact, psychological problems can be more deep-seated and potentially more severe. So there is an urgent necessity to release the dense energy blockages that cause the psychological problems.

"But, regardless of whether the cause is physical or psychological, the illness consequences are preventable," he said.

Clarifying this point, Sifu continued, "Say a person suspects he's got a heart problem. He goes for a medical checkup and the tests show no indications of the disease as the heart is normal. Two years later, however, when he returns for checkups, symptoms of the disease are found.

"But if a physical event has not yet developed into a diagnosable condition, then physicians say that there is nothing physically wrong, and medicine is unable to do anything for the illness. I'll say that by acting to remove and release the tensions blocking energy flow, the illness process is prevented."

I needed more first-hand evidence of the efficacy and potency of CFQ treatment in terms of its lasting effects. I needed to understand how the system dealt with energy that caused psychological disturbances and diseases, and how getting rid of trapped energy in the body can transform it.

One opportunity came when a stroke patient arrived at the Center with his wife. While the husband was attended to by Sifu, I introduced myself to the woman, Melissa, and asked her about her husband. The man was 73 years old, had suffered a stroke three years earlier, but had only come to receive CFQ treatment over the past six months.

Melissa told me that when her husband first came to the Center, his body was very heavy and he needed much help to get into the building. The stroke had paralyzed his entire left side, leaving fingers curled up. His hands and arms could only be lifted to 40 degrees below the shoulders. However, his condition changed after five treatment sessions.

His arms could now be fully extended and his fingers were totally mobile and he could comb his hair. His walking improved although he still had a limp. Melissa was elated with her husband's progress as his life was getting normalized. He was more energetic, had stopped drooling, his incontinence and constipation problems were completely gone. He was spending time exercising in the garden and reading newspapers and books. He could now do more for himself, was mentally alert and cheerful, and did not demand as much attention as before.

After the man's treatment was completed, I asked the wife what he did for a living. Before she could answer my question, the husband spoke up clearly, "I was formerly a telecom technician."

Melissa smiled in appreciation and remarked, "Wonderful, he can remember so well. What a change this has been!"

She spoke of the time wasted in the first two-and-one-half years after the stroke, when nothing they tried seemed to help him to recover. Not until coming to Sifu over the past six months.

I asked Sifu to clarify how tension energy led to strokes.

"The tension forces accumulated push on the central nervous system as well as stiffen the neck region. As this continues, the left side and the right side of the body are in a state of disequilibrium. If the pressure is greater on the left side of the body, eventually, there is a disastrous impact on the right brain hemisphere. When the stroke occurs there, the left side of the body becomes paralyzed and then quickly hardens. So paralysis is not just brain damage but originates from body tension."

"The energy system has obviously lost its equilibrium," I commented.

He added, "In actual fact, paralysis is probably a process whereby the body system voluntarily shuts down this physical function of the body in order to minimize the build-up of fatal tension. Otherwise, the continuous tension accumulation due to normal activity could bring a more disastrous or even terminal effect."

"Right, the body shuts down in order to survive," I interjected.

"In CFQ treatment, by releasing tension energy on the left side of the body, gradually blood capillaries rejuvenate in the brain as well," Sifu explained.

I questioned his work on another kind of paralysis, that caused by spinal cord injuries. He explained that damage to the spinal cord produced such a severe shock that it results in a burnt-out effect. Still, the nerves were not completely severed, otherwise there would have been instant death. The paralysis was akin to an electric wire short-circuiting, shutting down communication.

I mentioned the widely reported case of a well-known actor who became paralyzed after falling from a horse and who vows to walk again.

"In the case of a cervical neck injury, it is more problematic than lower injuries. Even so, the nerve fibers are still connected but the burnt-out effect will limit nerve function. However, the vital organs are still functioning."

I thought that perhaps transmitting luminous energy soon after the injury could have an opening effect for new-cell growth and repair. One's innate self-repair response would activate to heal the damage.

Curing the Impossible

On the next Sunday morning, I approached a middle-aged woman whom I had seen in the group practice that Sifu had earlier introduced as Meilee, a nurse. As we sat down to converse, I noticed that she had a bandage wrapped around her big toe. I asked her about her interest in CFQ. She first came to the Center on her niece's recommendation for treatment of high blood pressure and diabetes, and subsequently she was initiated into the energy practice.

I asked Meilee to explain her initiation into CFQ meditation.

"Sifu firmly believes that there must be a direct transmission of the Gold-Body energy to his students in order to initiate them. The process ensures a proper understanding of CFQ practice and energy principles."

She explained, "Sifu is able to connect with the student's energy pattern which is activated and purified. It is only during initiation that the Mantra is revealed to the student for its correct and protective application."

Pointing to her fingers, Meilee described a growth, the size of a raisin, that used to be on the side of one finger.

"I am diabetic, so I became a bit worried that it would turn septic. I thought of seeing a doctor, but when I approached Sifu he told me it was O.K., and to just keep practicing."

At first she was skeptical and used some medication since it was quite painful when touched. But after a while she felt bad for not trusting the Master and stopped her self-medication. Then very soon, the growth dried up and the scab just dropped off after a month.

I prompted Meilee to go on and she quickly pointed to her eye.

"One day on waking up, this left eye," she divulged, "really jolted me. Everything I looked at was distorted. Again blindness is something a diabetic worries about. Fear was in my heart and I went straight to see Sifu. He just laughed to dismiss it."

"He only said, 'Energy has so many ways of leaving the body.'"

"I went to the ophthalmologist to have her do a thorough check. But there was no growth or blood clot, nothing she could find wrong. I went back to Sifu, and he again reassured me that it would wear off by itself. True enough, this condition was gone after about three weeks."

After that, Meilee could see better and in a remarkably different way from before. Ordinary things looked different.

"Even trees look so very fresh, not filtered by something. It's very much clearer and colorful."

"So, once the healing crisis ended, everything has improved for you?" I asked.

Her face lit up as she disclosed that CFQ has not only resulted in a major change in her ability to heal her body, but had improved her practice of meditation and tai-chi disciplines, and even relationships and family life.

I returned the following day to speak to another man whose entire family practices CFQ. He explained how one member of his family had been transformed by it. His son, Kaydn, who was aged 17, would be leaving for the U.S. to enter college next month. As a child he had been sickly with sinus problems and breathlessness, which developed into asthma. The father recounted the family's attempts to search for medical help for the son but had never found a cure. So someone suggested seeing Sifu some two years back.

"Progress was slow at first," the father recalled, "but after a year Kaydn was better than before. He stopped for a year, and returned again last year as health problems seemed to recur too often. Treatment resumed and then the Master got him to practice meditation last year."

As I began to end the conversation with the father, he interjected, "Another thing about Kaydn changed."

"His academic performance in school was always average, and at best no more than above average. Last year, he took his high school completion exam and amazingly scored an unbelievable eight A's, or distinctions in all courses in the national exams. His twin brother who had few health problems compared to Kadyn and who had always performed better as a student, ended up with six distinctions," the father said.

Sifu's comment on the boy's case was that certainly the meditation, by removing the tension forces, by making the person more relaxed, by clearing the 'karma' that was blocking or shielding the person's intelligence, had made the young person healthier and brighter.

A young, vivacious woman in her late twenties caught my eye. I introduced myself and sat down to engage in a conversation with Chin-San. She described how she became involved in CFQ meditation. Ever since she was a child she had had gastro-intestinal problems and a poor appetite.

Some years ago other symptoms appeared, the most troublesome of which were breathlessness and long bouts of fatigue. In the morning, Chin-San felt too weak and nauseous to get up from her bed. She could only have her first meal of the day in the afternoon, and other than that she virtually stayed in bed for the entire day.

"Did you work?" I questioned.

"Yes, in an office. But by age 25 I had to quit. I didn't work for three years prior to seeing Master Yap."

"What did your doctors say was wrong with you?" I asked.

"No one seems to know. I sought help from all the specialists. They performed tests including X-Rays of my digestive tract but found no cause. They prescribed tranquilizers. I felt worse."

"Was there pain?" I inquired.

"No, but I felt very uncomfortable and weak constantly."

"Sounds like chronic fatigue syndrome to me." I said.

"Yes. I found that out later."

After three treatment sessions with Sifu, improvements were evident. After 20 sessions, Chin-San was initiated. That was a year ago.

"You look so lively and bubbly and beautiful now, it's hard to imagine you not being energetic and healthy," I beamed.

Smiling shyly, she said, "There's more."

Chin-San had been going steady prior to suffering the chronic fatigue and acute intestinal problems. Her marriage plans were called off indefinitely because of her deteriorating health condition. Three months after Sifu started treatment on her, her health condition changed completely, and she had her wedding. After that, she found a job as a kindergarten teacher.

Chin-San's sister also joined her at the Center. She recently had a third child. The first two children were never too healthy and the mother had great difficulties during the pregnancies. The third child was born a year after her sister and her husband had CFQ practice. The pregnancy was trouble-free and the baby was robust and healthy. Chin-San's happy face lit up even more.

"*Mei, mei!* The child is the most beautiful baby I have ever seen. And every feature is simply perfect."

Among the large gathering at the center, there were some 20 members of her family who are CFQ practitioners.

That same afternoon, I noticed a young man at the Center who had just completed his meditation. He introduced himself as Wei, a hospital administrator, and related the tale of his grandmother. His 'nanny' was diagnosed with brain cancer that had already spread into her lungs.

After assessments from the general hospital, she was straightaway referred for medical treatment. The radiologist found a few malignant large spots in the brain just behind the eyes. The doctors told Nanny that if not treated she might go blind.

But the grandson suspected far worse since the cancer was deep in the brain. When Wei checked with her physician, sure enough, it was the fourth and terminal stage. The attending nurse told him that the radiotherapy for Nanny was not meant to destroy cancer cells, since it was simply too far gone. The real purpose was to treat the skin lesions that she had.

Wei, eyes glistening and voice quivering, continued, "Nanny was not going to live for more than three months."

He asked Nanny to see Sifu which she initially refused, believing that only western standard treatment could cure her cancer.

Recalling the patient, Sifu remarked, "When she first came to see me, she was undergoing the first few sessions of radiotherapy. She had lost all her hair. She was short of breath because her lungs were also cancerous. She had no appetite, was weak and worried, and when she came to me her grandson had to help her walk."

Treatment for her started, twice a week for one month. After two sessions she felt much better and healthier. She started to have daily bowel movements. She continued with the radiation treatment until it was completed. When she returned to the hospital for a scheduled checkup three months later, the doctor, who had originally diagnosed her problem, was surprised to see her alive, amazed that she was feeling better, and looking much healthier.

"After a complete course of 20 sessions of CFQ treatment, that took two months, Nanny was literally glowing with health."

Nanny agreed to be initiated, after some persuasion from Wei.

Sifu added, "That was over six months ago. Now she has a full head of black hair and she no longer looks like a cancer patient."

The wrinkled black patches on her skin due to radiation therapy have also gone. Even other problems, such as rheumatism and depression have mostly disappeared.

"She is alert and healthy and looks much younger than a woman of her age."

I questioned Sifu about the tumor and wondered whether it was still there. He had cautioned Wei not to bother checking this out for the time being. It was immaterial whether the tumor had gone from her brain. Even if it had shrunken, the hospital might mistake the scars left as a problem.

"Or more dangerously, they might decide that since she is now better, she should receive the full treatment of chemotherapy which was originally not recommended because of the advanced stage of her problem. That means recommending all kinds of drastic treatment that might be more harmful!

"Yes, I can assure you that the problem is gone," asserted Sifu.

"But to prevent the cancer returning, Nanny needs to continue to meditate daily. That's all."

The next day when I called on Sifu, he excitedly said, "This morning I received a telephone call from Nanny. Last night was the first time that she suddenly found that her face was twitching and spontaneously making weird faces–strong pulls and jerks on her face. She was very worried, but I reassured her.

"Madam, that's a good sign. It means that the dense energy is activating. Feel assured that's all right, and let it move that way."

Sifu's ability to heal, and perhaps cure even medically incurable diseases, seemed astounding in impact and immediacy, but what was more important was to understand it in rational terms. I wanted to find what exactly he was doing and feeling as he performed his Gold-Body energy healing feats.

Knowing of his love of nature, I suggested we take a long stroll at the Botanical Gardens. This was a 30-hectare garden at the end of Waterfall Road, a short distance from the Center. The garden had hundreds of exotic and indigenous plants species, chattering rhesus monkeys, and a variety of lily and lotus ponds. On that day, there was also an orchid exhibition as an added attraction.

I appealed to Sifu to detail what he did during the healing process. "What happens when you send the energy down, opening it out, and sustain a state of deep relaxation?" I asked.

"This energy comes into contact with the troubled tissues to undergo a reorganization to be relaxed as well. And, yes always, I use the Mantra of the Gold-Body energy to tune into pure energy during healing. This is also the process of self-healing for the practitioner of CFQ," he said.

I sounded out the notion that the intention to heal was a starting point. He nodded that indeed, healing began with an intention to heal, tuning into the person, and establishing rapport with the individual.

"You don't even remember you are doing healing. Healing happens naturally."

The healer allowed the spontaneous movements experienced to direct the healing as they manifest as a whole pattern. The energy transmitted to the patient would activate the dense energies causing the problem.

"Until the healing is completed the unwinding movements will not stop. Even though the healer is moving, neither should there be a focus on moving."

I asked whether he visualized, saw energy, or the physical problem during healing,

"There is no need to expect anything specific. Because the movement itself will tell. Somewhere in the healer, the person knows what to do, without being quite conscious nor understanding how. Certainly, your radiant energy knows what it is doing."

Apparently, in the CFQ system of treatment, the Gold-Body energy 'knew' what to do from moment to moment. The purified energy of the healer is used to try to stir up the patient. This stimulation produces the effect of activation of trapped stale energy and the patient moves in accord with the energy excited.

"However, the healer continues to penetrate in-depth."

I probed him to elaborate on what penetration meant here.

"I skip the non-specific layers, and only work on the layers that have dense energies related to the patient's presenting problem. So I am very selective," Sifu said.

That was the case when treating the boy with the intense chronic pain. With the boy, by selecting and working only on the layers that caused the pain problem, Sifu could get rid of the problem faster. With that removed, the young patient quickly felt relieved.

But in his normal treatment, he would not be selective but straight-away go in without regard to which layer. He would simply penetrate. But the problem could not be totally or thoroughly treated in that way. In the case of the female patient, there was also a re-organization of the energy patterns.

"Thorough healing required remodeling or restructuring the body's energy pattern and stabilizing it," he clarified.

I felt Sifu was effectively re-balancing the patient's energy system. Then the body became much more relaxed.

"Yes, in future the kind of energy that a person accumulates in the daily process would also be different. It does not follow the previous 'pattern of upward suspension' of residual tension forces any longer. It is a more streamlined and balanced pattern.

"Bear in mind that it is not just giving energy, through waving one's hands to direct the energy in certain locations of the patient's body. I am also removing something or throwing that out," he said.

The healer could also spontaneously do body work such as massage, acupressure, or try to loosen the joints. In a more extreme case, Sifu is walking in a certain way, making dance-like steps around the person.

"That's also healing. And I find that, yes, whatever one does, there will be effects."

I made the comment that his Gold-Body energy was, likely, constantly being connected to the energy of the patient.

Sifu stated that in fact there was that connection. Sometimes he dislocated from it but only when it happened spontaneously. Then he would finish and detach from the patient. If he were to himself intentionally conclude, that would turn out to be premature, and he would somehow feel that something was not complete.

I hypothesized that because of that connection, whatever he did seemed to have an effect. During treatment, I saw him making movements that directly produced similar movements in the patient because of the energy connection. I asked how he sensed the patient's tension.

"The energy knows," he claimed. "But as one advances, one will better understand what one is doing.

"What problems you are able to heal is up to the limit and depth of working on yourself. You cannot go beyond what you yourself haven't attained. For example, after one or two years of practice, you can succeed in handling your health problems developed over the past five years. After that, you have enough purified energy in you to deal with others with similar problems. If, however, a patient comes in with a twenty-year problem, I'm afraid you'll not be able to handle that."

I asked whether the healing Gold-Body energy would become ineffective across a barrier such as distance.

"Not if you are purified," Sifu countered.

"Then there is less negative or denser energy that acts as a shield. The patient's physical presence is not required. Once you have become more purified, you are more closely connected to other people."

When pressed about what this state of purity was like, Sifu revealed that in the Gold-Body luminous state, one felt a sensation of being weightless or of being transparent.

"You go into meditation, and you feel the body is not there. In that light, you fully understand what it means. The experience goes beyond the meditation period. Even when you walk, you feel weightless. One feels boundless. The body has changed physically when the natural faculties become restored," he explained.

"This is another form of energy within, that exists in physical reality. You are not dreamy but fully aware. You are concerned about everything. You are firmly physical, yet you are not bothered by physical existence. Reality fails to become a hindrance to you. Yet at the same time, everything is so boundless and effortless."

I reflected that it sounded like a transcendent state experience with the body totally relaxed, but the mind fully alert and awake.

Sifu replied that when the energy was totally relaxed, the body and mind became one and totally in harmony.

"The mind, the body, and the whole system is fully vibrant. The body is without tension, and so can function much better in harmony with the mind. They function as one so that the full, perfect function of the mind is possible. Everything, including the brain, body, and thoughts is synchronized, carried together, and working together as one whole."

His description of this purified, luminous energy state appeared to be an apt characterization of a state of transcendental illumination. Further questioning would have to wait for a more opportune time.

Readiness to Heal

A day later, we sat on a bench shaded by huge rain forest trees at the edge of a small pond thick with large flat, floating lotus leaves. I wondered about how long it would take to begin doing healing work. Sifu admitted that some students, after several months of practice, had started healing others. Normally he would not encourage this until the novice healer has had three solid years of practice, necessary to understand how energy cleanses the body. But he would not prevent them if healing others happened spontaneously. Certainly, not if they were able to do something for others.

Sifu explained that in many current subtle energy healing systems, once the practitioners begin to feel some qi or energy sensations such as tingling in their hands, they are told that they can heal.

"On the question of qi sensations, most conventional energy systems believe that the more and intense they are, the better they can heal. Therefore, the practitioners will try to create, absorb, and store such sensations. In contrast, CFQ believes that sensations are merely bodily adjustments or energy wastes and residues such as heat, heaviness, and numbness which should leave the body," Sifu said.

Attempts to create or absorb these sensations will bring about a disastrous effect, which only becomes obvious much later on. Therefore, healers have to learn to release or let go of such sensations.

He cautioned, "Let them melt or dilute back into the pure cosmic energy. Eventually, all sensations will clear out. And then the practitioner experiences a luminous state of 'no sensations'. To be precise, one feels the transcendent sensations."

In CFQ, one could not effectively become a professional healer until after perhaps seven years of hard practice. But from the start, however, practitioners gained the benefits of self-healing as they unwound the tension forces during spontaneous movements.

"The training has vast potential for them to become true healers. Activating energy in others is part of the unwinding and letting go process. Reciting the Gold-Body Mantra and radiating energy becomes part of the merit of healing others. Practice itself is actually a healing process that lays the foundation of healing others."

He again questioned blind reliance on traditional ways of healing and meditation.

"A hundred years ago, people didn't have to rely or use much of their intellectual faculties. Practicing olden methods of bringing energy up toward the crown, or toward the forehead, helps to balance out the mental and physical aspects. Today, our lifestyle is so stressed out that energy that is drawn in automatically goes up. We draw energy up readily instead of it going down. If there is no specific emphasis to go down, then energy automatically goes up and gets trapped in the upper section becoming part of the problem, and increasing the probability of disease manifestation."

Sifu emphasized that in CFQ meditation, the natural sitting or relaxed standing position was preferred rather than sitting with legs crossed or in the traditional full 'lotus' posture. He also referred to the common use of mantras in many spiritual practices.

"Even using the right mantra, if they are not taught that where the mantra is 'placed' is important when reciting it, the mantra will also naturally go upward to the forehead. Here the mantra compounds the problem."

I recalled reading, from many sources, about meditation that emphasized focusing on the forehead, pineal gland or 'third eye' energy center in attempts to open it, and efforts to retain energy there.

"The energy will naturally go there, go upward, that's very natural," Sifu said. "It's incorrect to believe that the mantra should be recited from the head or in the mind. One must mentally bring it down to the lower abdomen. The correct way is to recite the mantra from the lower abdomen."

He questioned meditative systems that believed in building up energy in the pineal gland.

"They claim to be able to develop the 'third eye'. That meant seeing things others could not, or the ability to predict future events, and so on. But how accurate were such visions or predictions?

"It is simply not good enough if only some of these happened to turn out to be true. It must, at the least, be substantially true."

He added, "I read that some famous 'third-eye' masters are actually regular patients of mental hospitals."

He provided a different explanation of spiritual practice and its effects.

"When a person systematically cultivates or works with energy, the practitioner gradually learns to see or sense the forces that constitute the physical component, or that will eventually build up to give rise to future physical events. But such ability does not arise from opening a certain pressure point, *chakra*, or esoteric organ, as is popularly believed. Moreover, what is seen energetically has to be interpreted for its physical significance, and the accuracy of interpretation is dependent on one's energy system."

He went on, "A more 'purified' cultivator, or fully committed practitioner, is normally more accurate, since the danger of his own impure energy disturbance is reduced, or the risks of mistaking one's own karma for that of others are minimized. A person practicing acquisition techniques to open the third-eye is unlikely to have purified his energy."

Sifu emphasized again, "You need to let go to purify, and letting-go and acquisition are two opposing extremes. Moreover, acquiring and increasing the density of energy in the pineal gland makes a person confused, and likely to behave 'out-of-the-world' in time to come."

I again asked him whether the reason why energy needed to go down was because of the nature of our more stressful lives.

"Yes, tension energy is inward drawing, as well as upwardly suspending to become trapped in the body. These two things are the same. So when you bring tension down, it naturally radiates and goes out. There is a resulting opening effect to relax the whole body.

"Indeed, the Gold-Body energy takes time to cultivate and is not for the faint-hearted. The truth must be told even if the truth is not easily acceptable."

Facing reality can seem harsh. For instance, one must appreciate the fact that the slightest indication of a disease itself involves many long years of unhealthy energy accumulation in one's lifetime before it can become symptomatic.

"To work toward a cure, there are chunks of energy to clear out that are embedded in deep layers. So one needs to bear with the inconvenience and effort of clearing it out," Sifu explained.

He cited popular methods that involved visualization. Even though one was not taught to visualize, people naturally use their imagination to visualize.

"What we are also avoiding in cultivating Gold-Body energy is visualization. You are asked *not* to visualize. Visualization creates mental energy, which is also inward-drawing tension or karmic forming, ending with the tension blockages clogging up the main body."

Continuing, he cautioned about seemingly successful techniques that gave some temporary relief, but in reality only had a suppression effect.

"Say, you feel a body pain or a problem. The pain is there, and we say that pain is better than no pain when there is a problem. Now why is this so?

"In the first place, when there is some pain, things are not totally hopeless, it's still active and the problem is still sending warning signals. When things deteriorate further, no pain remains until the problem is renewed and pain intensifies.

"Now, if you do something such as take medication or ordinary therapy, you get relief and there's no more pain for the time being. But it's good for some time only because this can be a suppressing consequence," Sifu said.

"In fact, suppressing leads to the problem becoming inevitably harder, more condensed. It moves deeper inward. To clear it, there is only one path, that is to face it, and open it out from inside."

"In my Center, I do treatment continuously. For me, the worst feeling of all is knowing that while the patient is not the disease and the patient is treatable, the person won't or is unable to surrender, or let go enough for me to treat the problem. The patient must be co-operative for there to be a good chance of success."

Suddenly, I was conscious of the gathering darkness around us and the loud croaking of numerous tiny, green frogs in the pond. Soon the night insects would add to the cacophony. It was time to call it a night, but one that I would long remember. I had uncovered an energy healing approach that promised to match the challenges facing humanity in the next century.

Part Two

The Golden Light Lands

4

The Making of a Mystic

Going beyond the Ordinary
Shedding the Orthodox
In radiant Emptiness
Return to the Origin and Truth
The Self-nature reveals.

Calligraphy by Master Yap

Thus far, everything that I had seen and heard indicated that Sifu had truly become a remarkable master of energy healing. I had witnessed and observed the dancing Tao master as he performed his healing. I had interacted with his many patients and students as they recounted, in retrospect, how their ailments had melted away and their health was rapidly restored.

Conventional medicine had not responded to, or had given up on the array of diseases they suffered from. Just as dramatic, it appears that not only had symptoms of their suffering vanished, many other aspects of their lives had also benefitted from exposure to the healing energy.

As I reflected on these observations and experiences my respect for Sifu's monumental energy healing system was strongly reinforced. It was like no other that I had encountered. The practice seemed worthy of the lineage of the master Taoist-Buddhist practitioners of antiquity. A short two years earlier, when I first met him, he certainly struck me as a competent and earnest traditional healer, superior to the 'garden variety type'. But there was nothing especially unique or mystical about him. What had happened to produce this wondrous transformation in him?

The time had come to ask Sifu where his knowledge of the Gold-Body healing energy came from. Two days before my scheduled departure from Malaysia, we sat down in his meditation hall for him to narrate his life story, something he had put off, until now, despite a few gentle requests.

Over the past week, I had spent many hours with him each day. I was impressed with the enormous energy which he put into his work of treating patients. He employed no assistants in his work. His whole day was immersed in energy work.

Sifu lived an uncomplicated and simple life that revolved around energy healing that had benefitted several thousand patients. On a daily basis, he worked with energy 12 hours a day, and spent the evenings at home on his own meditation for several hours at a stretch or with his wife and two very young children. Small wonder that he seemed to know much about energy.

Uppermost in my mind was what had led to his illumination, and the profound, peak experience of 'Golden Light energy' that he hinted was a revelation of the source of the flow of knowledge that manifested as CFQ. How did he attain this state? Many have spent their whole lives searching for this elusive goal, but thus far, I have not met anyone who could describe it to me as a direct experience.

His childhood was spent living in a remote place in the hinterland of Penang Island. He was born in November 1956 under the zodiac sign of the Fire-Monkey, in a simple wooden hut at the edge of the jungle, away from the village houses, on the outskirts of the town. His grandparents were immigrants from China, and his parents managed to eke out a living working as impoverished rubber tree tappers. But his mother was a typical Hakka, a resilient Chinese immigrant group famed for stoic hard work, and eventually the family fortunes improved.

Until he was fifteen years old, Sifu lived on the jungle fringe, exposed to the wilderness, often going hungry. This was a hard time for all and he felt nutritionally deprived then. But he felt that as a boy, there were certain benefits growing up at the edge of a rain-forest. He was more sensitive, and psychically tuned to nature and the realities of life. His childhood memories included feeling protected because of a keen sense spotting cobras and other poisonous snakes.

Sifu recalled a dream he had and a vision of pursuing a spiritual interest. This could partly be explained by a prophetic statement attributed to his maternal grandfather, a Taoist monk, who died when the boy was nine.

The monk told the boy's mother, "This son of yours will earn a living involved in spiritual matters."

She accepted this prophecy as he was quite a famous Taoist monk renowned for his psychic ability.

True to the prediction, young Sifu was curious about all spiritual practices, often going around watching how local spirit mediums and healers worked in a trance, listening and talking with them. The young man was associated with a large group involved in martial arts training, and getting injured during training was common. He discovered a new talent in healing. By placing his hand on an injured part of his friends, it seemed to heal readily. By age 25, through his voluntary healing work, he had gained a certain reputation.

Pursuing his dream, he spared no effort to learn everything about traditional healing arts. He exposed himself to more meditation practices, following any proclaimed meditation masters in the region willing to teach him. He learned from those who claimed to be able to perceive demons, able to catch spirits, communicate with deities, etc. All in all, Sifu had learned ten types of meditation and Taoist approaches.

In the meantime, as a young adult expected to establish some vocation as a livelihood, he began a program of work and study with Coopers and Lybrand as an articled clerk to qualify as a CPA accountant. Not long after certification, in his late twenties, he started a firm as a public accountant and company auditor. Yet he was discontented with his profession and wished he was doing something else.

Sifu paid scant attention to his accounting work and continued his voluntary healing work with reasonable success in treating injuries, pain, the common flu, and asthma. While not knowing how lasting the effects were, he was convinced that it was more effective than available conventional methods. Healing seemed to be easy, and that led to more ambitious plans. He thought that it was time to become a healer full time. A final circumstance boosted his confidence to change vocation and quit his accountancy career. This incident was related to the mother of his girl friend Laileng. She is now his wife and they married in November 1989.

At that time, the mother had gone for a morning walk when she slipped and fell hard on her upper back. Something serious had been damaged since she appeared to be paralyzed. They did not want to move her too much in her condition and the hospital was too far away. Instead, she was brought home, and Sifu offered to do something for her.

He placed his hand between her shoulder blades, and very soon she reported that her body felt lighter, and she could move her body for the first time since the fall. Her family members were afraid to transfer her to a bed because of her paralyzed state.

However, the mother said she felt she could move by herself. Astonished, her family saw her shift her body and then get up to lie on the firm bed. She told her family it was unnecessary to call for a physician. Three days later, she was able to move about sufficiently to walk and wash her hair, and perform ablutions. That day, she went for an X-ray, and was told that a spinal vertebra had been badly fractured.

The damage was so severe that her doctors were completely mystified, not understanding how she could move at all, let alone walk. They suggested putting her in a hospital bed to be kept immobile but she refused. She felt no discomfort nor pain, and immediately went home. This was a major, successful healing story, convincing enough to be a turning point in Master Yap's life.

At the age of 33 years, he came up to Penang City, to set up his Energy Therapy Center. He did not have any specific treatment approach other than knowing many types of traditional energy healing, together with his experiences in healing others. Even then, right from the start as a healer, he was never short of patients to treat.

He recalled, for example, two female patients who had had mastectomies and then subsequently suffered a relapse that their doctors pronounced as terminal. His energy treatment seemed to have saved their lives. But as he went along, he gradually discovered how inadequate he was. He wanted to find out why he could not successfully treat certain cases. What else could be more effective, and what was preventing such patients from getting well?

Taoist healing is an oral tradition. Sifu felt that he had reached the limit of knowledge about Tao and energy therapy from all the known sources. Also, two years after becoming a professional healer, he was starting to develop health problems. His body became very stiff, his hair was falling out and turning grey. He had migraines, and problems with incontinent urination. The bottom line was that he was suffering a host of illnesses, and he had turned into a healer who was unable to heal himself.

Initiation into the Golden Light

Two-and-a-half years later, Sifu had his first major spiritual initiation. At that time, he was in touch with someone who practiced using mantras. So he tried the mantra out of curiosity, although he was never too serious about it.

And then one night, on a Sunday, he took Laileng to get something for dinner. It was a ten-minute drive away. He stopped on the side of the road, waiting for his wife who had gone in to pick up a takeout order.

Suddenly, he saw a whirlwind circling, and swirling the leaves and debris on the road in front of him. There was no cause for alarm, but for some unknown reason, on seeing that, he panicked–his heartbeat increased and palpitated. He waited calmly for Laileng to finish getting the food without saying anything to her when she came back.

As he drove home silently he started to shiver, and felt disoriented, but hung on until he finally reached their house without mishap. He felt a strong need to be by himself.

Sifu recalled, "I went in and locked the meditation room door, and as I chanted a mantra I went into spontaneous meditation. I felt that something was changing inside."

It was almost like being in a trance state, he said. He was moving very compulsively, but his mind was detached, and stayed away from the movements. They started at 8 p.m. and continued until 3 a. m. the next morning.

"I took out some joss sticks, lighted the incense, danced with them and 'tattooed' peculiar designs all over my body. I understood this to be an initiation by forces unseen," Sifu said.

Everything stopped as soon as the joss sticks burned out.

"After that, I went into the trance-like state again. I turned my body to face in different directions, bowing and apparently honoring the doorway, and corners of the room, as if some energy force had entered. I was doing one type of spontaneous movement for a while, and after that I turned as if praying toward the door again."

In the fluid process, he had aligned himself to what appeared as the eight sides of a hexagram figure. At each shift, he felt that something seemed to be released, and go out from him. He would then bow and pay homage again, and something else would come into his body. The powerful energy jolted his body again and again. This process was repeated 64 times, representing what he later understood and thought were the 64 energies of a hexagram symbol.

The hexagram meaning went back to six years earlier, first provided to him by an old man he had met then. This old man was supposed to be very wise, well known in that place as a living 'Loh-hun' or Taoist sage. People worshiped him as such. At that time, well over ninety, the sage saw Sifu, liked him, and discussed meditation with him.

Sifu told him that he had spent ten years practicing meditation and he could do some healing. Then the old man looked at the palm of his left hand, and pointed out an eight-sided hexagram pattern right along the major lines. Sifu revealed to me that the hexagram had faded, but was much clearer then. At that time, the hexagram shape was precise, very exact, and very clear.

The old man correctly predicted that the sign would become distorted as Sifu grew older. A hexagram on the palm was a strong sign of the healer, indeed as rare as, he said to him, probably one in a million. The sage predicted that he was to become a leading healer. Before he ended, he gave Sifu a mantra to recite.

This was a mantra on the hexagram, to invite the presence of its spiritual energy. For the past three years, he had recited this mantra even though he doubted its value. Perhaps, the 64 energy entities in the initiation represented the 64 forces generated by the hexagram. He sensed that the strong unwinding experience was a manifestation of karmic fruition, and had put him into a state of awakening.

I knew that the hexagram was a widely accepted protective esoteric symbol among Chinese people. It is commonly hung over doorways much like the Western horseshoe. In the ancient 'I Ching' text, considered to be one of the most ancient and authoritative of Chinese writings, the book of oracles is based on the 64 versions of the hexagram.

A seeker of truth or wisdom gets into a meditative state of mind to connect with time displayed in the Book of Changes or *I Ching* ('I' means chameleon) that marks each moment as a hexagram. It reveals not only the future but also the ethical values of one's actions attached to the oracular pronouncements.

As Sifu's initiation continued, it gathered even greater force and some new spontaneous tai-chi movements.

"I experienced the body being very strong, and very powerful. I could hold my breath for five minutes. So I began to think that I was invincible. I punched myself hard, but felt no pain. The sensation was pleasant, and felt like punching rubber," he said. He was in a dreamy trance-like state but was conscious of what went on. This state continued on for three full sleepless days.

But his health problems were not solved, even after this esoteric initiation. However, it opened a new dimension for him and his understanding of spontaneous healing increased after that event. He continued his healing work as before but the health problems remained unchanged.

He tried even harder, but felt disappointment since all the energy techniques he had learned fell short of the promised cure. Some of his patients became well, others did not. Sifu felt that the energy therapy he performed was simply not good enough.

He thought, "There must be something more than this."

Sifu, at age 36 years, was going to do things his way. He was ready to leave behind all his conceptions of healing and forge ahead with a new creation. This was also the period when I first met him. But I was unaware of this transitional initiation then, nor the next major initiation that he begun to describe. It was to be his first complete experience of the Gold-Body luminous energy state.

It was then about two-and-a-half years since his first initiation during the night of the hexagram. He still did not fully understand about energy.

One night, as he was doing his meditation, Sifu thought to himself, "I'll forget everything I have used as a healer and have been taught about energy healing up to this point.

"So I sat down, not wanting to do anything," he recalled. "It was 9 p.m. and I felt tired. I did not realize then that dropping all I had been taught was a form of letting go. Healing also is a form of letting go of one's energy. So probably the letting go phenomenon had been in formation all this while."

Sifu would not bother any longer with what he had learned, and just start fresh and find out what the truth was.

"Suddenly I felt a very strange sensation: Something was crawling, shifting, moving in my front and chest area. Minutes later, I realized that something was pushing from the back to cause the chest sensations. Muscles were shifting continuously, including energy shifts which were felt very physically.

"Like a flash, something seemed to open up with lightning force and my perception changed. A Golden Light shone, and poured out streaming from the heart region. I remembered very clearly that it was from the chest, specifically from the heart itself. I seemed to see the heart and something from there just shone out. I felt the Golden Light, and the intense heat that came with it. My consciousness went out into the light and I was carried away into it.

"Then the revelation came. Within the Golden Light, I was part of its consciousness, and the information began pouring through me. I was part of the information, but I was not aware of what I was.

"I saw all the knowledge that has since become the principles of CFQ. Crystal clear explanations. It was like the information was there, and I understood what it meant."

I thought to myself, "Ah, this is it, the amazing truth."

"Whatever I wanted to know came to me. It was all explained with perfect clarity," Sifu added.

I thought that this seemed like a spiritual experience of 'the medium is the message'.

That night, the luminous body state continued until 11 p.m. Sifu's experience, the light, the energy, and the information were all one and the same thing. When he tried to locate his body, he was aware only of the light still shining, and the information itself. After that it slowly faded away, and by 11 p.m. he was back into himself.

"The Mantra of the Gold-Body energy also came about during the night of the revelation. I was given the explanation of the Mantra itself, but I didn't know how to go about doing it. I still wasn't clear about how to practice with the Mantra. So I didn't bother about it."

"Ah," I thought, "Sounds that meant incredible, purified energy."

The next day the Mantra returned. At first, it seemed to recur in his mind, and then the source of the Mantra shifted outside from his body to somewhere around him. Next, the same chant appeared to come from within, and finally, he heard it coming from everywhere.

"The Mantra just kept repeating itself endlessly. In fact it was disturbing, because I did not know how to deal with it. The moment I wanted to forget and not participate, the Mantra would come in," Sifu said.

The whole day at work, the Mantra kept repeating itself, flowing on its own.

"That night, during my meditation, the insight came that the Mantra should be recited from the abdomen. The energy continued for about three days, and further information came naturally about how to meditate."

Earlier, after the preliminary initiation, Sifu had not seemed to understand thoroughly about the spontaneous healing movements.

"I just felt I had to move. When I did this or that during treatment, people also moved in response. But I didn't understand movements," Sifu recalled.

During the night of the Golden Light, he felt complete clarity about what he had to do, and about the energy phenomena. Today, whenever he is faced with a question about energy and meditation, he seemed to know what to say without forethought, and this came from the revelation itself.

Too much had happened too suddenly for Sifu to remember concretely whether all the CFQ knowledge came that night. One thing was certain. Since the revelation, whatever information or response he needed, invariably the answer or action that comes is spontaneous and crystal clear.

In a single golden night, a whole system of knowledge was brought in. He had become the Tao itself. Sifu had been initiated into a special rare state that the Ancients called, the '*Stillness of Heart*', in which one sees and interprets things as they are.

He said, "Sometimes, it is described as the state where one is, 'not thinking and not, not thinking.'"

Knowledge comes not from external sources or acquisition, but is derived from an intuitive wisdom manifested as "instinctive knowledge". Sifu's luminous metamorphosis and attainment seem to be what I had been searching for. He had described a connection with the Golden Light that I felt came from cultivating Heart energy. Here was an 'in vivo' model and a way to realize ancient truths which had been lost in the mists of time.

The Meaning of 'CFQ'

It was getting close to 10 p.m., and hunger pangs led to a routine but knotty choice that typically indulgent Penangites encounter nightly. Penang is famed for her rich, and spicy culinary arts and there is no place like it in Asia for outdoor food. This nightly spectacle is locally known as 'hawker food' heaven. It is a veritable plethora of heavenly aromas.

Sifu drove me in his Isuzu Trooper to Gurney Drive, one favorite site that I remembered. It faced the sea, once guarded by now ornamental cannons on what was left of 19th century Fort Cornwallis, the spot where Francis Light had the historic landing on the island. An endless selection of food stalls along the pedestrian sidewalk came alive after sunset.

But eating was not uppermost in my mind, nor did the throngs of people, sights, food smells, and sounds distract me. It was here that Sifu, in answer to my query, described the abbreviation 'CFQ' to be *'Chaoyi Fanhuan Qigong'* and satisfied part of my 'energy food' appetite.

"The word, *Chaoyi* means," Sifu said, "supra-mental, super-conscious or psychic; so CFQ meditation is supposed to develop a superfine 'Gold-Body' energy.

"The word, *Fanhuan* means rejuvenation, and so another purpose of CFQ is to rejuvenate the body to alleviate disease and aging. The term 'Qigong' is the art of developing energy (qi) and mind training."

Put together, CFQ was a means of developing and using primordial Tao energy for the prevention of and recovery from disease, and the rejuvenation of body, mind, and spirit. It was becoming clearer to me that the meditation could accomplish much more than what people normally would expect to get from regular Qigong.

I recalled seeing, on a wall facing the entrance of the Center, large scrolls with calligraphy of Sifu's poem about meditation. I sensed then that the purpose of CFQ went beyond the physical realm. Pulling out a translation of the poem that he had given to me earlier, I read the last three lines out loud:

Without uncertainty, hindrance, and Unbounded
Arise excellent Wisdom, excellent Realization
Excellent Suchness.

As we walked along the Esplanade lined with a thousand aromas challenging my senses, Sifu added that an integral part of meditation was the use of the 'Mantra' of the Gold-Body energy as I had already observed. He explained that in general, mantras were short and specific verses that were chanted because of their inherent intent toward some objective. They were analogous to phrases used in greeting or wishing people we meet with our good intentions, or prayers used to invoke blessings.

"Of course, good thoughts generate finer or good vibrations."

But, he stressed, "What is good is very subjective. It differs among individuals. A person may think that what he is thinking is good but it may not be necessarily good for others. Good but selfish thoughts can be very dense. Moreover, given the fact that we are so bogged down by dense vibrations and bad energies, having one good thought is accompanied by plenty of bad ones," Sifu doubted.

Thus, it is difficult to think of something that is specifically good and maintain that thought for any length of time.

"In CFQ, to represent goodness we think of the Mantra," he explained.

"What is the meaning of the Gold-Body Mantra?" I queried.

"The Mantra is made of three words commonly used in Oriental literature to describe anything that has Purity, Perfection, and Beauty. These qualities are always combined in the phrase. When used for our purpose, their meaning relates them naturally to everything that is pure, good, and compassionate, and anything that comes from truth, justice, beauty, and perfection. These qualities are implied.

"Good thoughts generate good vibrations and good vibrations are what we essentially need to melt away the dense forces and frequencies."

I recalled, "*A thing of beauty is a joy forever.* Or as Shelley wrote, '*Beauty is truth; Truth Beauty; That is all ye know on earth and all ye need to know.*'"

I surmised that the Mantra referred to pure energies of 'Metta', or Golden Compassionate Love.

He felt that for the time being it was best not to publicize the Mantra. The Mantra should not be taught to any person who had not learned the way of CFQ meditation.

"This required an initiation, a crucial, direct transmission of energy that is exchanged by the mentor to the student."

Sifu added, "The Mantra is to be repeated silently and in the most relaxed way while doing meditations. It is unnecessary to dwell on the meaning of the Mantra, nor should one visualize it. Since the surfacing and dissolving of tension forces during meditation give rise to stray thoughts and images, repeating the Mantra naturally casts out the tension forces to detach from them.

"Besides," he reaffirmed, "the act of repeating the Mantra itself ensures that we are aware of our vital vibrations, or Spirit, at all times."

The energy Mantra acted as a bridge for the meditator to access and use cosmic energy. Repetition increased the Mantra's power. In addition to using the Mantra during meditation, one should gradually repeat it any time or in any activity.

"The Mantra also enables the meditator to naturally tune in to the vibrations of other practitioners as the uniformity in the rate of vibration allowed the purified energy of each practitioner to converge into a unified field."

Energy Principles in CFQ Meditation

As I returned to the Center the following day, I felt it was time to review what was quintessential about CFQ. We met again to talk, this time at a cafeteria in the luxurious Golden Sands Hotel. We headed to an isolated corner with a view of the golden sunlit beach. Sifu began by saying that the meditation dealt with ultimate relaxation to regain perfection and what that involved.

A person's mental-behavioral state and health status are shaped by past actions, deeds, and their resultant effects. This is nature's law of causality or cause and effect, in a word, 'karma'.

One's past karma would be charged with the memory of its creation, as is one's experiences in life which are largely created by the memory in the energy. Karma, then, is not a consequence of luck, fate, or chance. Neither did it have anything to do with an omnipotent Creator sitting in judgment of man's deeds and actions.

Sifu said, "Karma is simply one's inherent tension energy and memories that obey the natural laws of energy.

"Everything that happens to a person," he explained, "has already taken place in the karmic energy patterns that the individual has created and become attached to the body."

This is the very cause of aging, disease, and death as the physical mechanisms of the body were prevented from its proper functioning.

"Karma," I gathered, "is the invisible 'super-glue' that bonds our past with our current lives. Karma also sets the trends that are predictive of what can happen in our future lives."

Sifu called his karma-cleansing method *'the method of ultimate relaxation,'* that is the only effective way to dissolve and flush away tension forces.

"It is the ultimate letting-go technique. By letting go, the body would not be deprived of energy, but filled with purer energy of fine vibrations. That's the Gold-Body radiant energy."

He affirmed that CFQ practice went beyond physical and mental health. "In the advanced stage of meditation, the purpose of cultivation was *the luminous, weightless, bodiless state of expanded consciousness, a state known as being One with the Tao,*" Sifu declared.

"This was precisely how the word 'Qigong' came into being. 'Qi' is not merely breath as it is normally interpreted, but the word is a metaphor for air, that symbolizes what advanced cultivators experienced as the non-existence of self.

"One feels so joyous and relaxed, and as light as thin air."

"So," I mused, "perhaps CFQ is a means to 'lighten-up' until one literally shines with a golden hue."

Sifu's notions reminded me of what the Buddha teaches about *Prajna-paramita* or the way of intuitive wisdom.

Meditation was also meant to develop self-healing. Healing was a process of getting rid of diseases, through ridding the body of dense, karmic-forming tension forces.

"In so doing," he pronounced, "we also free ourselves of the forces that bring undesirable conditions to us. In other words, we get healthier. Prolonged practice enables us to be able to heal others. Rejuvenation is also a benefit of practice."

However, he cautioned that things were not altogether rosy. Everything that the practitioner worked on, including old health problems that seemed to have been cured, would resurface. This was frightening, given that we had so many problems before, and in an average adult, everything was already in the deteriorated state. Repairing the body often entailed suffering.

"For those who were willing to take the challenge *such sufferings are nothing compared to the reward we will get,*" Sifu said.

He assured that, "After three years of practice, the practitioner may move into the legendary stage called *hatching and bone-changing,* a transforming marker toward cultivating the Gold-Body state."

This aspiration was described in Taoist lore, but few contemporary methods had claimed success.

Sifu expressed confidence that this goal should occur naturally to practitioners. He again cautioned that this was a state of tremendous pain to go through. But after this breakthrough, a person could be truly considered as an advanced cultivator.

"Eventually," he smiled confidently, "more and more people will join in cultivating CFQ. We literally see that this luminous energy is vibrated outward and it affects people and the surrounding. It affects the world. As it goes on, more will move in."

At last, I thought that I had seen for myself a contemporary way of cultivating health and spiritual awakening, characterized by cosmic consciousness and instinctive knowledge. All along, my intuition about the meaning of the Golden Light had paved the way and shaped the events that have led me back to South-East Asia and Penang.

This transforming mission now appeared in the realm of the possible. But I felt that it was still no more than a remote possibility. Another piece of the puzzle had to fall into place. I was scheduled to continue on my itinerary, this time to Burma, where I hoped I could gain a deepening of personal insights, and an immersion in the origins of ancient truths that I felt were missing thus far. But these truths were somehow very much linked to Sifu's healing approach.

I would go with my wife, Pat, who had arrived in Penang the day before. That night, Sifu dropped into our hotel to greet her as she had requested some healing from him. She had bad lower back pain and insomnia for the past few days.

He asked Pat to sit comfortably on the edge of a chair, and began his energy transmission treatment. He began to move his arms and soon, she started to sway forward and sideways. After a few minutes, her limp arms slid off her lap, and her neck began to droop sideways. Her legs stretched out as the feet were raised off the ground. As I watched, her legs straightened out parallel to the carpeted floor, and at right angles from her torso. Some force was pulling and almost levitating her off the chair. Then her figure stopped moving.

Looking back on what Sifu had said about CFQ treatment, I knew that he was dealing with the detrimental forces within her body. Pat's body movements were simply the way that the dense energies were moving out from her body. He had used the Mantra of Golden Light to detach and to define the healing energy developed, to radiate 'Metta', or the beneficial and loving energies, to drive out the tension forces.

He placed his hands on her shoulders for a few seconds, ending with some slapping motions. I could see that Pat was looking drowsy, and could barely keep her eyes open. She mumbled some excuses about calling it a night, and flopped into the bed fast asleep. Sifu extended good wishes for a safe journey. I said I would stay in touch with him when I returned to Canada.

The next morning, Pat woke up looking fresh and said she had not had such a sound and deep sleep for weeks. We were ready to move on.

5

The Fabulous Golden Peninsula

Traveling to Burma was a long-cherished wish, first stirred during childhood in Penang, when my mother told tales about her spending seven years of her childhood in Rangoon, before being taken back to the ancestral village in China. The Burmese connection gained momentum when Pat inadvertently traced the whereabouts of her grandmother's relatives who lived in Burma two generations ago.

But first, we stopped over in Chiengmai, in northern Thailand, to visit friends for a few days. A short distance away, across the Golden Triangle, lay Burma, but this part of the border was sealed to foreign nationals. The usual so-near-yet-so-far feeling returned, but this time I could enter Burma legally, by flying to the official gateway city, Yangon, or Rangoon as we know it. In Burma, I would be able to see for myself and learn more about the Buddhist roots of CFQ meditation and its Golden Light.

Landing in Rangoon airport was a shocker–conditions quickly reminded me of a childhood time in colonial Malaya in the 1940's. Despite 50 years of sovereignty, Rangoon, a decaying city of four million, had made few efforts to improve or even maintain its appearance since the British left in 1948. Incredibly, everything had come to a standstill, and Rangoon rests in a acute state of decay and pervasive neglect, an anomaly that is totally unlike the economic miracles common in South-East Asia today.

But I was in Burma for a singular reason, and there was no place like it in the world. I wanted to discover the fabulous *'Suvannabhumi,'* the legendary Golden Peninsula, chronicled by one of the mightiest philosopher sovereigns in history. He was Asoka, the first emperor of a unified northern India who renounced warfare and converted to Buddhism in the 3rd century B.C.

Asoka was born a little over a hundred years after the death of Alexander the Great and was, like him, one of the greatest and fiercest conquerors in history. In 250 B.C., he proclaimed his universal peace mission from his imperial capital in Pataliputra City that was also close to the site of the Buddha's enlightenment. He initiated the world-wide transmission of the Buddha's teachings which amounted to a humanitarian revolution and the equivalent of a Bill of Rights for all.

One of the earliest of nine missions of elder monks sent by the Emperor to spread the *Dharma*, or the teachings of the enlightened Buddha, was carried eastward to the Golden Peninsula, which scholars today identify as a region stretching from present-day Burma and Thailand, to the easternmost corners of the Indochina sub-continent. Evidence of the existence of early golden kingdoms in distant lands westward from India have survived through numerous stone inscriptions engraved on rocks and pillars edified in numerous ancient sites.

There was much exchange between ancient Greek and early Buddhist thought and philosophy. A great patron of Buddhism in India, some fifty years after Asoka's death, was the saintly, Buddhist Greek King Menander, ruler of the Bactrian kingdom in Central Asia in present day Afghanistan. Through the influence of Greek kings and monks in Gandhara, there appeared for the first time, the making of images of the Golden Sage with the countenance of the sun-god Apollo.

By this time, toward the beginning of the Christian era, two forms of Buddhism flourished side by side in India–*Theravada*, and a new movement, *Mahayana*. Through Asoka, Theravada developed into the Southern Buddhist culture of present-day Southeast Asian countries. Mahayana, from India, became a Northern movement as it spread to Central Asia and further to China during the reign of Emperor Mingti (58-75 A.D.).

The Golden Chalice

Our first day in Rangoon was spent in joyous reunion embracing and discovering our newly found family members. It was a homecoming of family that had been separated at birth and came together after living individual lifetimes spanning several generations and continents.

As twilight descended cooling the air, Uncle U Maung, the patriarch of the Burmese family, instructed us to don simple native sarongs to walk barefooted to enter the Golden Pagoda, or the *Shwe Dagon*, perhaps the most impressive Buddhist shrine and living monument in the world. Even from a distance, the magnificent magical pagoda, situated on a hill, dominated the skyline with the glimmer of pure gold.

According to legends, the sacred site dated back 2,500 years, from the time of Asoka but frequent earthquakes meant that the ancient pagoda had been built and rebuilt many times. However, inscriptions dating from the 11th century recorded the visits of the Kings of Pagan, from the first Burman kingdom. The golden dome rose 326 feet from its base, built on a gigantic 14-acre platform which itself was like a small temple city.

Entering the southern entrance, the stairway is flanked by a pair of grinning leogryphs, mythological animals that are half-lion, half-griffin. We climbed a wide, two-lane stairway which was more like a bazaar.

I walked clockwise around the towering, glowing Shwe Dagon and at each turn, there was an incredible cluster and assortment of smaller, ornate pagodas with golden spires, statues, ornately designed temples, mysterious images, and countless dazzling shrines.

Yet, touched by the golden light of the main pagoda, they all seemed to fit together in a surrealistic fashion. Meandering through the various structures, I felt an extraordinary consciousness of peace and elation, experienced on rare occasions in remembered meditative states.

I gazed through a pavilion at devotees facing 28 images representing the 28 previous incarnations of the Buddha, themselves facing the great Golden Pagoda. The marble and alabaster statues all represented the same consciousness or energy that, in the lifetime of Prince Siddhartha, became enlightened to Buddhahood.

In Theravada doctrine, the *arhant*, or realized being, on attainment of enlightenment, enters nirvana without delay. Theravada believes in only a single historical Buddha–the enlightened Siddhartha. Mahayana believes there have been countless Buddhas before the historic one, with more to come. Hellenistic notions of Greek kings claiming to be the people's spiritual savior, and of celestial beings and gods that intervene to aid suffering humanity, were probably reinforced by the Buddhist concept of the *Bodhisattva*.

This is an enlightened, bodiless being, whose selflessness is embodied in the vow not to cross over into Nirvana, until all beings are liberated. Some Bodhisattvas were named after Olympian gods who were added to the Mahayanist Buddhist pantheon. A Mahayana believer invokes blessings by simply reciting a mantra of the name of a favored celestial Bodhisattva. Mahayana forecast that the next Buddha to be born on earth, in the remote future, is named *Matreiya*.

In Buddhism, rebirth is an evolutionary process that continues through myriad states of spiritual development until entry into Nirvana. This is the ultimate goal which is a return to the One, or cosmic consciousness, ending rebirth.

In Buddhist thought, the energy that is transformed from birth to birth is analogous to a lighted candle, which just before being snuffed out, lights a fresh candle. Only some sort of transformed energy is perpetuated and that continues in rebirth. In keeping with the continuum of Buddhist cosmic energy, stars also expire in a similar way. Stars expand, brighten, and burn out to collapse in red dwarfs or black holes to explode all over again.

The Enlightened Sage, however, taught that every being is part of the whole, but there is no part of a being or any aspect of a personal identity that can be called the soul. The world of becoming is made of shadowy forms without any substance, and is merely a virtual reality.

The only permanent reality and truth is the state of enlightenment, or Buddhahood, the ultimate goal that everyone eventually attains. Or in quantum energy terms, all matter, after countless eons of time, converts into pure energy or consciousness.

Karma is central to rebirth as well as explaining all changes that take place in life. Karma is the universal law of causation such that every cognition, behavior, action, and deed produce concomitant effects or results. Each person is, alone, responsible for what happens in his or her life. Since causes and effects are endless, and energy is indestructible, they can be played out in this life as well as future ones.

It dawned on me that the mystery of karma in one's life, stars, galaxies, and perhaps the universe, could be understood in energy terms. Sifu's CFQ way could well be the answer. Furthermore, since each being is part of the whole, every action of each part affects the whole. So individual karma impacts collective karma, which in turn influences the individual.

Indeed karma keeps the wheel of life turning, and the world going around. The Golden Sage taught that through the wheel of Dharma (his teachings of karmic cleansing by removing the defilements of craving, greed, fear and ignorance of who we are), the person becomes emancipated and free of karma. The liberated person experiences the wisdom of cosmic heart perfection and awakens to the Pure Heart energy.

"Enlightenment in human existence," I thought, "comes through the cultivation of a karmic cleansing practice to be free of karma accumulated in every cycle of rebirth."

For the moment, I felt that it was important to connect with what I saw and all that I experienced in the midst of the Golden Pagoda. The devotees sat with feet tucked sideways on the tiled platform, with radiant, rapturous faces, and prayerful hands touching together. Hundreds of tiny, ancient bells were delicately tingling and chiming in the gentle breeze. The whole uplifting scene felt like being suspended in some huge baroque theater, with a philharmonic orchestra moving in unison under a maestro playing heavenly rapturous music.

The Shwe Dagon is indeed a most precious, almost living, wonder of the world, that is a splendorous monument to the eternal grandeur of the human spirit. Since its humbler beginnings in antiquity, succeeding Burmese kings had added and improved on the fabulous pagoda. Over the past five centuries, Burmese royalty had donated tons of gold, and thousands of precious stones.

The pagoda's solid form is built up of several enormous parts rising first in terraces, starting from a square base which elevates to circular upper elements. Going beyond the bell-shaped mid-section, the massive structure displays moldings and bands of lotus-shaped petals, topped by a banana bud before reaching the seven-tiered umbrella fringed by hundreds of tiny 'hti' or bells. The uppermost tier itself is covered with hanging gold and silver bells and jeweled ornaments.

The entire pagoda is sheathed in gold leaf and the lotus and banana bud portion are studded with a colossal 21,000 bricks of solid gold.

"That alone is literally looking at a billion dollars," I noted.

Above the *hti*, is a jeweled vane resting on a hollow golden orb with 10,000 diamonds, rubies and sapphires. The topmost vane with its flag turns with the wind. Finally, the orb is tipped with a single, gigantic 76-carat diamond.

I realized that here in one immense and spectacular sacred site, the Light of Perfection that shone through the ages in the Golden Peninsula continues to manifest its living presence.

I stood still to take in and savor the unbounded energy of the Shwe Dagon soaring and merging into the darkened sky above. It struck me that this wondrous energy that I felt breezing through me must be one and the same as the Golden Light experienced by Sifu in his initiation into the Gold-Body State.

But something was missing from the whole experience in the Shwe Dagon. The site contained more history than I could absorb clearly when so condensed. To know timelessness, I needed to see and trek, as it were, the interplay of the phenomenal world recounted in slower motion separated by time and space. In this sense, something is lost when a spectacular masterpiece of antiquity, to cover the blemishes of aging, has to be refurbished too often.

Whatever sublime energies and beliefs had been awakened thus far, I felt that I would benefit from connecting with ancient sites in their natural state. I figured that a lot more lay ahead of us.

There were still two other distinguished places that had to be visited outside of Rangoon. We received some instructions from Uncle Maung. He gave us his business card that we could refer to for introductions during our travels up-country where the family had tea plantations. On the card, I saw the plantation logotype showing a tea-cup besides the words, *Golden Chalice*.

Pagan: Ancient Kingdom Ruins

Our first stop was to the deserted city of Pagan in central Burma. Pagan was the first mighty Burman kingdom, established in the early 9th century long after the decline of the *Suvannabhumi* period. The ascension of King Anawratha, considered the greatest of all Burmese kings, to the Pagan throne in 1044 A.D., inspired the Golden Age of Burmese history.

Over the next two hundred years, a string of Pagan kings constructed and glorified the fabulous capital city, with each king vying to out-do his predecessor by adding even more dazzling temples. Shortly after the imminent onslaught of Kublai Khan's Tartar hordes, the kingdom collapsed, and Burma broke up into small, weak states. Marco Polo was at the great Khan's court, and witnessed the preparations for war with Pagan.

The deserted city of Pagan is truly amazing, and one of the world's archaeological wonders. It lies on a dry flat plain, that stretches back from a curve in the Irrawaddy River. Its dry climate ensures that the near thousand-year-old ruins are unusually well preserved.

Even though Pagan had been abandoned for many centuries, the tropical jungles had not reclaimed it, unlike the famed *Angkor Wat* ruins in neighboring Cambodia. Not only is Pagan better preserved from the decaying influence of jungles than any ancient monuments anywhere else in South-East Asia, she has some of the finest structures ever built. Within an area of 25 square miles, there are the collective relics of 5,000 temples and pagodas. But most, while not damaged by weather or time, have become no more than decaying heaps of reddish stones, long ago plundered or flattened by earthquakes.

In every direction that you look, stand scores of pagodas, and temples of different sizes and shapes. It is as if all the great cathedrals of medieval Europe were rounded up and miraculously relocated and reassembled all together in one spot. All my senses were excited to produce a vision of uncomparable splendor.

We had found accommodations at the Thiripitsaya Hotel, close to the exotic Pagan ruins. The bungalows and main lodge area, built during British colonial times, turned out to be a fitting base to explore the temples. Hla Maung, the tour guide we engaged for the next three days, had arrived, and we were to get around the various Pagan sites by horse cart.

As we sat on his coach, he rattled off, in English, a sampling of temples that we would see, Burmese names that sounded to me as pleasing as the tingling bells that hung from the pagoda spires—*Mingalazedi, Shwezigon, Salomon, Mahabodhi, Gawdawpalin, and Htilominlo.*

Hla Maung was an excellent guide who spoke an Indian-accented English. He pointed out the various styles and shapes of the monuments–a blend of Mon, Indian, Chinese, and Burman. Pagodas were solid structures, while temples were hollowed to allow the pilgrims to enter a dark cool interior and meditate before the image of the Golden Light. Indeed, Pagan temple interiors resemble towering Gothic cathedrals.

Pagan's most famous and well-preserved monument, and also my favorite, is the magnificent and venerable Ananda Temple, named after the Buddha's most beloved disciple and cousin. This architectural masterpiece was constructed at the beginning of the second Millennium, and is one of the region's few remaining active golden temples.

The temple architecture is North Indian, and has a colossal, central and almost solid square base, shaped like a gigantic wedding cake. On top, are diminishing terraces, golden spires, and a 180-foot, bell-shaped, gilded pagoda of Burmese origin.

The enormous white bulk resembles a snow-clad mountain, standing like a solitary peak with her golden spire gleaming, catching the last rays of the sun. Ananda's appearance is symbolic of the sacred mythical Mount Meru in the Himalayas, said to be the center of the Universe, and the temple's dark, cave-like interior hollowed out of the solid base is suggestive of the glorious, living Void of Nirvana. Enshrined within each niche of the enormous cube of central masonry, are four colossal standing Buddhas, each 30 feet high.

I entered each one of the sacred caves, roofed by 40-foot radiating arches, gazing at the exalted faces of the Enlightened Ones, each suffused by an enigmatic half-smile radiating beneficence toward the four cardinal points. The only light came high above, through narrow openings to the exterior that allowed a focused beam of light descending to penetrate into the heart of the mountain-cave temple.

It was through Sanskrit, the language of ancient India, and its vernacular dialect, *Pali,* that Buddhism spread to the Golden Peninsula. Indian Sanskrit is a descendent language of the Proto Indo-Europeans who first emerged from the steppes of the Caucasus in southern Russia around 5500 B.C. Their language is also the root language of Greek, Latin, Celt, and almost all European languages.

A millennium and a half later, their descendants, the Kurgans, set out westward to Europe, while another Caucasian branch moved east to the Indus Valley. The latter's descendants eventually controlled the main valleys of the northern half of ancient India. One of them was born as Sakyamuni or Siddhartha Gautama–the historic Buddha and the Light of Asia.

The death blow for Buddhism in India came in 1199 A.D., when Moslem Turks and Afghans swept down the Ganges valley sacking the great monasteries, universities and shrines, which were the last remaining strongholds of Buddhist culture. Pagan also became a center of Buddhist learning with the arrival of refugee Indian scholars from the famed Nalanda University, the cultural heart of Buddhism. Fifty years earlier, Thatbinnyu Temple, the tallest monument was erected in Pagan. We had kept visiting this 200-foot temple to the last, since the ancient site provided the ultimate vision. It was the ideal spot to watch the sun set over the pagoda, as the dusty plains lining the Irrawaddy River, turned a golden red. Thatbinnyu had a shape of two gigantic cubes, piled one on top of the other. We climbed a maze of steps that snaked their way to exterior steps before entering the upper floor leading to a huge seated sublime Buddha facing east.

Here, the symmetry of four colossal Buddhas in the Ananda Temple was replaced with one single, gigantic sculpture located centrally in the Thatbinnyu Temple. The lower roofs are flat, providing usable terraces outside. A set of internal, claustrophobic stairs leads to the uppermost terrace outdoors, to provide a spectacular view below the entire temple site overlooking the river with distant hills beyond.

Waiting at the terraced roof for the sun to set over the hills, Hla Maung pointed at a Burmese pagoda or *stupa*, rising up from the red soil. He narrated the story of its symbolic meaning.

"In 543 B.C., during the time of the Buddha's imminent death after 45 years of spiritual teaching, weeping disciples asked who would guide them after he entered Nirvana."

The Eternal Buddha then described how they could remember him, and from this the various components of the pagoda took shape.

Taking his coarse robe, he folded it into a perfect cube, and placed it on the ground. Next, he placed in the middle of the cube, his inverted begging bowl, and vertically over it, his walking stick with the bottom end touching the bowl.

Standing up, the Golden Teacher referred to his five fingers holding up the stick, as the five virtues to remember him by.

"These are, honoring the Dharma teachings, the *Sangha* (or monastic order), one's parents, teachers, and all living beings."

He had formed the familiar Burmese stupa, using his folded robe, inverted bowl, walking stick, and hands. Finally, as a crowning touch, he held his umbrella over the stupa to signify taking refuge in him.

That same night, we returned to the Ananda Temple. This was the beginning of the Buddhist 'Lent' a prolonged period of spiritual retreat that begins on a full moon to commemorate the Buddha's first sermon some 2,500 years ago. The temple was built to signify the endless wisdom of the Buddha. The full moon of July cast a magical light over the sandy road to the temple grounds.

Golden hues seemed to emanate from every direction. Soon I felt a breeze that stirred and tingled through my entire body. I felt light and buoyant and could not help smiling in elation as the star-lit silhouette of the Ananda pagoda became clear.

Two ancient-looking temple caretakers, a couple, allowed us entry into a small shrine housing an exquisite jade Buddha, in the midst of the most beautiful wall murals painted. We knew from Hla Maung that the old couple were renowned for their skill in traditional Burmese massage. That night, we were their only clients. Going back to the hotel in the creaking horse cart, riding leisurely over the sandy trail, and passing temple shadows lit only by a bright full moon, that was a perfect ending to a perfect day.

The Road Back from Mandalay

Much more happened in the week that was spent away from Rangoon. Mandalay, Maymyo, and ancient deserted cities, long romanticized by Kipling, Orwell, and Hollywood movies, lay ahead. We rented a car and a driver-guide to seek out many historic places to enrich appreciation of Burma and her heritage. Before moving on from Pagan, we had one final day trip to Mount Popa, 30 miles away.

This Burmese Golden Mountain is the home of 36 'nats', Burmese magical spirits, whose life-size statues are displayed in the Popa village at the foot of the mountain. When King Anawratha first propagated Buddhism to Burmese, as was common in other converted countries, local beliefs were assimilated in this most tolerant of religions. The Golden Metta became the 37th 'nat', but one that the Burmese love.

Then there was an hour-long trek up the precipitous peak of Mount Popa to a Shangri-la complex of pagodas, monasteries, and shrines. Right on the craggy mountain top, which provided a breathtaking view of the flat plain below, we joined the huge crowds heading toward a large monastery. Seeing the bright decorations and noisy crowd, I assumed that some festival was under way.

"No, you are lucky," Hla Maung explained.

There was a funeral service going on for the revered abbot of the monastery, and this was regarded as a wonderful, propitious event for all who participated. I wanted to protest, but before I could say a word, a space on the rows of occupied benches was already provided for us. We silently sat down, joining hundreds seated in the roofed courtyard.

What happened next was totally unlike what is normally expected in a Western funeral service. Strangely, people did not look somber, sad, or teary during the eulogy which paid homage to the deceased abbot. The colorful eulogy was delivered by a beautifully costumed woman, singing praises and dancing on a stage, with a full orchestra of Burmese musical instruments.

An open casket, covered with a flimsy veil, was placed at the front below the stage. But it was brightly decorated as if it were part of a festival procession. And that was what happened after the stage show. Monks lifted the pall to transfer it to an inner chamber, with the crowd following and forming a long procession.

The final part of the service involved viewing the body of the abbot. Pandemonium broke out as it was practically impossible for the massive throng of people to file into the small room in an orderly fashion. Yet, as soon as they saw that we were foreign visitors, they gave way to us. We found ourselves escorted into the chamber, and to my consternation, invited to snap photographs of the casket close-up.

As I hesitated, one of the monks said, "No, it's not offensive to us, and taking our master's photograph will bring you much blessings and good karma."

Over the long ride back to Pagan on the back of a truck, I ruminated on what I had seen and felt. The abbot's face looked very old, but surprisingly his disciples had told me that he was about sixty. I recalled what Sifu had said about how accumulated noxious energy leads to premature aging and death.

Monks and meditators practicing acquisition methods could draw in and store tremendous energy in the navel 'dan tian' and chakras in the solar plexus, and forehead. Drawing inward such dense mental or etheric energies into the body could strengthen paranormal abilities, after spending years practicing this way.

"But in the end," I recalled Sifu saying, "they would lead to attachment, unwillingness to let go, and would be karmic forming. Gold-Body energy, on the other hand, is of fine vibration, of the highest quality, and with the lowest risk of side effects. CFQ believes in pure, Gold-Body energy to transform ourselves into the *dan-tian* of the cosmic."

Burma's long history can lay claim to upholding the ancient wisdom taught by the Buddha. In India, three months after the '*parinirvana*' or passing away of the Enlightened Sage, 500 *arhants* or enlightened disciples, held the First Council to protect and preserve the purity of the legacy, with Ananda leading, and reciting the unwritten Dharma teachings. About 200 years later, the Third Council was held under the patronage of Asoka. When Buddhism expired in India, future councils were held in countries outside of India where the Dharma had taken root, in Sri Lanka, Burma, and Thailand. The Fifth Great Council was held in 1871 in Mandalay, the Burmese capital established by King Mindon. In 1954, Buddhists from all over the world met in Rangoon for the Sixth Great Council to celebrate the 2,500th anniversary of the golden Buddha's demise.

Mandalay is the Burmese heartland, the 'Golden City' built by the last dynasty before it ended with the British annexation in 1886. I liked easygoing Mandalay a lot more than Rangoon. A spectacular view of the city of Mandalay can be seen from the summit of the 770-foot high Mandalay Hill, in an otherwise flat city. Dominating the view is the huge, burnt-down Mandalay Palace, with its remaining walls, surrounded by a royal moat, and remnants of a distinctively roofed watchtower. Climbing up the hill on stone steps with a covered stairway provides a pleasant stroll, with many resting points.

Close to the top, a huge golden image, with one outstretched arm, marks a spot where the Buddha and his disciple Ananda were said to have paused on Mandalay Hill. In a lower temple, is housed the 'Peshawar Buddha Relics', three bones of the Buddha. The relics were authenticated by King Asoka, who had formerly enshrined them in the revered wondrous Hellenistic-designed pagoda in Peshawar.

We headed back to Rangoon, but could not resist thinking of returning, having been smitten by Mandalay with its pagoda bells tingling in the wind.

By the old Moulmein Pagoda,
lookin' lazy at the sea,
There's a Burma girl a settin',
and I know she thinks o' me,
For the wind is in the palm-trees,
and the temple-bells they say:
'Come you back, come you back to Mandalay!'

Kipling

Celestial Light

Uncle Maung met us at the dilapidated Rangoon airport. On the way home, there seemed to be heightened tension in the air, as the wide, tree-lined roads were deserted. Soon I saw, hidden close to side alleys, trucks with armed soldiers in battle fatigues.

It was July 19, a national holiday to commemorate the assassination of the martyred hero, Aung San, some fifty years earlier. But the universally detested and brutal military regime today was prepared for possible trouble and demonstrations in the streets. It highlighted the plight of the people's heroine who was under house arrest.

She was none other than Aung San Shu Chi, the martyr's daughter. Her efforts to free her people had brought world acclaim and a Nobel Peace Prize, but the regime has vowed never to give up power to the democratically elected Nobel laureate.

The repressive government had quelled all protests with brute force, killing thousands, but the soft, gentle voice of Aung San Shu Chi as she stood up in the Shwe Dagon remained a beacon of inspiration and hope. The regime has rapidly degenerated into military repression with disastrous consequences and widespread, abject poverty that even the customarily tolerant Burmese are revolting against.

A planned visit to the campus of the University of Rangoon had to be canceled. I told Uncle Maung that there was one more place I wanted to visit before leaving Rangoon. This was the famous Mahasi Meditation Center, founded by Burma's greatest meditation teacher, Mahasi Sayadaw, in the late 1940's. The famed Burmese method of insight, or Vipassana meditation, had also spread abroad to Thailand and the West.

Here at the renowned Center, I had hoped to meet some of the contemporary meditation masters. When I was introduced to the old man seated in the administrative office, he sadly reported that since the government crackdown, the resident masters had been removed. He could only provide some pamphlets of lectures by the late Mahasi. Permission was granted to wander around the two-acre Meditation Center. There were still meditation classes, as I saw some women, dressed in white, practicing mindfulness as they walked on the veranda in slow motion.

Reminiscing over all I had seen thus far, I was acutely conscious of having connected with the wisdom of the Golden Sage, and his experience of the enlightened state. In the Ancient world, that new Golden Light became a beacon that brought enlightenment to multitudes living in practically all of the major civilizations of the period–Greek, Indian, Far Eastern, and Indochinese.

It was here in the Golden Peninsula that the Light was first disseminated from its birthplace in present-day Nepal. In the Shwe Dagon and the wondrous temples of Pagan, I experienced this most precious legacy whose form and presence were so tangible that my doubting, skeptical mind had to stop denying its reality. It was, simply, pure light and golden energy that felt as close as a heart-beat away.

If the golden energy is real, I thought, so must be the energy of our physical bodies. I recollected Sifu's reminder to have an open mind toward the notion of energy.

"The energies are real, but most people have not learned how to be aware of them." Sifu stated that when dealing with energies trapped in the body system, through meditation, such energies become as physical as those that come through our sense organs. It dawned on me that the energy of sub-atomic matter that physicists studied mathematically could be personally discovered and directly experienced.

CFQ energy meditation matches the essence of what insight meditation professed. The ultimate goal in letting go is total relaxation. By using super-conscious, Gold-Body energy, as well as letting go, we remove the karmic forces of disease causation attached to us.

When impure energies are released, a joyous state of alertness, free from the bondage of physical body is attained. One's original nature, the cosmic or boundless, Golden Buddha Light, will shine through.

It was time to depart from Burma and return to Canada. At the airport, hanging on to our newly found family, we expressed fond farewells and hopes of meeting again in Burma, and elsewhere in the world. It had been two weeks of unique, and never-to-be-forgotten experiences in the heart of the Golden Peninsula.

For two thousand years, along the mighty Irrawaddy River, inspired Buddhist kings and prolific dynasties have created earthly versions of celestial visions, from the Golden Shwe Dagon, to the temples of Pagan, and the palaces of Mandalay. Journeying to Pagan had indeed connected me with a liberating energy pointing to a perfection that needs only faith and trust to pursue.

On the plane, I eased back still ruminating on some of the feelings I had about sights seen of Pagan and Burma, mingled with thoughts of the events in Penang and Sifu's Gold-Body energy state. It dawned on me that the periods of my life that were best and precious to me were spent exploring a life purpose as a seeker of enlightenment. I was filled with optimism that I had finally found that path.

Storm clouds had shrouded the ascending plane but the sunlight displayed an iridescent rainbow beyond the distant hills. Looking down from the plane, I caught one last sight of the heart of Rangoon which took my breath away and that will forever remain in my mind. I had gasped in immediate recognition when I caught a glimpse of the out-of-this-world 'stately dome' below me. Flood gates restraining one's imagination suddenly vaporized pouring forth a fantasy of wonderment, much like Coleridge's fabulous Xanadu in 'Kubla Khan.'

As I peered through the clouds, a long way down, my vision zoomed in on a gleaming golden symmetrical dot that flashed and winked in the sunlight. It was the Shwe Dagon Pagoda still visible miles below, radiating light. Then, a few seconds later, the glittering radiance was gone.

Part Three

Northern Light

6

Northwest Passage

In the spring of the following year in Canada, Sifu had accepted my invitation to come over to introduce meditation and energy healing to friends and a western audience. Personally, I thought that his presence on my home ground would stimulate further understanding of a unique, if not revolutionary approach, to meditation. For the first time, I could appreciate an energy causation model of healing and consciousness expansion. I recalled asking him to clear up some confusion about the ambiguity of the energy concept since different sources he addressed seemed to have different conflicting meanings of it. For example, both practitioners of Sifu's Gold-Body state and conventional Taoism regard energy as central in their practices.

I asked how the body's *qi* energy was different from Gold-Body energy.

"Qi is more consistent with, shall I say, the etheric component of energy," he responded.

"Etheric means it has more of the physical aspect, much like what people perceive as the aura or the subtle bio-energy around the body. It's closer to the physical, but different from mental energy that arises from thoughts. This is the common usage or interpretation of what qi means."

The Chinese term qi meant energy, but then had different terms for different types of energy. Ordinary Qigong did not clearly state what type of qi was acquired during training. CFQ is concerned with radiant cosmic energy similar to the pure energy of quantum physics, and not the other more impure forms of qi energy with specific identities.

"The Taoist word for cosmic energy is '*khun-yen qi*'. Also the cultivation of the Gold-Body state is a purification practice to best return to cosmic consciousness or pure energy."

"I am appreciative of why the Ancients use the word *qi*, instead of any other word," the Master revealed.

"Qi is the same word for air. In the advanced stage of meditation, the body becomes so relaxed that one is no longer confined to the physical body, so that one cannot even find the boundaries of the physical body. One is simply part of everything, the cosmic, and totally free. That free state, in ancient times, had no word to describe it. The closest equivalent is air, free and unrestricted."

He added, "But Qigong has been misinterpreted and misunderstood, and today people think that the purpose is to, 'absorb the pure energy from air'. I say that's all wrong."

In line with CFQ, such energy also has impurities. Certain training methods can certainly strengthen such energy fields in the body. But a problem or diseased area in the body often has a stronger magnetic field than a healthy one. So a strong field measured does not necessarily mean that a person is healthier. What is most important is balance, that is, that the energy must flow smoothly and harmoniously.

Ancient Taoist masters claimed to teach the secrets of how to be in full control of disease and aging and ultimately the 'transformation from the mortal body' and the development of the Tao or cosmic consciousness. 'Transformation' is often used to describe a magical change in terms of physical health and knowledge. The benefits include, 'return to youthful appearance', invulnerability to all diseases, supernormal feats, and healing ability. A person who has gone through such a transforming state is called an immortal *Sien*, the word for a demigod.

These claims sounded much like the alchemy studied in the Middle Ages aimed at changing base metals to gold and to discover immortality. Western alchemy had close links, through the Arabs, to China and even modern psychology. The Chinese added 'medicine' to the alchemy that was simultaneously being developed in pre-Christian times. Chinese alchemy, like traditional Taoism, sought to discover the Way of perfection and health. In European alchemy this evolved into the medieval pursuit of the philosopher's stone.

There is something archetypal in the symbolism of alchemy. Jungian psychology shows that it appealed to the basic psychological tendencies of the mind and humanity itself. Jung certainly drew from Eastern philosophical concepts and practices which he couched in Western scientific terms. For example, his notions of archetypal images, collective unconscious, and synchronicity of events were thinly disguised attempts to make the Oriental law of karma more specific and palatable to Western minds.

One could say that karma, a deeply embedded universal belief in the East, is indeed in the collective unconscious of people from India to the Far East. Jung broke away from his mentor Freud, because of his belief in Man's inherent, flawed nature. For Jung, the human psyche is perfectible because we are an integral aspect of the cosmic energy of perfection. This would be the ultimate archetype of a universal collective unconscious.

Eastern spiritual paths and meditation practices aim to experience the Tao or the way to the state of cosmic consciousness. I had long thought that these were nothing more than myths and folklore.

But Sifu describes it as a state of Golden Light, of *'seeing oneself, free from the physical body, shining into the Eternal.'*

From this Gold-Body energy state, one accesses 'instinctive knowledge,' as opposed to ordinary externally imposed knowledge, dissolving into the cosmic self and becoming part of the storehouse of eternal knowledge and intuitive wisdom. The journey that had surfaced thus far gave me a glimpse of that Gold-Body luminous state of transparence.

Sifu was to spend three weeks with me in July of 1995. This was to be his first trip and exposure to North America. Our collaborative efforts would have a kind of yin-yang balance. When I first met him on my return to the East in Penang, he was my student in Western psychological science. When he came to the West, arriving in Canada, I would become his student in Eastern healing practices. I am a Western-trained academic, well versed in research and theory, while he is self-taught, and experienced in Eastern esoteric healing skills.

I was also curious to see how the energy he brought would influence people here, and how well his Gold-Body energy transmission techniques in healing would work in a completely unfamiliar territory. He was also curious about how receptive people here would be to his system of healing and meditation.

I was finally to get my wish to receive further instruction and exposure to this new perspective. At stake, was Western credibility, my own cultivation and advancement in Gold-Body meditation, whose principles I had yet to fully grasp and whose health benefits were still unclear.

Canadian Loyalist Valley

The plane from Boston landed at Fredericton Airport. As a line of passengers formed a queue for immigration, I caught sight of the slim and fit form of Sifu, who flashed a broad smile in recognition. The Customs clearance process took longer than usual despite his carrying only a tote bag and a medium size suitcase. Perhaps the female Customs officer was suspicious of someone unfamiliar with a sun-darkened complexion carrying a Malaysian passport, and coming from the region where illicit drugs could be transported from the Golden Triangle.

As she began her routine questions and glanced at his shining eyes and guileless smile, she faltered, her hands trembled and she dropped her pen. She looked excited and nervous, and I wondered whether Sifu was teasing her energy in some way. Unable to continue, she abruptly passed him to a male counterpart who took him to another room and shut the door.

It was another 25 minutes before he emerged, and walked through the exit where I was anxiously waiting. He smiled to reassure me, and without any sign of annoyance, explained that besides interrogation, Customs had done a strip-body and luggage search before letting him go.

"They were just doing their job," Sifu commented to dismiss the unpleasant incident.

This was hardly the reception I had in mind for his first trip to Canada. However, travelers no longer have to suffer such personal indignities in Fredericton as international flights stopped flying here a few months after he returned to Malaysia. Perhaps he cured the malady in Fredericton's airport.

Driving home from the airport on that warm July day, we chatted about the last time we had seen each other. I told him about the family reunion in Burma and now here he was meeting me at home in Canada. I briefly described the location of Fredericton, a small town in the southern neck of the woods in picturesque New Brunswick that is a seven-hour car drive north of Boston.

I gave Sifu a brief version of the history of the province. Beginning in the early 1600's, the French from Brittany tried to establish the first European settlement in the Maritime region which they called 'Acadie', a descriptive Micmac Indian word. The Acadians enjoyed a friendly relationship with the indigenous cultures but soon the English arrived and called the territory, Nova Scotia.

Nova Scotia was sparsely populated until after the American Revolutionary War of Independence in 1776, when tens of thousands of 'Loyalists', fearing persecution, poured in from the thirteen American colonies. These were converted Americans who picked George III over George Washington.

In the spring and fall of 1783, after the British Colonial army accepted its defeat, British evacuation fleets brought 15,000 English,

Irish and Scottish Loyalists from New York City, together with remnants of the British Army, to settle in the St John River valley.

This sudden, large influx of boat people two hundred years earlier led to the creation of the province of New Brunswick out of Nova Scotia in 1784. The harbor of Saint John was linked to the fertile soil and woodlands of the interior by the St John River valley where Fredericton was one of the earliest settlements. Since its beginning, Fredericton had two distinct features—its being the capital city of New Brunswick, and the site of the University of New Brunswick, the oldest campus in Canada.

As we arrived at the doorstep of my split-entry house, my expressions of welcome were reiterated by my wife, Pat, who was waiting for us. A movement from the white birch tree in front of the house caught my eye. It was a little chickadee bird with an unusual yellow breast fluttering upward. It landed on the edge of the gabled roof, and then decided to peer down and scrutinize us as we walked underneath it.

"Thanks for your welcome," I smiled.

Pat took Sifu directly to her garden because of his avid interest in horticulture.

Over the days he spent in Fredericton, this was his favorite spot. He was delighted by the explosion of colors from the host of lilies flourishing in the garden. The day before he had left home to fly here, he noticed that among all the orchid plants in bloom, one stood out. He thought it remarkable that one of his Cattleya orchids had seven stems of exquisite yellow flowers instead of the usual three-flowered stem.

Sifu had arrived on this continent in the seventh month of the year. If these were all coincidences, it must have some meaning. Nodding, he said that in Taoist practice, 7 was a number that signified a change of state, rebirth, and completion.

"For example, a person takes 7, or 7 times 7, that is, 49 days, to be reborn into a new or different plane of existence."

"The Buddha received Enlightenment after sitting under a tree for 49 days," I recalled.

"A Taoist attempting to create a spiritual event or auspicious change always made use of multiples of 7, in terms of dates or ceremonies," Sifu added.

"Yes, and the 7-year itch was made famous by Hollywood."

"For you to mature in CFQ cultivation to become the most potent healer you can be, will also take seven years," ended Sifu.

I asked him to elaborate further about coincidences that often occurred in everyday life. For example, I would wonder about some friend whom I had not seen in years and then coincidentally, the following day would meet him.

He replied, "Once his energy field is in the vicinity, your alignment to him will manifest to 'see' your friend. At the energy level, you are already connected with others. As the energy from your friend draws physically closer and closer, it comes down to your conscious awareness. Energy is bringing it to your knowledge or awareness."

I suggested that mental thoughts and beliefs have immense energy that can influence our bodies and behaviors.

"Apparently, lots of things happen that go beyond our physical consciousness. Students come to me saying, 'Oh, last night, I had some problem and you were there!' They feel I am there, but in most of the cases, I am not aware that I was. Of course, I am aware of the energy when they practice," Sifu said.

I felt that this was just a small illustration of the notion that our energy vibrations were everywhere rather than confined to our physical bodies.

"First," he explained, "to believe in such things is to create an opening. Otherwise, right off the start, you are cut off from that possibility. You will then be unable to develop or use the energy."

"We seem to be drawn toward certain people, places, and practices repeatedly," I began.

"A possible explanation," I speculated, "is that on the energy time-scale, such re-connections remind us of who we really are, our core being."

Sifu, drawing from his own practice, referred to having a number of very profound, very real, vivid moving experiences which unfolded as a spiritual enlightenment. He explained that one's hopes, thoughts, beliefs, actions, and experiences all have mental energy components which are stored as energy forces in the whole person.

These forces form electromagnetic fields within and in the space around us. They are also connected to other energy fields, and influence physical matter and events outside our body. Under the right conditions, these forces are activated and react to external changes and connections.

"Cultivating the Gold-Body energy is a means of effectively resolving problematic situations we encounter."

Sifu cited an example, an incident that happened to Lian, a new student of his who was driving home at night in the heavy rain. Suddenly the headlights flickered, and dimmed. He panicked but decided to keep moving while figuring out what to do.

So he kept driving, determined to go all the way home. The car battery had just enough power left to keep a small glove compartment light on. Finally, he approached his house reaching the front metal gate. To his surprise it was wide open, since the gate, normally, was locked electrically. He turned the car in, and the moment he reached the end of the drive-way, the engine died. Somehow he had sensed how much energy was left and had turned the car in just in time.

"All the time he was reciting his Mantra," Sifu noted.

I silently thought about chance coincidences to account for this episode.

"Look," I said to him. "Can you explain this again? It's quite easy to accept that the mind can influence the body, heal it, get rid of pain, and so on. But how does energy affect the external, physical world?"

Sifu replied, "There is a basic assumption to understand how. For anything to happen, first things must happen energetically; then only do physical events take place. Before an event occurs, it must be attracted to us because of our energy pattern and function. In every instance, anything that happens to us, it's because of our own energy and force field within our body that creates changes in events."

Continuing, he said, "For one who practices CFQ, all these forces or energy will begin to alter. Changing these forces means that the person will create a different course of experience. Things will happen differently. The normal energy or electromagnetic forces that attract impending events are now changed to new possibilities."

Through sufficient unwinding of such forces, the person may not even be aware that problems have been prevented, since they do not develop.

"However, on hindsight, one can detect having escaped from a narrow accident. Here the person has not reached the stage of totally clearing out the problem—otherwise the near miss won't even happen. But the practitioner has reached the stage of changing it. So that's why he was able to prevent that from happening."

Some partial mishap still happens, but without any real, negative outcome. But if the energy pattern is totally unwound, nothing untoward will happen at all—not even the car breaking down as in the previous case mentioned.

I said I still did not understand clearly why unwinding would purify the energy to reduce the severity of a problem.

"O.K., say the person is supposed to meet with an accident in a month's time. By then the energy forces and the magnetic field forces have developed to create the events leading up to the accident. Now embark into CFQ practice, and the forces are weakened. Probably the person may still meet with the accident, but it's superficial, and certainly not fatal.

"Again, whatever external events that happen, even when they seem totally unconnected, they have become attracted to us because of our tension pattern. By purifying the tension, by releasing it, the denser or undesirable event will not happen."

In psychological terms, I reacted, if the person did not practice meditation, he would not have been subconsciously sensitized to the imminent changes ahead and would be less prepared to face them. The person might also attempt to set up futile defense mechanisms and roadblocks to resolving the obstacles. This in turn could worsen the problem when it occurred.

"Simply put," Sifu commented, "the body's attached forces store the seeds that have a causal relationship with future events occurring to the person. The changes that will occur in our lives have already happened at the energy level which are very much our responsibility. Everything that we think, feel, and do ultimately has some effect on our physical bodies, mind, and spirit. This is the ancient law of karma giving rise to events and which creates desirable as well as undesirable experiences happening to us."

The Energy Connection

I took Sifu for a quick tour of Fredericton, just about the tiniest provincial capital in Canada with a stable population of 45,000 within its city limits. As we crossed the old former railroad bridge on foot, we could see the most visible landmark, the historic Christ Church Cathedral. The massive stone structure, with its distinct, copper-roofed, soaring spire, was first constructed in 1845. Once inside the cathedral, one quickly feels transported into a world of serene intimacy, surrounded by the rich, interior woodworking, butternut wood paneling and the east-west light reflected from vividly colored, stained glass windows.

Friends had arrived at the house to be introduced to the Master. I told Sifu that his presence here in Fredericton was no accident. I disclosed to him that I felt that my life had established new and permanent roots in the western 'new world' since the birth of my grandchildren. They not only have my heritage, but merely looking into the depths of their wondrous eyes reveals windows into mine and their maternal ancestry, a mingling of their indigenous, Acadian, and Loyalist-Gaelic forebears.

I feel that we belong to energy clusters with still potent affinities to form a kind of 'spiritual energy family' that may extend beyond physical boundaries and the isolating separateness of space and time. Within ancestral family members, we unknowingly or unconsciously exchange energy intended for each other.

Sifu was scheduled to give a public lecture on alternative healing that Friday afternoon. This would also give those who were unable to attend the weekend workshop the opportunity to hear him talk in the Psychology Building, at the University of New Brunswick. Many local professionals attending were providers of alternative health services.

Sifu began by saying that the Eastern approach to health and exercise is very different from what is currently understood in the West. Eastern approaches emphasize relaxation and putting the body into what he described as a 'soft state' through quiet meditation.

This is in contrast to strenuous exercise–as exemplified by the Jane Fonda 'burn and sweat' style. Movement is encouraged in his health system, but this is not the same as exercise, which itself is not necessarily good for health. What has to be done is to use internal energy to make oneself unwind the tension trapped in the body.

After stating his belief of the root causes of all pain and disease, he asked for a volunteer to demonstrate his relaxation method. The woman who stepped forward was asked to sit on a low chair with her feet placed on the ground and knees apart at shoulder width.

Sifu then moved around her, speaking quietly and encouraging her to relax and make her body loose and soft. He stood behind her so that she could not see him as he slowly waved his hands and arms at her.

Although he was never closer than two feet from her, she began to sway and move as if commanded by his fingers. She too responded to him as if he was a puppeteer moving her with invisible strings. At other times, her head jerked vigorously and her breathing became more labored.

Toward the end of the exercise, she bent her body over until her head was close to the ground. When he finished, she got up firmly with a big smile, and walked back to her seat with a relaxed gait.

Karen, a nurse, stood up to explain that she had received a similar relaxation treatment from Sifu the day before. She told the audience that when she first met him, her shoulders were so tense that they felt as if they had an 'iron bar across them.' After one session, she said the pain had disappeared, she felt completely relaxed and had had the best sleep in years.

Sifu assured the audience that anyone interested can learn his technique and thus help themselves. Confirming that while CFQ relaxation training looked simple, it was in fact quite profound. Unwinding to dissolve the detrimental energies or forces to release them from the body took time. But three to six months of practice would bring noticeable results and overall improvement in health. He told the audience that he had effectively treated several thousand people over the past seven years.

Another benefit of meditation in the advanced stage, he claimed, is the ability to shift the meditator to a luminous body state with a consciousness which brings peace together with 'joyous alertness'. The consequences of achieving this state, he added, include invulnerability to disease and youthful vitality.

That evening I had a chance to ask Sifu to elaborate on an issue he brought up about meditation. He had remarked that exercise would not necessarily improve health. I pointed out that research had indicated, although not unequivocally, that people who exercise had reduced risk of heart disease as well as a greater psychological well-being. Also, as a person ages, there is a loss of muscle strength as nerves die, and muscle cells are rapidly replaced by fat cells. Consequently health deteriorates and the elderly move slowly because muscle cells react slowly.

"Exercise is thought to revive new nerve connections to regain physical mobility," I said.

Sifu responded by describing the ideal healthy state. "Ancient oriental medical texts referred to the optimal 'cotton body' texture, in which the entire body is filled with a musculature that is ever soft and loose."

That was best for blood circulation without obstructions for perfect body functioning.

"It's like cotton. It feels soft and the person feels that the body is weightless. Once the person can bring the body system to reach that stage, complete body and cell regulation is not a problem at all. There's nothing to hinder the regeneration."

I knew that Sifu was referring to the complete removal of all energy blockages in one's system, exchanging one's stale energy with the flow of Nature's pure cosmic energy. But few have achieved this optimal state since it is a long, continuous process that takes years of practice. But that was the direction and CFQ is a path to do that, he said.

"Isn't movement and exercise suggested as a way of enhancing cell growth similar to CFQ practice?" I queried.

"On the contrary," he denied.

"Vigorous muscle activity and movements, while exercising, create a kind of tension. The tension acquired prevents muscles from regenerating properly. Tension is the major risk factor that ages the cells. Sure, the muscles are there and they are meant to be moved, but meditation is effortless and there are minimal, spontaneous movements."

Sifu remarked that there was no clear correlation between strenuous exercise to either achieve or maintain health. He gave an example of a stroke patient, whose body was paralyzed and hardened. The patient went to a physiotherapist to exercise and stretch the muscles.

"I find that an emphasis on exercising muscles may make the problem worse. When the patient recovers from stroke, the muscles and limbs may be weak but they can still move. But when they exercise too hard, the limbs become hardened, very stiff, and in no time, that further limits mobility in the weakened part.

"Of course, having no activity will also increase tension and harden muscles. But, with those who were receiving treatment from me, even patients who do not engage in exercise do not have hardened paralyzed limbs, and muscles remain supple."

I was surprised to hear this perspective about exercise coming from Sifu, formerly a kung-fu and martial arts instructor.

"So the basic factor is neither exercise or rest but something else?" I asked.

He replied, "It is to be relaxed and that allows for muscles to regenerate."

The body is moving anyway. One cannot stop involuntary movements such as the heart-beat. Physical movement is good to some extent to keep the mind occupied and to activate the muscles, whereas strenuous movement always does more harm than good. Popular belief is that the right type and large amounts of exercise are important. Sifu's perspective is that exertion is itself a warning sign since excessive strain causes internal damage.

"Here," I pointed out, "most people think of relaxing as not doing anything or resting."

He replied that by CFQ definition, that was not good enough. That was why the purpose was ultimate relaxation, going beyond the normal forms of relaxation.

I added that when a person was too caught up in work there would be thoughts of going for a vacation to relax.

"Taking a holiday is creating another form of stress and adds on another layer of stress, albeit less than the previous activity.

"Also taking a rest does not do anything for the existing tension or stress already present. Nor does oversleeping, since the mind starts to wander, and becomes dreamy, and such mental activity can also become tension producing. Relaxation is meant to remove the tension that has gone into and accumulated in the body."

"Many meditation techniques have demonstrated the ability to reduce stress," I pointed out.

He said, "That is still insufficient to melt away the tension. True there is a certain level of relaxation, as indicated by slower heart rate and slow brain wave frequencies. But after the relaxation is over or when meditation stops, the tension remains the same.

"In our energy meditation, that accumulated tension is gradually removed as well. Admittedly, it is difficult to measure the whole-body relaxation energy state. So I rely on practitioners who report it's all very real, as the layers and layers of tension can be felt concretely as each comes out. The muscles loosen as the tension opens out and is released from the body."

I turned to another issue.

"You've described illnesses that can be removed by releasing tensions. What about diseases caused by bacteria, viruses, toxic pollutants, and chemicals?"

"O.K., take harmful microbes that go into the body. The body's blood and immune system will be activated to straightaway attack and neutralize or remove the microbes," Sifu replied. If the body is not able to do so, that's because of poor circulation or whatever other functions are implicated, so that the body soon is infected, he said.

I pointed out that different people react or vary in succumbing to infections. This means that the immune system competence is different.

"From the CFQ perspective, it depends on the degree of tension forces hindering the body," Sifu replied.

Some viruses, like the HIV virus, trick the T-cells so that essentially the immunologic functions collapse. Perhaps, the noxious energies dull the communication between the immunologic organs creating havoc for their cell-mediated immunity, I noted.

Sifu, in a steady, firm tone reiterated, "The first basic principle here is to trust the body system as the most perfect system. All humans have a perfect system, and so there should not be any differential immune system between us. We should all be able to ward off strong infections."

When there are massive tension forces present in the body and when that person becomes infected, it creates a surge of new tension, adding further to it.

"But if the body is able to release the tension, it will be all right," Sifu said.

"So, meditation is meant to restore the body to its high level of optimal immunity?" I reiterated.

"Don't use the word immunity," he replied. "Believe simply that without the tension, the body is perfectly able to take care of itself and the infection."

He went on to say that it was the same for toxic chemicals absorbed.

"They may even be carcinogenic, but the degree of harm also varies with the person expose to the same amount. That's again because all the body functions–the quality of circulation, and waste removal systems, for example–vary according to the tension."

A person who is more relaxed should be able to handle tension in a better way, he suggested. The body will be able to cleanse off the toxins and the toxic effects coming from the chemicals. Up to a certain extent, a relaxed person will be able to deal with it.

"What about addictions?" I asked.

"Biological factors such as using drugs, alcohol, and cigarettes that produce inducements and changes in the body also cause tensions from such addictions."

The body initially, after absorbing a certain amount of nicotine, say, gets used to it, and craves it. Wanting itself, in the mind, is tension-producing by nature. So releasing the tension will reduce and end the craving and yearning for the chemical.

"The more 'wants' a person has, even 'good' ones, the more the person is clouded by the dense forces of wanting this, or wanting that," Sifu said.

"The practice of meditation can dilute the 'wants' to become more open to the higher vibrational energies, that paradoxically will lead to the realization of ambitions. Wanting itself creates tension that shields the positive energy to become neutralized."

What we think becomes karma, with the energy of making it happen the way we want if we are not tensed up or too absorbed by the desire.

7

Tao Energy Initiation

Sifu stood facing his workshop audience of thirty-four people. Most were local professionals or practitioners in alternative medicine while others were practicing meditation, tai-chi, and other disciplines. He described the CFQ energy conception of life. For life to survive, each organism is equipped with a sophisticated system to absorb cosmic energy readily to enhance its functioning. The energy supplied is often not completely used up and residual energy is transformed and stored in the body. These forces are found in the chakras or specific energy centers; the places where the joints meet; and the physical locations of motor and sensory activities, as well as from injuries or infections.

Sifu held up a plain sheet of paper to demonstrate the effect of tension forces on the body.

"Our body," he began, "in its healthy natural state, is analogous to a perfectly smooth and clean surface. Watch what happens when I close my fingers on the paper and forcefully squeeze it tight. The paper creases, folds, and squashes into a paper ball. In the similar way, continual escalation of tension forces, produced by energy transformed into the body system, has a compressing effect that causes muscle stiffness, hardening, lumps, and knots in the body.

"Within the accumulation of tension forces, the natural healthy functions of the physical body are obstructed, and as the process sets in, chronic diseases and aging result."

He emphasized the right way to relax during meditation.

"All types of contemporary meditative and Taoist practices claimed that they practice relaxation.

"But as they get into actual cultivation, it is more like ending up with relaxing one third of the time and unable to let go after that. In other words, the method itself produces a build-up of tension forces instead of its declared purpose to let go.

"Functionally, it is not easy to let go and to release," he explained.

"If you think too hard of letting go, for example, you are not letting go. When you're too intent, that itself is tension. So in the CFQ system, active thinking or visualization is avoided. You understand the principles and do the minimal."

Loosened limbs are a pre-requisite for letting go. As the tension gets unwound, the body 'opens-out', elongating the muscles all the way to the tips of all the limbs.

"If the legs are folded," Sifu noted, "such effects are obstructed. This causes an energy rebound and develops as an acquisition process."

"So posture itself is very important. Since letting go is so difficult, in practice we have to ensure that the body is consistently relaxed and hangs loose."

When meditators started grasping at desirable experiences, they accumulated even more, and letting go was forgotten. That was true when they began to sense something they liked. They became over-joyous and grew attached to it. So the person would cling to such phenomena, holding on to them, hoping to re-experience them again next time and never let go of it.

"Over the years of meditation, instead of being freer, one becomes more attached and farther away from the truth," Sifu said.

That was the danger especially if one did not have a good teacher around who had gone through and understood the process completely. Sifu explained that meditation was facilitated by the direct transfer of Gold-Body energy from mentor to students. This process of energy transmission marked the initiation of students into meditation.

"The purpose of initiation is to activate and re-model the student's energy pattern."

"A mantra is useful because there is a relationship between thoughts and energy vibration. Thoughts are energies, basically mental energy. Thoughts harness the cosmic energy whose vibrations have been stepped downward," Sifu said.

"The Mantra not only defines the energy developed but protects the meditator from the possible overwhelming effect of negative forces.

"It serves as a protection and helps to produce good results in any endeavor," he reassured me.

The protective power of mantras was based on the assumption that certain vibrational thoughts and sounds could ward off evil, in the same way that a priest, of whatever religious persuasion, might exorcize evil spirits and harmful influences through invoking the name of some higher being.

Sifu explained that the energy cultivated in meditation was Gold-Body energy.

"First, you don't have to voice the words when reciting the Mantra. Second, you don't have to think of the meaning of the Mantra because it's all implied. And this is one of the qualities of psychic energy in contrast with mental energy. Mental energy involves active thinking. You must keep thinking of what's good, whereas here, you are not making any thoughts. You just repeat the Mantra. That's the minimum thing you need to do.

"It is effortless and you only have to give it a little 'space,'" I thought.

Sifu emphasized again the purpose of the Gold-Body energy Mantra.

"Primarily, a mantra is a way for us to focus our thoughts. The principle of CFQ practice is not to do anything. The least thing you can do probably is to repeat a reflex-like thought, such as a mantra. This helps us to be more focused to generate the right kind of vibration.

"In meditation, tension energy will start to move and manifests as external movement. The movement itself, however, is not your true energy. Movements are caused by the energy that one does not want. They are from dense energy and not part of one's self. The spirit is always crystal clear and always radiant, and not affected by the movements. It is the Mantra itself."

Someone in our group asked about the relationship between the Mantra and psychic energy. Sifu nodded saying that the good that is implied in the Mantra generates psychic energy.

"Does this purified or psychic energy come from the external environment?" someone else asked.

"It is cosmic energy and so can be found everywhere," he replied. "The cosmic energy available is used in the same manner that one uses it for all forms of thoughts, whether good or bad. All these happen without our knowledge. But now with the Mantra, we are participating and we are doing something for a special intention.

"We are making the energy more specific by focusing on only one type of purified energy. We don't want anything else but this particular form of psychic energy. The purity of the Gold-Body energy is the same as, or next to, cosmic energy."

Buddhist thought considered cosmic energy as 'Empty' or 'Void', since it was too pure to have an identity and will not compute within our system. In addition to using the Mantra during meditation, the practitioners should gradually repeat it at any time or in any activity that they were involved in.

"Repeating the Mantra is a form of blessing to all life forms and helps to dilute the dense forces within and around them. This is the *Metta* or loving kindness in Buddhism and enhances our merits."

Experiencing Psychic Energy

The late morning of the first day of the workshop was reserved for the introduction to the practice of meditation. Sifu began a run-through of how to do it.

"Goldbody energy meditation stresses simplicity."

He again cautioned them not to use the cross-legged, lotus or semi-lotus position.

"The process begins with abdominal breathing, at the same time focusing on the lower abdominal area. By awareness, one gradually dissolves and loosens up the tension from the abdomen to hip region. Since the tension forces are all interconnected, dissolving them in this region will cause a snowballing effect in other parts of the body.

"Second," Sifu added, "relaxing means opening out, i.e., the movement or releasing of forces from inside out. Third, the 'loving kindness' generated by the Mantra helps to release the Heart energy, very important in neutralizing the attaching effect of forces."

He directed each person in the audience to sit in a relaxed position, with feet firmly on the ground, body and spine vertically straight, and hands resting on the lap.

"Breathe into your stomach by inhaling to expand the abdomen and exhaling to contract the abdomen. Do this gently. Over a period of time, you should be able to do abdominal breathing naturally.

"Now direct seventy per cent of your awareness to the abdomen and hip area, and focus inward if possible. The remainder of your attention should be on awareness of your whole body and the surroundings.

"Remember, awareness is not concentration."

Sifu raised his arms stretching and extending his fingers toward the group.

"Repeat the Mantra silently. Put in minimum effort, just enough to ensure continuous flow."

One may tie in the Mantra with the rhythm of breathing.

"You need not visualize, just understand it as such. Involuntary movements and vibrations will manifest as the tension forces unwind.

"Allow these movements to happen and to continue. On the other hand, don't indulge in these movements; simply be aware of them and stay detached," Sifu urged.

Gradually, each participant began to move and stretch his or her body. He moved from person to person, rhythmically waving his hands as he went along. More people began to make loosening movements. I could sense the air getting thicker and warmer and charged with electricity.

From time to time, he would remind them to, "Be like a child, free and easy. Let go completely. Be aware of the abdomen, and repeat your Mantra."

After twenty-five minutes, Sifu ended the meditation. The group was told to open their eyes and slap their bodies vigorously. He described various effects that could occur during the meditation as the tension forces broke up.

"Vibrations that start in the legs will gradually spread all over the body and hands. Tension or stiffness results from the surfacing of tension forces. There are sensations of heat, cold, numbness, etc., depending on the impurities flushed out. Other physical movements can occur like rocking back and forth, or side to side, due to the release of forces by movements.

"Do not restrict the movements, but at the same time don't get carried away by the movements. Always keep your awareness with you."

Restlessness, stray thoughts and emotions can also surface. The energy forces within are the basis of thoughts, the release of which causes the unwinding effect. The thoughts are allowed to manifest naturally. But one needs to detach by going into the Mantra. Reactions naturally draw one's attention to them and the person may tend to enjoy, exaggerate or fight them.

"This you should avoid. Draw your awareness back to your abdomen and continue with your Mantra. At the same time, be mindful of the reactions. The speed of progress and types of reactions encountered differ individually. Disregard the reactions of others that you may notice around you during the group practice.

"Progress depends on an individual's ability to let go; so avoid enthusiasm and remove your ego. Do not attempt to hold on to a 'perfect' posture."

Now and then, practitioners should check their posture to ensure that they do not put in any strength. They should remove the strength from their necks, shoulders, arms, fingers, backs, and legs.

"If the tension forces surfacing from within are too strong to let go, let it be.

"Keep the flow of energy downward. If you suddenly discover that your vibrations clearly go far and wide, and feel that you are no longer alone, and the surroundings seem to be part of you, you have found your spirit, your purest and most vital vibration. That means you have developed some ability to influence things around you.

"But make sure you do not imagine yourself into such feeling," he cautioned.

After an hour's lunch break, we returned to the campus and reassembled to begin standing meditation. In comparison to sitting meditation, standing created a stronger downward flushing effect in dissolving the forces. Also, the effort in standing enhanced the commanding power in the energy cultivated.

The group spread out in the room standing and facing Sifu, getting ready to begin. The space was bright and sunlit as the glassed wall provided a panoramic view of the city and the St. John River Valley. As in sitting meditation, he told the group to breathe into the stomach and repeat the Mantra.

"Let the body go limp, hang loose, and let go," he exhorted.

Whatever they experienced, they were to remain detached and alert.

"Focus on your abdomen and breathe into it. Aware of your abdomen, feel loose, let loose, and be carefree."

After a while, people began to move slowly–neck, shoulders, back, and waist and legs. Sifu had both arms raised as he radiated and transmitted the Heart energy to everyone in the entire room. The air had a different quality of solidity and felt sticky. I felt the tingling sensations, the heaviness in my arms and hands. My body swayed back and forth from my seat. I felt the tension pushing down in my abdomen, unwinding and being released while flowing down the legs. My body was relaxed and stayed loose and the mind was calm and observant.

Finally, Sifu said, "Fresh and alert, fresh and alert, wake up and open your eyes."

At the end of the day, the participants shared and described what they had experienced. One member mentioned that during the meditation, he became restless, and his thoughts were too scattered. He made some jerking movements and toward the end he felt emotionally drained.

Sifu responded, "This is the primary pattern of tension. But by adhering to the letting-go principle and the Mantra, one allows them to unwind and leave the body."

Another person reported that he began to doze off and did not recall what had happened after that until he awakened at the end of the meditation. Sifu explained that the surfacing of tension forces created a shield which could cut off one's consciousness.

"This is a 'clicking out' effect. While many meditation practices dwell on the blanking out effect, CFQ works through such an effect into the *state of joyous alertness.*"

Only when one is able to work through such obstacles will one find how the 'good' energies' break out the 'bad energies' and dissolve them away.

A female participant asked about the numbness and loss of sensation in her legs. Sifu answered that the legs were the major outlets for the broken-down forces, and the outward flow of forces also released and affected the muscles and tendons of the limbs. The impurities in the broken-down tension slowed down at the limbs causing numbness and discomfort.

"When such sensations occur, don't get up abruptly. Shake the legs a little and continue to meditate until the discomfort disappears."

Another member felt alarmed by the violent, involuntary movements that she experienced.

"This is due to the release of some of the denser forces from the muscles."

This has nothing to do with the trance state or tales of demon possession. Shamans get into trance to deliberately contact and consult whatever forces will help them to resolve problems and to divine or 'see' the future.

"In energy meditation, no effort is expended for such purposes, and the practitioners retain full awareness of their minds. Allow the forces to unwind by physical movements, but ensure that you do not participate by enjoying it too much, exaggerate it, or try to vary it."

Sifu added his observation of a person who was doing a lot of posturing with tilting and twisting movements during the sitting meditation.

"As one gets progressively more relaxed, the tension forces within have to surface."

The body is comprised of complicated and uneven tension forces which unwind at different rates, therefore giving rise to weird and crooked postures. It will take some time before one will be able to sit right or still.

He continued with other possible CFQ reactions.

"Also, visions, vivid pictures of places and objects, as well as faces and entities may appear in one's imagination. They appear even more vivid than seen with normal physical sight, and the perception is combined with a feeling of a physical presence. They are all illusions at this stage, so do not feel attached. They will soon disappear," Sifu said.

"Others may see people, deities, or whatever intelligent beings who appear able and willing to communicate with you. They may offer you plenty of things or ideas. Do not take them for real; they are just the manifestation of your tension forces, which form part of your memory and imagination.

"If you ignore them you will see how they dissipate from whichever part of your body they came from. The common tricks they play on you are temptations and fear. Sometimes when sweet talk fails, they turn into grotesque beings to frighten you. You are safe with your Mantra and detached attitude."

The psychic energy cultivated by meditation, he claimed, radiated and influenced the surrounding environment naturally. Repeating the Mantra allowed the student to naturally tune in to the vibrations of the mentor and also enabled every cultivator to use the psychic energy to contribute to the growth of a unified field to receive its protection.

That evening I sought Sifu's views about the energy connection between people who came to the workshop. I pointed out the idea that a cluster of energies interacting together becomes an energy family. He nodded, voicing that our identity was comprised of all these various family energies with all the inherent conflicts when family members interact.

"There is an interchange, and your energy becomes enriched in that respect. Now in the our method, you can see the energy changes within you happening more physically."

I expressed the belief that raising the consciousness of one individual means that the whole family's energy would have been purified a notch higher.

Sifu cautioned on doing too much in the physical realm, because of the physical consequences to the practitioner. Interfering in the lives of others could lead to an imbalance in one's own life and practice. He agreed however, that anybody who came for help should receive something and be helped to the best of one's ability. Such acts of healing prevent a hindrance arising in one's energy system in the practice of letting go.

I pointed out that, "Helping also raised the practitioner's energy level. The more we use it for that purpose, the stronger became that purity."

He agreed saying, "Healing not only helps to improve the quality of energy. Healing also helps in the cultivation of the Path."

It was time to call it a night. But I knew that uncovering how energy works had just begun.

8

Harnessing Tao Energy

Early next morning, we stood on the upper deck behind my house over-looking the garden. We had just completed 30 minutes of vigorous and exhilarating standing meditation. I asked Sifu to explain how a group spiritual belief worked, i.e., a gathering to ask for protection, help, and blessings from highly evolved spiritual beings.

"Once you have a belief in that being, you find that you can tune into the right vibration and this somehow creates a series of changes that's all within yourself," he replied.

The connection has to be made by the supplicant, that is, the individual makes an effort to tune in and then changes happen in the energy system of the individual. I thought perhaps, a giant pure thought had the power to activate changes sought by desperate individuals.

"So," I said, "someone asks God for help. Does a God up there actually hear the plea?"

He said, "First, pure energy, by whatever name you choose to call the higher being, cannot be expected to come down to the level of human thoughts and feelings. You don't expect your 'God' to help in the same way that, say, a human therapist would. There is no such thing as a personal touch or direct communication from God."

The blessings from that source is a blanket vibration–if one believes in an ultimate Him or Her, it causes a series of reactions. But such reactions all happen within the person in line with that individual's energy system.

"What about the energy system that has been created in each person's lifetime. How real is this energy?" I asked Sifu.

"Even after physical death, this energy continues to live on, in some form of existence. This energy is essentially consciousness. I cannot provide you with proof of such existence, but I honestly believe that this is what happens. I draw from my CFQ practice where I experience certain out-of-body states.

"In the dying state, I believe all the tension forces in the body, the karma, the various energy patterns, and memories are all activated at the same time."

I said, "So, it's a replay of all of one's life events?"

He nodded, "Such replay can take place over split seconds—everything is replayed. But of course, to the deceased person, he or she does not feel the difference in time. Everything plays on."

It may take weeks or months to witness one's entire life and everything that was done in physical life. Once it is finished, the energy leaves the physical body, but it is still energy that is filled with identity. It follows the effects of the replayed pattern.

"For instance, the dying person who is fighting to survive, still has a yearning to live on. So, it may be so strong that straightaway it takes on a cosmic rebirth, carrying with it all the energy patterns to the new birth."

For the person who is not aware that he has indeed died, the replay will make sure that these forces are freed from the body. The energy will still be wandering, but has no relation with living persons. It has no awareness of what will happen next."

I surmised that existence is just like a dream-state—it just moves on and on, and does not know where to go as the mind cannot reason clearly.

Sifu's beliefs made me think about concepts of heaven and hell. He felt that for one who had such a belief system, and it was strong enough, the non-physical energy will spend some time in that heaven or hell. It seems like whatever was left of one's personal identity continued to be essentially played out.

"But," I asked, "in relation to CFQ goals, how would things be different?"

He answered, "The energy meditation practice is a purification. There is a process of a time-release of all the impure forces during meditation. For the practitioner, it is also a replay of the kind of tension forces as in the dying process, except that it is not instant and abrupt, but occurs over a period of time during cultivation.

"It is also a mild form of replay, even when we are alive in physical form, as the impure forces take its own sweet time to leave the body."

Continuing, he said, "But each time, something leaves the body, the person gets healthier."

As more and more of these forces leave the body, the energy system automatically interchanges with the pure positive energy of the cosmic. The dense forces are reduced even further, and ultimately one is free from them.

"Then straightaway, it's the enlightened state, whereby one is no longer affected by the dense forces that have been previously created by us."

Sifu elaborated, "One is no longer bothered by whether one is existing or living. It doesn't make any difference. It's so pure, all our thoughts, functions, and actions will be based on purity."

He went on, "There is no desire for rebirth. You are not moved to want to. That's why the term 'Unmoved Heart' is used, as you will not be moved by any desire. Your consciousness will function as purity. To you, they are all one indistinguishable, perfect purity. You are back with the cosmic."

The second day of the workshop continued with further practice and explanations of meditation and participants' questions on their reactions during their practice. The role of spontaneous involuntary movements and their meaning in the CFQ principle of unwinding was discussed.

Sifu asserted that he had studied extensively the origins of such movements in other forms of spontaneous Qigong and in trance-states and concluded that there was no spirit possession involved. Involuntary movements resulted from the need to unwind the forces within. The crude and coarser forces unwound and dissipated through physical usage.

"By allowing the forces to move the physical body spontaneously, rapid improvement in health results."

In the CFQ method of detachment, under no circumstances was there any loss of consciousness. He added a further point about the trance state.

"True, many other practices make use of moving phenomena. O.K., movements can happen if you excite and activate an energy system. This happens whether you inadvertently increase the degree of tension, as in most other cases, or you reduce the degree of excitation as in CFQ. But it is easier to create a movement phenomenon through deliberate encouragement.

"I mean, excite or get the participants to heighten it, boost them up, and people will become hysterical. So things get carried away and everyone will move. But this will only increase the degree of tension."

Those who practiced other Taoist or Qigong methods involving spontaneous movements, after a period of moving intentionally, felt they had acquired qi and were getting more energy into the body. They became excited by unrestrained movements. But this led to more acquisition of energy and more tension accretion in the body. In the trance state, the moment the person got excited, he or she had so much faith in it that it actually increased the degree of tension as it brought the energy higher.

"After a while, the person is knocked out of mind and one's spirit no longer exists. The person would be whatever he or she imagines. That is trance, the out-of-mind state. They think and believe they have reached special states.

"In meditation, the physically harder type of movements that we do are to bring the energy down. Then it is more difficult to make the person move. The movements allow the tension to leak out, but here stopping the movements is like waterproofing to prevent a leak."

It was the noon hour of the second day, and time for a short break. We drove home for lunch–a short five minutes away from the workshop site. As we sat on the deck overlooking the garden, I asked Sifu about Taoist practices in China.

He revealed that historically, several types of spontaneous Qigong were banned in China.

"The fact was a lot of practitioners ran into trouble. These people have their theories of why there are spontaneous movements."

Some claimed that they came because there was spiritual guidance. Others believed that the meridian channels cleared up so that movements became manifested.

"My position is that these explanations are not close enough to the truth," Sifu said.

"In meditation, movements come because of the unwinding effect of tension energy. This tension energy has formed into force centers in the body. It has direction and strength and whatever it is–that's the way it has to be moved out. At different stages, the movements are different."

Sifu explained that with spontaneous movements, on the negative side, practitioners might develop a tendency to move and talk in a manner unacceptable to most people.

"It appears to observers that they are possessed and the movements look frightening."

On the other hand, meditation or inward-drawing Qigong without spontaneous movements, if it is not properly practiced, will manifest differently. The danger here is that practitioners may feel withdrawn from society lapsing into a kind of depression.

"In both types of Qigong," he added, "the problems are quite the same and lead practitioners astray."

When involved with energy, one must understand the laws of energy itself: How one creates it, how to create a purer state of energy, how not to complicate the energy, and what is beneficial and what is not.

"All these are very important and clearly dealt with in meditation."

Back in the workshop, someone asked the Master to describe the nature of the Gold-Body energy, in terms of how it felt, and how it worked in the body.

"I will start off by first explaining the disease-causing energies. As this condensed energy is melted, we can actually feel the density, tension, and heaviness. As it melts off further, probably you feel the tearing sensations, the pain, and things running out like electrical sensations all over the body."

Sifu went on. "There are also magnetic fields so that in the process of practice you feel the magnetism running through."

Again, all these are dense energies, and one feels numbness, heaviness everywhere. Heat is only one of the sensations of impurities surfacing. There is also cold, and itching. Rashes may also develop. There could be diarrhoea, or purging because the dense energies are opened to be flushed out. All these are the properties of bad energy.

"When you are able to dissolve them, then you feel their presence."

At this point, the practitioner had yet to feel the good energies coming through. They were still too subtle but that did not mean it was not powerful.

Interrupting, I said, "Can you describe what this subtle Gold-Body energy is like?"

"As we go along. Now, as you progress and become more advanced along the line of cultivation, you'll find there is a contrast between good and bad energy. For example, the bad energy may appear to you like clouds, since in deep meditation, despite being wide awake and alert, your functional pattern is very slow. But you must make sure that you stay wide awake and alert.

"This is important. That alertness grounds you there. You must know that you are there. That alertness is your spirit, all right?"

So the impure energies felt cloud-like or dense. One might see different colors, normally the darker shades of various colors–red, blue, and green.

"But the colors that appear to you are not totally pure or good. All these are part of the physical body and you feel the physical sensations of the energy that are present there.

"In addition, there are also the vibrations that are peaceful but much less tangible. It is almost non-existent yet this psychic energy feels very real. It does not feel quite real because it has gone through us and is no longer totally pure. But psychic energy is the opposite of the dense energy whose sensations you can readily sense. You feel the psychic luminous body energy as it radiates through you."

"Of course," he ended, "now and then, the dense energies will be quite mobile and intrude so that the practitioner again senses the impurities in the impure or not totally pure energy. So one is constantly shifting, moving, and changing in and out of the experience of Gold-Body energy."

Letting Go Your ALL

That evening, Sifu provided some personal feedback on my meditation. I felt that the workshop in Fredericton had a significant impact that advanced my understanding of meditation.

I said, "Coming back to my practice this afternoon, when you spoke to me, I finally realized that, 'Let-go and hang-loose,' is literally hanging loose so that the body is very limp and relaxed. At the same time whatever movements to come are allowed. I felt that the movements are more effective to relieve tension in this way."

He again emphasized that CFQ was the opposite of what we think of as exercising.

"When exercising, you know what you want to do; then there will be exertion which means strength is applied. All this hardens the body and builds up tension."

In meditation, the body was allowed to go limp. While this was done in an effortless way, the movements themselves could be very strong. It also went in cycles. Sometimes, it became toned down in vigorousness and as one progressed, the movements became more graceful.

"For us, the application of strength while performing any movement constitutes a component of the ego. Ego means holding back to be strong. One feels strong and wants to hold on."

This apparently was a hindrance and a deterrent to the practice of meditation.

"Some of my students studying Buddhism in the past were never too clear about it until now. The unwinding effect can give such new insights of previous issues and problems. That's because, in the past, they have created the energy," Sifu said.

"Hmm, so it's old energy that they are in contact with," I commented. "Why would it be better or clearer this time around when they unwind?"

Sifu said, "In the first place, what you have created previously from studying may not be true because of this being acquired knowledge. That itself may prevent the truth from coming through to you. Conscious knowledge is also judgmental."

"If you have a way to remove such judgment itself, certainly you are closer to the truth," he continued.

"In meditation, when you unwind it, you'll find that the truth just comes in. The truth is everywhere, but the truth is prevented from your knowledge because you have acquired some kind of conscious knowledge."

I probed, "Let me see whether I understand you correctly. With the CFQ letting go technique, using a new perspective, we are more relaxed, we are more open. So that when we go back to previous or earlier information studied, our new perspective provides a truer understanding of the old information?"

"The technique will make us more sensitive and more aware of what things are happening. That includes the truth of what has happened. Thus we can easily pick up the vibration and just know that. We are more conscious of what truth is," he asserted.

"Zen people like to say, 'Go beyond letting go, and beyond not letting go.' CFQ goes for that state of letting go, and not letting go as well. If one is too concerned with letting go, eventually, that itself is not truly letting go," Sifu added.

"Letting go is natural; it is just like that. The cultivator doesn't have to be too concerned about letting go. First have the idea that one doesn't need to acquire anything to start off. That's the best form of letting go. How much to let go and what letting go means, let them come to you in your practice," he suggested.

"In fact, 'Just be what is,' is a good expression of the Tao and advanced stage of letting go. Gradually when the energy gets more refined, the person does not have to bother to let go. It is automatic, and built into one's system."

The individual is then closer to the source, the universal mind.

"Essentially, just watch from there. One does not have to do anything at all. In other words, you have to purify your energy until you are in the state of purity," Sifu explained.

"Purity is effortlessness. You are one with cosmic energy or the Tao. You do not have to bother with letting go."

He wanted to check out my meditation, that I began over the past year.

"Tell me what is different about today's practice session?"

I replied, "In my normal meditation, I blend CFQ with other practices. I first do quick stretching followed by a fifteen-minute standing meditation. I move but not always spontaneously, for example, I include Tai-chi movements as well."

He said, "That's not totally letting go. As you advance in your practice, the movements will be looser and freer. Evidently, your practice has not been regular or smooth enough. But you are also making progress and moving into the borderline of the transformation stage. I will defer explaining and describing this term to a later time.

"I noticed," Sifu continued, "that your body was kind of extended out from the interior. Things are being pushed out from inside. That's good. When it manifests in that way, your body feels stiffer. Things have got to stretch outward."

He explained there was a kind of ball-like force or energy centered around the hip at the back and the front lower abdomen. That was why I had moved the way I did, pushing backward and forward in that manner. This is the initial stage before moving into the more advanced stage.

"In subsequent progress, the tension can be felt strongly as it becomes more apparent," Sifu said. "As the practitioner goes further, such forces feel rubbery. They have solidified as part of one's physical body."

"My practice at this point is a composite of many things that I do," I responded.

Shaking his head, Sifu said, "That itself can be a problem. In terms of energy, the simpler the things you do, the more straightforward it is. Energy is highly sensitive to the thoughts themselves, to whatever we do. The cosmic energy that is converted is then screened through.

"I can see, as well, you're experiencing many physical sensations and changes."

Sifu gave some examples. A lump could be reduced to half its size in an hour's session. It depended on the stage of healing—and if it was not ready, it would not happen that way. Something physical might just pop up suddenly.

"So immediately after a session, one might have rashes appearing. Or the practitioner might come with a bout of flu that clears up right after the practice session. One felt the physical sensations, the muscles might bulge out, things seemed to jerk and shake the body."

I remembered talking to Fon, one of Sifu's senior students in Penang. I asked him to expand on how meditation had helped in his life context. He was an engineer by profession but also a martial arts instructor. He reiterated the significance of letting go, which was not only adhered to during meditation, but was to be cultivated twenty-four hours a day.

"Even during sleep," he stressed, "Let go of everything."

The aim was to prevent creating a troubled mind. "The correct way is to practice from the inside. It is an inside type of practice even while one's hands are moving. You focus inside and on what's inside."

"Similarly, in Tai-chi practice, movements are external and relaxed, but always the practitioner is taught not to let the energy move out. This is the wrong way of cultivating."

Sensing my skepticism, Fon disclosed further, "People all want to create more strength. People like to have heavy, powerful muscles and demonstrate an external show of power and strength. I call this type of training and martial arts, 'muscle exercise', aimed at puffing practitioners up externally."

Fon admitted that many martial arts teachers suffered from health problems. As a Wushu (kung-fu) martial arts instructor himself, he had his share. Before he came to Sifu, he had jaundice and a swollen pancreas.

"Practitioners who cultivate correctly, have smiling faces rather than tense faces. They look pleasant and relaxed. They smile sweetly, and that indicates that they can lower their blood circulation. One is totally centered and relaxed in every movement. This is the Tao."

I asked Sifu to elaborate on attaining the state that he called 'instinctual knowledge'.

"Let the energy guide you along. I can only point the direction. No matter how much you try to understand conceptually, and whatever you learn from hearing others or from books, they are the basis of acquired knowledge. At this time, knowledge actually goes from outside inward. It changes when you have unwound much more completely."

"After that," he added, "I want you to forget totally what I say and what you think you have learned from me. Then the inner knowledge that comes up from within will also somehow click with the outside knowledge and this is subjectively experienced as instinctive knowledge."

But the Tao was clear to me and this was the Gold-Body energy state.

He commented saying, "At that point, you have let go sufficiently so that your ordinary self is gone. You are not attached and essentially become identified with the universal self."

It is better to just do it and forget about doing it. And that itself is letting go.

"As a matter of fact, if you think you have somewhere to go, you are making too much effort and not letting go enough. Let go of all conceptualizations of attainment and then just keep going."

"Yes, keep going," Sifu repeated.

Part Four

Energy Psychophysiology

9

Tao Energy Transmission

It was obvious that Sifu had sparked a resonant chord with participants in Fredericton. He was to stay for another five days in the city before leaving with me for a scheduled visit to the Monroe Institute in Virginia. His demonstrations of CFQ treatment during the workshop led to the desire of many to request personal healing sessions. Over the next five days, some sixty people came with their ailments to seek help from him.

People came with their pain and illnesses and the emotional problems of living. One couple was Cindy and Dick. He had had a stroke ten years earlier that left one arm and leg paralyzed. After a couple of treatment sessions, Dick reported that his damaged hand and fingers had become more flexible and mobile. Interestingly, some nine months later, Cindy gave birth to a healthy baby girl. The couple had tried previously for several years to have a child but conception didn't happen until the Master's arrival. It was an extraordinary coincidence.

Tanya, a nutritionist, who had spoken up during the workshop approached me to ask whether Sifu could help her son. "Logan, who is ten years old has Down's Syndrome," she said.

I tried to discourage her, saying that this was a genetic disease, and at his age probably impossible to reverse. Besides, Sifu was leaving in a few days. She would not take no for an answer, until finally he relented and agreed to treat the boy for five sessions.

Tanya brought Logan and Jim, his younger brother, to Sifu. Jim, aged eight, had a large patch of scar tissue on his chest from a childhood accident that had resulted in a severe third degree burn. Besides his Down's syndrome, Logan had two serious physical problems. He had juvenile diabetes that required daily insulin shots, and his eyesight was poor due to cataracts. Three months back, one cataract had been removed and the lens replaced. Surgery for the other cataract eye was scheduled for the following month.

After the second session with Sifu, Tanya could see changes in her two children. Jim showed immediate improvement as his scarred tissue felt much softer and looked healthier. Logan's appearance had also changed–his posture looked 'lighter' and he moved and walked with a co-ordination and balance that his mother had never seen before. He also became more cheerful in temperament. By the fifth and last session, the parent noticed two dramatic changes in her son.

The first related to his diabetes. Tanya noticed from the daily tests, that the blood sugar levels had begun to stabilize. When they did fluctuate, she did not do what she normally did, which was to adjust the insulin dosage. She found that, even without increasing insulin, the sugar level returned to a stable level by itself. Diabetic control had improved.

The second change was in Logan's vision. When he was looking at something or reading, his head was not as lopsided as before. The boy had a characteristic way of tilting his head in order to see better with the eye that had the cataract removed. But now his head was more evenly positioned as if he could see through the other affected eye. Could it be that the bad eye was clearing up by itself?

Tanya had occasion to speak to the eye specialist, who flatly dismissed the notion of cataracts suddenly clearing up, and said that no alternative medical procedure that could do so exists. The surgery would go on as scheduled. A month later, she called with great excitement and wanted to visit me. She had taken Logan for his cataract surgery a few days earlier.

The doctor upon examining his eyes was astounded pronouncing that indeed the cataract had cleared up enough that surgery was not required. The surgery was canceled indefinitely. Tanya was totally elated.

"Wow! I am truly impressed." I concluded.

I remembered Sifu saying that we must trust that the body is sophisticated enough to deal with every problem, once the obstruction by tension forces is removed.

"To summarize," he said, "diseases are manifestations of problems caused by the accumulation of forces. In other words, they are the victims, not the perpetrators. Illness symptoms are the complaints, or 'cries of help' of the victim of disease. To give relief is to soothe or quiet the victims. The effective healer must pursue the bullies that cause the suffering. Tension force is the bully or culprit that causes all diseases.

"The basic rule in CFQ treatment is to bring unhealthy energy down by creating an opening and radiating effect, so that the person becomes more relaxed."

I surmised that fundamentally a healthy body and mind are rooted in a balanced energy system in which energy flows radiantly. Physiological risk factors as well as psychological disturbances create an imbalance in energy flow leading to physical disease and emotional dysfunction.

"Cure is a slow process, so people in the meantime need relief medications. The need for surgery, however, must be carefully assessed."

Surgery 'shocked' the body and did violence to it. Every part of the body served its function and unnecessary removal could create more harm than good. But this did not mean that the person should shy away if a real need arose. A carefully assessed surgery could remove and prevent further damage to the body and save a life. I asked whether energy treatment worked because of the power of belief.

"It is just being somehow open. Yes, open and not actively disbelieving. This notion of non-disbelief is hard to understand," Sifu replied.

A person who does not say a word during treatment may be harboring a strong disbelief or distrust rather than being simply a nonbeliever. Belief in the treatment is not required. A person who is in a coma can be treated even though he is unconscious.

"In all cases, energy meditation heals and works," he revealed.

I recalled that he had worked with animals, treating race horses. He turned to describe how he did it.

"Four horses were brought to my attention, down with tendon and knee injuries. One had a bleeding problem. The horse owner had kept them from racing for a year, refusing to put them down. Out of desperation, I was called in to treat them. After ten weekly sessions, three of them were ready to return to the races. The remaining horse, who had an acute tendon problem, is progressing well and will take more time to recover.

"Here are my observations of physical changes as the horses recover from their injuries. After three sessions of energy transmission, the coat becomes brighter. After eight sessions, the coat turns darker and glittering bright. One light brown horse turned into a red horse. Wrinkles and skin folds in the horses disappear, and enlarged blood vessels subside.

"The race horse trainer, who initially was indifferent to me, after witnessing these changes, has become very co-operative."

He commented, "Now they look like race-horses!"

So whether human or animal, standing or moving, it seemed that his treatment was physiologically effective. All that was required was a cooperative attitude on their part.

"Even for the person who believes and is highly co-operative, he still has to face some discomfort in the disease-freeing process. But in this case, he can be reassured that it's all right and he is more at ease and relaxed with the process. So the unwinding effect is speeded up and goes smoother."

"Yes," I nodded. "We know that physician-patient psychological factors influence recovery from illness–such as a positive relationship and confidence to adhere to the treatment regimen."

Sifu admitted that he had cases of people who were literally bundled up by well-intended friends and pushed into a chair for him to treat. And more often than not, they felt unbearable pain and discomfort.

"For such a patient, one has to work through the energy of the disbelief itself. The energy that was meant for healing becomes more like destructive energy."

"Healing is a partnership," he concluded. "Without that, the situation would be similar to the refusal of a drowning person to hang on to the rope extended by the healer."

Resistance to Energy Healing

I thought Sifu would like a change of scenery to take a look at the Atlantic coastal areas. I decided to take him to St. Andrews, a popular coastal resort, about a ninety-minute drive away through quiet, winding, rural roads. We resumed talking about how one's rigid beliefs can be counter-productive to health. He gave some examples.

"Let's say someone has the problem of rheumatism. The Chinese '*sinseh*' or traditional herbal doctor, even the local medical doctors, give the conventional wisdom saying, 'It's wind and water getting into your system that's causing the problem.'"

"But I say to this patient, 'No, rheumatism is actually tension accumulated in the body, drawn inward so that the tissues are glued together. If you drop your fear of exposure to the elements of wind and water, that itself will help to reduce your rheumatism attacks.' But they are unconvinced and continue to suffer the pain rather than follow my suggestions or go through treatment."

He commented on another source of misinformation. "There are Qigong healers who themselves are ignorant of how and why healing works. These healers claim that they give nourishing qi to cure disease. Also, they professed that the moment they give this qi to the person, it will stay permanently in the body, and so the patient will remain powerful and healthy.

"Nothing is further from the truth! But to change this widespread erroneous belief is not easy," he admitted.

After lunch, we had the afternoon to spend on Deer Island, located next to Campobello Island–President Franklin Delano Roosevelt's summer retreat. I resumed conversation, pointed out the problem of acceptance of any new idea, invention, or therapy by the public.

"In healthcare, people conform to the orthodox medical views and are skeptical and distrustful of traditional and new approaches," I said.

Sifu agreed that indeed rigid beliefs complicated the problem. Another common situation was people walking into his clinic with a complaint such as a backache.

"When I check the energy of the patients, it's not unusual to find not only the presenting problem, but also several other minor problems that they may not be fully aware of. But I tell them that my treatment is for every chronic problem that they have."

Continuing he sighed, "After some sessions of treatment, there is improvement, enough for the old problem to have subsided. But by then, they have forgotten that they came initially for treatment of backache. Now, they complain of finger numbness, or maybe a stiff neck. They had these problems before, but in relation to the backache, they were not as intense. So they complain that the treatment has not helped them and they quit coming."

He reiterated another fact.

"In standard medical treatment, if injections or pills are taken, patients forget that with chronic problems, it takes years too. The same pain and problem still persist, but they say that it's cured."

"For example, a person with stroke. I tell such patients that I need one year to treat them, once a week for 30 minutes. So over a year that adds up to 50 sessions but in the process they can be walking, jumping, and their limbs regain at least 80 per cent mobility and use."

"Yes, people who go to alternative medicine often have a skeptical and impatient attitude yet expect an instant cure," I commented.

Sifu said, "One of the main problems which I face is the holistic nature of healing. I tend to see the correlations between past problems as well as potential problems and current existing problems. So in treatment, I wish to bring previous illnesses or symptoms out to the surface and clear them one after the other. This brings tremendous benefits to the patients, and I take great care and pride to do this."

But few appreciate this and continue to grumble over having gone through all the discomforts. He cited the example of one female patient in her early sixties. She had her menopause 15 years earlier, and after a dozen energy treatments she unexpectedly regained her normal menstrual cycle. She became extremely annoyed at the Master for causing this inconvenience.

"Then there was a jealous husband who confronted me for apparently making his wife look younger and prettier. The man, with gangland connections, sent his thugs to threaten me. Fortunately, it ended before things went out of control. The husband confessed that he just wanted to make sure that I had no ulterior motives regarding his wife!"

I said, "Most people, when they have medical problems, ignore their responsibility that they had done something to cause it."

Sifu agreed. "They protest that it's not because of the way they think, or behave, or anything to do with them. When I tell them they have to take some time each day to remove disease-causing tension forces, and so on, they stop listening. It is the same problem for treatment."

Sifu described another story in which strong resistance to treatment led to unfortunate outcomes. This was a middle-aged man, actually a relative, who was totally skeptical about his energy healing.

"He denied that he had cancer that was diagnosed by his physicians, and went around looking for a herbal cure. He blamed his symptoms on rheumatism. But his pain was then so severe that he would cry throughout the night. He could not eat or move his bowels, and lost a lot of weight."

Eventually, when his problem was unbearable, he finally came to Sifu for treatment three times a week. After the second week, he had a purging. His appetite returned and he could eat again. He slept through the night without discomfort.

Sifu added, "Earlier, I had told him that if he wanted to continue benefitting from my treatment, he must stop all herbal medication and not take any enriching food supplements. But as he got better he wanted to get stronger, to add more weight. So he ignored my advice."

Then one day, after a month-and-a-half, the problem erupted again. Complications surfaced, he was shivering and in pain again. He called Sifu, who advised him to return to the hospital.

"After that," he said to him, "If you still want my treatment, come back only on the promise that you stay away from the herbal remedies and tonics. This is doing more harm than good. What is strengthening your body is also strengthening the cancer cells as well."

The man chose not to go back. He went off to China to seek treatment and died a year-and-a-half later, Sifu reported.

Sadly he felt that the patient's cancer was a curable situation.

"But such patients, once they feel better will stop listening. Instead, they will search for more familiar ways or follow what others say will cure them. Again their beliefs of what works clash with my therapy."

Mission Impossible

Sifu went on to explain how one's emotional disposition, attitudes, and societal beliefs about cancer have made a curable disease vastly more resistant to recovery.

"It's just like the old lady, Nanny. She is the terminal brain cancer patient who had recovered completely when you last spoke to her grandson Wei."

"What has happened to her since then?" I inquired.

"About a year after treatment, she heard from a friend of hers who had cancer. The friend underwent only a brief regimen of chemotherapy after which her physician assured her that she was cured."

Sifu pointed out that Nanny's friend probably had some small growth or tumor developing, which was not necessarily malignant.

"The growth can be naturally removed without invasive toxic treatment."

However, her physician recommended chemotherapy. She bragged to Nanny that she did not have to do anything else to get well.

When Nanny heard this, she wanted to stop her meditation.

"I told her she must continue on with the practice for at least three years. She was very angry with me for insisting."

"She resented the practice?" I asked.

"Yes! When she talked about energy practice to stay free from cancer to her friends, they all laughed at her. That added to her resentment. But Nanny had forgotten how severe her cancer was and that her doctors had given up on her. They did not prescribe chemotherapy then because she was not expected to survive through her radiotherapy."

"So what happened next?" I asked.

"Her grandson, who knew better, insisted and made sure she kept up the energy practice which she did with a lot of reluctance and grumbling."

"Such patients should best stick to standard medical treatment and be done with it," Sifu concluded.

In Nanny's case, despite her cranky attitude, she survived a total of 18 months.

He added, "I notice in cancer patients treated by me, such as Nanny, that in the last few weeks of dying, they suffered little pain or struggle. They continued to eat and have bowel movements until the end.

"Nanny, for example did not use morphine at all."

Sifu reminded me about the case of Tony, another cancer patient who was from Hong Kong.

"Do you remember what happened to him?" he asked.

Two years earlier, I had stopped briefly in Hong Kong to visit with friends. I mentioned to Kristine, a close relative, about Sifu's healing. Some months later, unbeknownst to me, Kristine had encouraged her friend, Tony, who was at the final stage of terminal cancer to see Sifu..

Tony aged 40 years had surgery for colon cancer, and part of the large intestine was removed. For three years, there were no obvious problems. Then as his breathing became difficult, he went for a checkup and the diagnosis was that the cancer cells had spread including multiple cancer spots in his lungs. Tony knew that this meant fourth stage terminal cancer.

He was told that without treatment the cancer cells would grow and spread rapidly. Treatment recommended would give him another three months and at best six months to live. Either way it was a matter of time. Tony decided that he would rather live without the pain of undergoing treatment.

Kristine pushed him to travel to the Center in Malaysia for treatment. After two days with Sifu, Tony seemed to open up and energy returned to him. He was initiated into the energy practice after the fifth session as he appeared to have become physically revived. He started to move spontaneously, but only a little because of the dense energies in his sick body. But he continued treatment as well as practice. A week later, his voice became stronger and his breathing deeper and unblocked. He flew back to Hong Kong, but even with some regression, he was still better than before treatment.

It was also obvious that he still had a half-hearted attitude and was skeptical and doubtful about meditation. Tony did not return until two months later, when treatment was overdue. During treatment, Sifu managed to put him into more movements.

"By the end of the week, he was very happy with his recovery. He went back to Hong Kong having survived the cancer for three months.

"Despite this, my cancer patient was unable to understand what I was saying because it was so contrary to his beliefs and expectations," Sifu recalled.

Tony had great difficulty accepting that anything so intangible, light and gentle, could cure terminal diseases. It was five months later before he came back for the third time. Sifu recounted the effects of the third treatment.

"He had certainly outlived his physician's prediction since it had been over nine months since I first treated him..

"Evidence of recovery was beyond question, but the patient did not return for the required treatment. Overall, he survived some 15 months."

Complete cure required daily unwinding and proper meditation. The expected symptoms of further unwinding of the dense energies such as body aches, coughing, etc. had to be tolerated.

"Furthermore," Sifu added, "the daily hassles of living should be interpreted in the right manner. Above all, at this weakened stage, the patient must continue to maintain emotional equilibrium, stay relaxed, and keep up the practice of sending in healing relaxation energy."

Raising some doubts, I asked, "Aren't the initial benefits of energy meditation simply the effects of the person's positive beliefs in healing which by themselves have no lasting effect. In short, simply a placebo effect?"

"No, I must correct such a misconception," he said. "For most diseases that are not immediately life-threatening, CFQ energy treatment and meditation are indeed long-lasting. I have severe diabetic patients whose problems have not resurfaced even after seven years. That's after undergoing six months of treatment, with no recurrence of the disease at all."

"I have treated patients with severe back pain due to slipped disc sciatica, who after three months of treatment have shown no trace of the problem for five years.

"Medically such lasting cures are impossible.

Sifu continued, "But when you refer to terminal cases where the patients are given no more than a few months to live by their doctors, the need for the patient's active co-operation and responsibility is substantially greater. The physician has already given up any hope of recommending any treatment.

"Even so, with CFQ treatment, such cancer patients had their lives prolonged. They looked and felt healthier in every way. But it is imperative that such patients, after initial recovery, understand the pressures ahead."

He went on to describe the devastating effects on the patient of society's deep fear of cancer and expectations of how the disease should be treated.

"Cancer is a taboo word. The fear of cancer is so great that people think of cancer as a death sentence. Health professionals look at the cancer patient in remission and advise, 'Oh you're really sick, so we'll treat every symptom that occurs. You have got to take strong medication or accept surgery, otherwise how can you get well? Or you must take enriching supplements or eat better to become healthy.'"

Sifu concluded, "Everywhere they go, cancer patients get the same reactions from well-meaning people. But the cancer persists–the real danger is the constant or consistent exposure to false ways of dealing with the disease. No wonder the patient becomes confused or gives up. I strongly uphold that these beliefs prevent long-lasting and complete cure."

I agreed with Sifu that it is our emotional reactions and responses that determine whether we succumb to our disease's consequences. When emotional equilibrium is permanently tipped off balance, that inevitably results in shortened lifespans.

It was past 7 p.m. before we began our trip back to Fredericton. I asked Sifu how professionals and health-care workers, who work with sick people on a daily basis, can stay healthy.

"It begins with one's consciousness of perceptions and thoughts and how they relate to energy. Low quality thoughts are denser by nature and more prone to causing illness than higher quality thoughts. Loving thoughts have minimal negative karmic effect."

On the other hand, hostility and hatred of others have a great negative karmic effect that is very heavy and dense energetically. One's worst enemy, and the greatest creator of tension, is negative emotions such as fear, anxiety, and hatred.

"A balanced mind and body produce calm and peaceful states of consciousness," I commented.

"The key to health is to be relaxed, and relaxation is defined as–to be in harmony with nature and in tune with Tao," Sifu said.

"Energetically, the individual is not his or her own perception or self-image. We are basically all the same. Our vibrations interchange freely. We are all connected to the same and constant source of radiant energy that is health-sustaining to ourselves and others."

We had reached the outskirts of Fredericton. I thought about the trip planned for the next day. We were to drive to Portland, Maine, to catch a plane to Charlottesville, Virginia. This was to be Sifu's first ever visit to the United States.

10

Lighting up Virginia

I brought Sifu along to the conference at the Monroe Institute with the intention of having him listen to Western technologically oriented methods of working with consciousness and energy. My experience is that our physical bodies are merely the densest part of who we are and an adventure lies ahead to discover and perceive our energy selves. Sifu was also invited to conduct a workshop on his special healing technique.

That first evening in Charlottesville, Sifu and I strolled over valleys with panoramic views of the Blue Ridge Mountains and headed toward the river bank. I described to him the Monroe Institute's mission to help people learn more about their energy selves using sound-frequency techniques to induce meditative states of consciousness.

I talked about my two-hour address to Institute members scheduled for the next morning. I explained to Sifu how it felt to be in a state of complete brain hemispheric synchronization.

"It's very much like a meditative state when one is physically fully relaxed, with the mind open and alert. One is no longer troubled by external and bodily sensory input nor feels restricted by time and space."

Future evolution of life on earth depends on humanity's consciousness and ability to balance intellect with survival instincts. It is this deeper awareness of the connectedness of self and others that brings matters of the brain and heart together to deal with life's challenges, and to sustain planetary life. Peace in our hearts will then also be reflected in our environments.

I said to Sifu, "That awareness, for instance, would bring to an end the escalating armed conflicts plaguing the world today and the 'studied indifference' to the plight of millions of war traumatized children."

The fundamental question of the seat of human consciousness remains a mystery. Neuroscientists, after more than a century of searching, have concluded that there is no specific place in the brain where consciousness is located. Unquestionably, their assumptions about the source of consciousness are in doubt. But what the brain does continually, whether awake or asleep, is to make images, which are purely mental constructions, even when the stimuli are from external reality. Like a rainbow, our consciousness and perceptions of external reality have no objective reality which can be measured.

"Presumably we all see the same colors of the rainbow. But they are all merely reflections of one form of energy to another," I said.

I knew from previous discussion with Sifu, that he also firmly asserted that neither consciousness nor mind was located solely in the brain.

"No, it's not in the mind or brain. It's all in the energy. We are comprised of a composite, or sum total of energies, beginning with the inherent energy from parents and past karma.

"These will define the kinds of energy which become the experiences one will face through life."

"So you're saying that our mind is just a concept or a quality, rather than being the intrinsic aspect of consciousness?" I responded.

"Shall I say that the mind or brain itself is more like a display screen of the intrinsic energy that is our essence? It is a special faculty located in a special place, whereby whatever energy activation occurring is brought to your awareness."

"And you also disagree that consciousness is in the brain?" I queried.

Sifu guided me saying,"Okay, say we study or read a book. That reading itself involves the absorption of energy since in the act of reading, energy is absorbed through the eyes, as you interpret its meaning, and experience various emotional reactions. All the organs including the eyes, various areas of the brain, the head, other body parts, and eventually the heart are affected. The energizing effect from reading a book is stored all over such areas, and not just the brain."

He elaborated, "Perhaps, in the heart section, as you get excited by what you read, you feel the muscles in that area tensed up or aroused. So these are all energies drawn from the act of reading, that form the memory of the reading itself.

"Of course, when recalling the memory, the energy within all these places becomes activated, and manifests in the thoughts. You think that your consciousness comes only from the brain, but that's not necessarily true.

"For people who are more energy-sensitive, they, when recalling some event, can detect an energy flow in certain specific places over the entire body."

Apparently what drove the brain was the vital energy in the body, and the brain was just a specific component. Still feeling dissatisfied with this explanation, I pointed out that the brain stored information much like computer hardware storing data.

"To begin," he explained, "it's helpful not to disbelieve in energy, but to be open-minded enough to allow for this possibility. By being open to understand this energy system, the individual can personally discover this truth–these data are not stored in the brain. When I go into meditation I feel, see, and understand its true nature. I also see it in patients," Sifu said.

He expanded this notion, saying, "Consciousness is in the energy, and one's energy is everywhere in the body. When you unwind the energy forces, such information resurfaces like pages of material in a book opening up. The words may originate from the left side of the body, or maybe on the right side. It can be in the stomach, it can be anywhere."

"The energy can even be outside the body, "I nodded.

Psychophysiology of Energy Healing

On the second day of the conference, we had a tour of the research laboratory facilities and a review of the research conducted at the Institute. I told Sifu that he might be curious about a study looking at brain wave changes of meditators in the research lab. I wanted to dwell on the electro-cortical activity of meditation and the kinds of changes in brain frequencies that are of relevance for Gold-Body energy healing.

Contemporary wisdom suggests that a higher or purer energy state is associated with higher rates of vibration. A purer state of consciousness, presumably, is endowed with corresponding purer energy and correlates with faster bursts of cortical frequencies. I suspected that in this brain state, detachment from ordinary processing of information was complete to allow for an inner-world processing that was more relaxed, insightful, spontaneous and of greater potent symbolic meaning.

Mystical experiences are associated with slow frequency bursts in the central cortical activity that is accompanied by a progression of higher-powered and faster-synchronous beta. The sudden appearance of gamma frequencies appears to be the transition to the transcendent state. This is defined as an awareness and perception beyond one's normal ego-self limits into a universal knowing and awareness. Subjective reports of 'out-of-body' experiences, a sense of merging with other people, and ecstatic feelings of rapture are common.

I thought about Sifu's teachings that regarded the most essential core of life as something beyond the physical to the 'Heart energy' center. As energy beings, a proper understanding and cultivation of energy principles meant the difference between an optimal healthy existence and pre-mature aging and disease.

Certainly, the electromagnetic fields that envelop the body have long been known to exist, and are measurable by magnetometers. It has also been established that during shifts in higher states of consciousness, the person's external electromagnetic field progressively increases in frequency and power that coincides with internal cortical changes. They suggest that the energy component of the body extends beyond brain and skin boundaries.

"What is needed," I pointed out to Sifu, "is a breakthrough involving not only detecting and regulating electro-cortical changes within the brain but also grasping how the entire energy body electromagnetically functions to regulate health."

Sifu's brief talk on meditation and healing demonstration to the audience during the third day of the conference generated enormous interest by delegates. He explained how meditation would benefit them. For energy psychotherapists and massage therapies, such as acupuncture, reflexology, reiki, and body massage, it was imperative that they should expand their understanding beyond their own specific area.

"In the past, when I first offered healing on a voluntary basis, I also used such healing techniques but without much understanding. Apparently, it works with some patients," Sifu explained.

"But, I didn't know what was being given to the patient, what makes the energy work, and what makes the patient well."

Sifu said, "But now with a full understanding of CFQ principles, there has been a tremendous increase in effectiveness. I can see that energy is about sending relaxation energy. It should open from inside out. Things open and are let go. Once you understand this, the quality of energy will certainly change. Those who follow other methods of healing will, after practicing CFQ, also develop something more.

"The diligent practitioner instinctively had the appropriate knowledge, even after a few months of CFQ meditation."

But they could use healing in their own way without necessarily labeling it as energy meditation or CFQ.

"That is not important," Sifu said. "Instead of holding on to preconceived ideas they have been trained on, now they are more open. They appreciate and know why they work in a particular way, instead of what others say."

Someone in the audience asked about experiencing beneficial energy. This was Kathina, a healer, who earlier had volunteered to be the recipient of Master Yap's transmitted healing energy. At the end of fifteen minutes, her aching neck and back pain had vanished. Kathina, also an astrologer, was speaking about the possibility of a Golden Age of energy in the new millennium.

Sifu cautioned, "Many practitioners erroneously believe that energy is omnipotent; that the more energy the better. But at times it may not be totally good for the person."

"In meditative states," Sifu commented, "one might see, for example, colors and also sense various heightened bodily sensations. When there is some color, the energy experienced is no longer the purest form."

But colors differs in purity, and lighter shades that one feels happier with are the purer forms of energy. Those that are darker, denser, and cause discomfort, attach to the body and are impure, or less pure energies. If one feels happy with it, and it doesn't create too much discomfort, or it is not disturbing that much, then it is purer regardless of the color. This is also the case with electrical impulses. Electrical sensations are all impure. But they differ again in the density of impurity.

"There is a belief that all that one needs to do is transmit energy, and the more energy given to the patient the better. Of course, that belief can harness some energy, and give something to the patient who will feel some benefit. But in the long run, it will turn into adversity," said Sifu.

Kathina nodded and raised the issue of transmitting energy in group healing.

He gave a direct reply. "There is something transferred for sure. Prayer is the energy created by belief. The energy has been created and directed to the subject of prayer. The belief automatically harnesses the cosmic energy.

"Cosmic energy being so pure, so vibrant, and so fine, it is easily shaken by any thought pattern, and for that matter any belief. Faith is good enough to convert it. It steps down and goes to the target subjects without their knowledge."

There is a transfer of energy without anyone knowing. However, the intention of the prayer is good enough.

But he cautioned, "Whether that energy transmitted is of lasting benefit to the subject is a question mark."

Sifu agreed that healing could be done a thousand miles away. Energy being finer than physical matter, it could move any distance. It was not subjected to the limitations of physical objects.

He declared, "Energy is finer than light–it's ultra-light, and moves instantaneously. So there's nothing strange that the energy can be easily transmitted over vast distances. Prayer is mental energy tilting toward good, and will work along that line. If you are imposing such energy on the problem, the patient will feel well temporarily. But it's not a cure, only relief."

Apparently, the cause of the problem remained since it had not been dissolved, so the problem resurfaced again.

"But then with new stimulation, eventually the problem gets worse. That's because stimulation is tension that is added to the existing dense energy," Sifu explained.

Sifu, in the past couple of days, had given me much understanding based on his wonderful grasp of healing and energy. In the misty cool of the Virginian sunrise, I woke up suddenly and quickly scribbled what had stuck in my consciousness:

Open your Heart energy,
Dissolve the tension forces.
Bring down unbounded Golden Light.

The following day, Sifu was approached by some conference participants for treatment. There was one female college student who suffered from chronic fatigue with frequent stomach upsets. After a few sessions, her condition improved and her fatigue was gone. Another was a twelve-year-old girl with attention deficit problems, and her parents appeared gratified by the observed changes.

Sifu noticed Kathina, who was working with two AIDS patients. He could see that she was extremely empathetic and was trying very hard. But he felt she had become overly emotional by becoming too involved with them.

"She was filled with depressed emotions, and there is a lot of hidden sadness in her. I left her a note giving a strong suggestion that she must release that negative emotion for her own benefit," he said.

A healer should work with full sincerity, but after that forget totally. To do otherwise is to be stuck with the patient's plight itself, and that is harmful to the healer. I would approach Kathina on this matter later on as I sensed a special connection to her.

That evening, Sifu announced that we would meditate together for the first time.

"In this session, I will put you into a deeper state of meditation," he said. "What I mean by that is that I will try to rearrange your energy pattern for you; bring it down deeper, and this will generally penetrate deeper to release and radiate outward. This is going to excite the tension forces from within the body more vigorously."

Thirty minutes later, I shared with Sifu what I had experienced during the meditation. I felt that during the practice, a force was pushing from the abdomen down as well as from behind, and right through to the ground.

Sifu explained, "Yes, take note of the phrase, 'pushed down.' It is really not pushed down. Pushing down requires an effort. But of course I have worked for you in your meditation and you feel that it is pushing down. Very often things melt off and they just go down naturally."

Continuing he said, "Two kinds of forces are actually happening here. First, you have the tension force which is, by nature, 'upward suspending' in relation to the torso. And now we have introduced sufficient healing energy, generated by the Mantra that has a downward flushing effect.

"Downward flushing does not mean that effort is involved. It is effortless. But these two forces come through together and they create the effect of melting away the suspending force. And because the suspending force clings on in the process of being flushed down, you feel that it is being pushed down."

I interjected that a better word to describe the sensation was being pulled down.

"O.K. If you feel that it is pulling down, the predominant sensation is the healing energy. With the pushing down sensation, the tension sensation is more predominant. One force will produce an equal and opposite force. That means the tension force is as strong or almost as strong as the healing force. Together it creates the right effect. But we are not participating by not using any effort."

Sifu concluded his observations of my meditation. "Primarily, this session has occurred in the way that I desired for you. I wanted to let you feel the deeper, inner tension forces, how they melt off, come out, surface, radiate away, and finally go down. In the process of feeling that, you have felt the forces to be quite heavy and very sticky. Indeed, the transformation can be entirely physical.

"In your case, I could clearly see the changes occurring externally as well. Your body was bouncing and 'fighting' back and forth. That is the melting process of deep tension forces. So you have now experienced being carried one step deeper into relaxation," he said.

He added, "But there is also the radiating effect that is more subtle, opening up from everywhere in you. It is okay not to feel it clearly for the time being.

"Whatever it is, let it flow down that way. It is simply letting go."

This was to be our last evening at the Institute. I needed to know what experiencing a pure energy state was like.

I asked Sifu, "Once we become purer and purer, do we stop having vivid imagery, see colors, or feel electrical sensations?"

"Yes," he conceded, "you have a profound knowing that you are part of the cosmic. You feel very light, very tranquil, and very peaceful. But you are wide awake and alert. You are part of everything and you are not bothered about anything. It is a totally effortless state of being."

"So at that point," he went on, "it's not seeing any manifestations such as physical, electrical, or colorful sensations. But there will still be other manifestations in terms of external forces that can move your body around. The letting go and karmic cleansing process continues. Of course, this is again effortless."

He elaborated further. "The pure energy works on external forces naturally, but at this stage there is a contrast effect. The contrast comes from working on refining the energies progressively. Yes, bear in mind that as you refine it further, you are moving more and more inward."

Each time a certain level of tension is released, one actually feels that it is quite difficult. As it gets released, it becomes very heavy. As it moves downward and outward, slowly it becomes lighter and lighter and then it goes away.

"Then as you shift further into the purified state, you may have a brief wondrous experience or moment of being almost at one with the cosmic," Sifu added.

But this phenomenon will further work inward to dissolve another spot of dense forces and one feels the heaviness again.

"So cultivation of the path is not necessarily a continuous, joyous state. Even when you reach a deeper layer, the dense forces are still very dense, and it doesn't mean it's finer. In fact, it can be even more dense than at the beginning of practice.

"But the difference is that now you're connected more with the purer energy after having released more layers. You feel more assurance that this is dense energy. It's there, but you don't know how it was formed in the first place."

Now, more pure things or energy are at one's disposal. The body itself feels very light in, as well as, out of meditation. For the rest of the day after meditation, one feels very fresh and alert.

"Eventually," Sifu concluded, "practice is extended to every hour of the day. At all times, the Mantra is there with you and you can make use of it. And at all times, you're letting go and you are fully aware of any phenomenon as soon as that comes in."

The conference in Virginia was coming to an end. Now the experiences on Western soil had reinforced and validated much that Sifu taught. I was ready to be a cultivator of the Tao or Metta Way, a path that would take me face to face with the quest for the 'Golden Light'.

11

The Psychology of Resilience

Six months had passed since Sifu left Canada to return home. I was concerned with what effect the Gold-Body energy had on me and what difference it would make. I felt sure that I could see how such changes would be played out through whatever expected events, as well as unpredicted changes, unfolded in the months ahead.

A new location for these formations was warranted. I wanted also to return to Boulder, Colorado, to contact friends I had not seen for years. I felt that the Southwestern region would be ideal for a variety of reasons. As it turned out, through the co-operation of Jonathan, a psychologist, and Mary who lived in San Marcos, Texas, I had shelter for a couple of months at the local university there. It was in Southwest Texas State, located close enough for me to get to New Mexico, and Colorado. Soon I discovered that the origins of Texas were older than colonial American history. The history of American independence originated not only from British colonies on the Atlantic seaboard, but in Texas.

Mary and Jon took good care of us in San Marcos. We toured the huge and sprawling campus located on a hill. The campus had grown from its former Teachers College, which had the distinction of being the alma mater of President Lyndon B. Johnson. Conversations easily led to many recollections of my student life in Boulder, Colorado, more than

25 years earlier. Jon, also a college student then, shared with me some of his struggles as well.

It was obvious that the 'Zeitgeist' that influenced college life back in the late 1960's was not only different and unparalleled, but continues to foment society today. The focal event of the Vietnam War galvanized a variety of consciousness and social movements and a growing distrust of rigid orthodoxy and established institutions. In the '60's generation, like some never forgotten music of one's youth, a liberating energy had been set on course. But the momentum of that expanded global conscience seemed to have faltered and stalled.

Jon and Mary reminded me of another American couple, from Boulder, Colorado, who joined the Peace Corps during the Vietnam War, and were posted to Malaysia where I was teaching. It was through these American friends' influence that I ended up going to school in the United States. Jon had a penchant for driving his Mercedes Benz, something he acquired from his youthful years in Germany. I thought about my young dreams of driving that '57 olive green Jaguar.

I told Mary about my engagement in Chicago, just before leaving Canada to head out to Texas. Kathina, whom I had met in Virginia, joined us for a retreat weekend about experiencing healing energy. The Chicago workshop group of twelve had a variety of reasons for attending, ranging from alternative healing to spiritual growth. Most were looking for another way to deal with their physical and psychological pains. The meditative experiences and manifestations of healing energy evidently produced insights and a cathartic release.

Kathina was delighted. She announced that her own severe migraine was gone after several months of energy meditation practice. One couple felt that they had gained in one weekend of energy psychotherapy what had taken three years of conventional therapy to accomplish. All had some aspect of their expectations met.

In Texas, as a 'international scholar' living on campus, I was obligated to present a couple of lectures related to human rights. I started off by stressing that the global prevention of psychopathology, social problems, and protection of children should be at the fore-front of professional efforts.

The origins of mental disorders and disease or the fundamental noxious agent is basically trauma-inducing stress and violence, and the pathology carrier is the perpetrator's egocentric consciousness of self preservation. Children, dramatically, have become the target of despicable violence domestically, nationally, and world-wide. In the past decade, global exploitation, greed, intolerance, and injustice have led to numerous armed conflicts from the Americas, Eastern Europe, Middle East, Africa, and Asia killing hundreds of thousands and displacing, disabling, terrorizing and traumatizing millions of children. And as the century turns, each day, thousands of children continue to suffer without hope or help from an indifferent world.

Toward the end of my visit, a final lecture was arranged, this time to a wider audience on campus at the LBJ Auditorium. I mulled over what I wanted to talk about and figured that drugs and sex would grab the interest of any audience. I recalled mentioning to Sifu my association with child rights groups in South-East Asia involved confronting the escalating, global expansion of the sexual exploitation of children. A global pandemic of drug use and HIV infection that affect the health and safety of youths threaten the stability and economies of nations.

I described the trafficking of children—treated, like in the drug trade, as human commodities for exploitation, to be bought and sold for profit. Child victims, seen as the latest 'hot' consumer commodity, were paid to perform sexual acts which were taped and disseminated as video pornography. Those who become infected with AIDS are discarded or left to fend for themselves. The predators come from near and far, and the authorities either are silent or condone it, in the name of tourism, entertainment, and national development.

"While legal sanctions, political will, and other interventions are being brought in to prevent the widespread problem, what could be done to help child victims recover from their trauma?" I challenged.

"I feel," I said, "that these children need resilience or inner strengths and skills to face the trauma and shock which are also manifested in physical and behavioral problems. To become resilient, they need much support and resources to return to a harmonious consciousness. This will in turn rekindle a commitment to themselves and to life. These children had gone through hell but had survived."

Sifu emphasized the impact of these haunting experiences, pointing to the traumatic memories that were energetically stored and solidified in the physical body.

"The energy becomes very hard and letting go of the past is difficult. To remove or 'tear off these old pages' of fearful experiences in the victim's life history is not easy to do effectively."

I thought another way was to help open 'new pages' that promotes child resilience and to avoid the influence of the nightmarish 'old pages'. To optimize their health they must first return to a calm and peaceful state by undoing the trauma trapped in their physical and energy systems.

"The most important solution is unconditional love expressed by care-givers, or those who work closely with these children. Love will dilute the central emotion felt by exploited children that revolves around hatred of others, resentment, and a feeling of utter destruction, toward both self and everything. The direct solution to nullify the intense negative emotions is with the energy of love. This is the starting point to recovery," I stated.

"Recovery means," Sifu suggested, "opening new pages or ways by showering children with love. Surround them with beauty from nature as well as decorative crafts and objects."

He went on, "The love, concern, and tolerance modeled by helpers will break through the children's distrust and ensure that the old trauma would not hinder the anticipated change to a better future.

They need encouragement to love others, and should be taught concern for self and others."

"Helping others is therapeutic, and is a central trait of children who are naturally resilient," I agreed. "The energy of love or connectedness heals trauma."

I remember the story of Kim, when a single tragic moment in her life, enshrined in a wire service photo, came close to marking the end of the Vietnam War. In 1972, the world watched the evening news of an American napalm air strike, and reacted with horror, anguish, and sorrow for a nine-year old naked Vietnamese girl, screaming and running from the cloud of explosion, with clothes burnt off, skin peeling and hanging from a naked body and limbs.

Miraculously, Kim survived the ordeal and war trauma, but spent courageous years of physical and emotional pain from the burns and terror. Then as a young adult receiving treatment in Germany, she defected, and was offered asylum in Canada.

In the U.S., she met up with the major players of that historic picture–the camera and news reporters, and the doctors who had healed her, all living in Los Angeles. There were moving scenes with tears of joy, release, and gratitude. There were also healing scenes of mutual forgiveness, and awe, as she met the American officer who ordered the bombing. When she spoke to veterans, they were touched, and that included many veterans injured and still haunted by lost comrades and mortified by the never-forgotten horrors of the war.

Kim is now happily married with a child of her own and living in Toronto. The disfiguring scar tissue that covered 90 per cent of her shoulders, back, and arms, and the intermittent pain from damaged nerve endings will remain forever, but her resilient spirit shines through to sustain healthy, exuberant functioning. Recently, she was honored with a U.N. Ambassador of Goodwill award.

But for many less fortunate traumatized children, reactions to abuse and fear can last into adulthood. The post-traumatic fearful reactions become "hot-wired" to the emotional brain or limbic system perpetuating fight-or-flight emotional responses instead of being mediated or balanced by the rational thinking of the pre-frontal cortex.

I felt that the abuse and sexual trauma had become rooted in the energy system as psychological disturbances. For a breakthrough in the healing process, the trauma-based energy blockages must be released and resilience rebuilt in the long road to recovery. I was optimistic that energy healing methods could help to heal these child survivors striving to let go of their daunting past, in order to thrive as adults.

Sifu turned to the issue of helping the care-givers themselves.

"For the adult energy helper, remember the interchange notion of energy transmission, that is, 'Everyone radiates.' Shower your audience, and your children with love. The CFQ mantra is a love mantra. Tune into this to radiate love. Let the adults feel what you mean so that they can impart it to the children they care for."

I also wanted to address in my lecture, the nature of the human spirit and its inherent healing powers, the very source of the protective power of resilience.

Transcending Self, Transforming Society

My purpose was to suggest that as we seek the truth of our being, we are confronted with the reality of the connectedness of all life. As we uncover the truth of who we are, we also discover that our state of health and well-being is closely associated with the well-being of others. Understanding and working to change oneself is crucial for society to be transformed.

I began by recounting my student days in Boulder, Colorado when college students confronted a true 'fight or flight' scenario, grappling with the anguish of a troubled society in the midst of the unpopular Vietnam War. I looked at the back wall of the auditorium which has a large picture of a gloomy LBJ, the president beaten by an unwinnable war.

Looking at the audience, I said, "We know little of the inner world of the human spirit and consciousness. Psychology and medicine need to factor in this non-physical creative energy dimension into the health equation.

"While decades of life have been added to the human lifespan in the past fifty years, health quality has not necessarily improved much. Cancer, circulatory diseases, and depressive disorders continue to rage. New strains of bacteria and viruses are creating un-treatable strains of old diseases, as well as sprouting new ones."

Meanwhile, the arsenal of chemicals and overused antibiotics is depleted and ineffectual.

"Promotion of resilience in the population is urgent—it is an essential protective factor to grow and thrive in the midst of unhealthy environments.

"How does one access the wisdom of the human body?" I probed.

"There is awareness that as we sit quietly and allow our consciousness to shut down stimulations drawn in by the five senses, and shift away from thoughts coming from the sixth sense (or the mind), we become conscious of something else that is qualitatively different from the six senses.

"In a deep state of relaxation, we can experience the healing energy, something that exists in us, but that we know little about."

Many Eastern practices and belief systems can help us understand how to get there. I reminded my audience that the scientific revolution began by demonstrating that what is apparent from ordinary sensing, is not real or true at all.

"Anyone driving across the unending Texas terrain, as I did, looking at an apparent, absolutely flat Gulf Coastal Plains, could easily mistake the entire world to be flat. Galileo, at the University of Padua, showed that the sun did not revolve around the earth, contradicting what we daily observe of the sun rising in the east and setting in the west. The earth is spinning endlessly on its axis, even though we feel that it is completely stationary.

"We cannot ignore what we see, but neither can we accept the world according to our five senses as the absolute reality," I said emphatically.

"Physical objects are purely mechanical arrangements of matter in motion. The astounding discoveries of the laws of energy in quantum physics are insights of physical reality that are just as valid to understand the nature of human life."

I showed slides of EEG brain states, using computerized brain mapping technology, to illustrate what appears to be going on during shifts in consciousness.

"In the transcendent state, a higher vibrational brain pattern appears as we become detached from our time/space life dimensions experiencing a profound sense of peace."

In 1970, psychologist Abraham Maslow, the co-founder of humanistic and transpersonal psychology, studied the lives of exceptional and healthy people who described their peak experiences. Those experiences sounded very much like the stuff of transcendent states. William James, the father of American psychology long ago, was indeed transformed by such states.

"During this state, the person experiences an inner harmony, and perceives truths that profoundly alter perceptions of oneself and the world dramatically."

"Current evidence," I pointed out, "also clearly support Maslow's contention that individuals can thrive in physically unhealthy environments. The healthiest individual is one who is committed to transcendent goals such as helping others, and lives to pursue transcendent values' such as truth, beauty, justice, goodness, wholeness, and playfulness. The ultimate is transcendence itself, or the pursuit of cosmic identification."

I attempted to show how Maslow's model of the healthy personality duplicates the core characteristics that are significant in the experience of meditative self-transcendence. Studies of deep meditative states indicate that the transcendent shift has several distinct characteristics.

"There is an affective quality, or an infusion of love of truth, beauty, and justice. This is the experience of the tranquility of '*Metta*' or loving-kindness and joyous alertness. Second, there is also a deeper sense of knowing and understanding reality," I explained.

Psychologically, one's earlier disease-prone profile, derived from early conditioning, limiting self-perception, and stress-provoking responses to reality, can be effectively discarded. There can be freedom from the dualistic problems of the mind and the heart, as detachment from the contents of one's thoughts develops to enhance emotional equilibrium.

"Third, there is loss of separateness and an awareness of universal consciousness. There is an opening to become more detached from one's normal self, and develop a profound sense of connection with the external world, culminating with a sense of deep empathy or motivation to help relieve the suffering of others in society."

I concluded by proposing a shift in future direction of medical science to enable each person to thrive in today's complex, stressful world.

"Practitioners," I proposed, "can rise to the challenge of optimizing health in the 'whole person' rather than instead of brain or body parts, of studying optimistic rather than negative emotions, resilience rather than disease-proneness, and self-healing rather than a treatment orientation."

To accomplish this, the insights of both Eastern and Western medical science, arts, and practices can be commingled, with the potential to create a revolution in human consciousness and healthy living.

Just before leaving Texas, I had one more task to do in Austin, having been invited by Mary to present meditation techniques to her friends. This was a non-college, meditation study group interested in energy transmission.

I drew the audience's attention to a curious finding. A review of epidemiological studies shows an ubiquitous, mathematical U-shaped function between the level of any specific, beneficial health factor, and the proportion in the general population dying from a disease.

The relationship, for example, between high serum cholesterol in blood and heart disease is often not linear. In fact, people with average cholesterol levels are more likely to live longer, compared to those with abnormally high and low levels.

People, for some reason, do not appreciate the message that, 'too much of a good thing is bad for you.' But this rule of nature, termed 'hormesis,' that substances which are toxic in high doses are beneficial in small doses, is well known. Similarly, in studying the benefits of exercising, dieting, or following a healthy lifestyle regimen, doing more is not better.

"But the alternative is not simply to do everything in moderation. The problem issue has to do with a deeply-rooted societal value for acquisition, of 'more is better' whether it be for more information, working endlessly, getting more things done faster, or craving fame, fortune, and possessions. "

"Today America is enjoying an era of unprecedented prosperity. Yet the number who are victims of violent crime, are sick without medical coverage, or grow up in poverty continue to accelerate.

"Maslow's motivational model of needs provides a distinction between the acquisition and letting go approaches," I explained.

Acquisition methods are necessary to meet deficit needs of the ordinary self. The goals pursued are to meet the demanding needs of family, work, and social life. It seems that many needs here are insatiable to the extent of being detrimental, when pursued beyond health limits. "Only by adhering to a letting-go approach, can the needs of the 'higher self', that values transcendent goals, be possibly realized. By letting go of one's lower self, the practitioner enters a state of freedom and this will awaken his/her true or higher self. The Buddha is a consummate model of completely letting go, that is, to exist in an effortless state of being."

I tried to convey, in a nutshell, what I believed to be essential in meditation, so that my audience could use the information as principles or evaluation criteria throughout their own meditation.

Swaying rhythmically, I said, "Tension energy released during meditation often manifests as involuntary or spontaneous movements. When one layer of tension is removed in this way, deeper layers of disease-causing tension will surface and be cleansed."

Eastern philosophy and medical science also believe that the mind is not located in any one organ or physical location, but resides in the entire person.

"It is the energy aspect that is crucial to one's core being, going beyond the mind itself," I asserted.

However, it is claimed that the most critical is the Heart energy center, located around the heart region. This challenges neuroscience claiming that the brain, and not the heart, is the seat of feelings, thoughts, and memories.

"Greek philosophers like Aristotle, and the ancient Egyptians associated the mind with the heart. When a pharaoh was mummified for the afterlife, the heart and other body organs were preserved, but the brain was discarded."

"In a totally relaxed state," I ended, "the natural exchange of one's energy with the pure cosmic energy, or cosmic identification, is enhanced."

Finally we fell silent, and sat comfortably together in meditation.

Part Five

Meso-American Jade

12

Southwestern Graffiti

Hexagram 37

The Sequence: He who is injured without,
Of a certainty draws back into his family.
Hence there follows the hexagram of The Family.
The Judgment: The Family.
The perseverance of the woman furthers.

The Book of *I Ching*

After eight weeks, my stay in Texas was nearing its end. During the final days, we traveled around the flat terrain of the southern plains, once in the remote past a vast inland sea. As we took to the road, it was soon obvious that the total Texas highway mileage easily ranks first in America. From the Central Plains, the rocky terrain extends westward to the Rocky Mountains where it hikes up to 6,000 feet in Denver, Colorado. We would soon be leaving for the mile-high city.

But first, we headed south to the Gulf Coast along the coastal line to the resort islands of Padre and Mustang. Swinging further west, we drove along the border of Mexico to savor the Spanish ambience and the dry, tropical terrain. We reached Brownsville, the southernmost city of Texas that is located on the Rio Grande.

I recalled reading a story about some of the area's founding history. Hernan Cortes, the Spanish conquistador in 1519, had conquered Mexico from the Indians. In 1540, Francisco de Coronado set out from Mexico City to search for gold north of the Rio Grande heading for present-day New Mexico. His quest was the treasures of the pueblo Zuni tribes in the fabled Seven Golden Cities of the Cibola. Despite Coronado's intense exploration, going as far north as Kansas, the expedition ended in failure.

Whatever precious treasures the Zuni Indians possessed were not measured in earthly precious metals or jewels, I thought. Like many ancient sites in South-East Asia, it is the treasures of the Heart that can be found emanating in the golden cities of ancient kingdoms.

From Brownsville, I looked in the direction of Matamoros on the far shore of the Rio Grande. I suddenly felt that somehow my own journey in the great plains would be incomplete without including Mexico. Reflecting on the period of residence in Texas, I perceived a definite shift and acceleration on the path journeying toward the Gold-Body energy state. Getting away from familiar ground and territory certainly helped to break off habitual thought patterns. As each step unfolded, the journey expanded naturally to the next step.

I had the illuminating thought that there is a Gold-Body energy connection to proven mind-body dynamics instrumental in holistic health. But the radiant golden hue goes beyond simply understanding mind and personality to one's spirit. I felt a sense of excitement and wonderment anticipating transforming events that lay ahead.

It was time to go to Boulder for a nostalgic visit, a homecoming of sorts. From Austin, the Texas highways, even the rural ones, were spacious and four-lane throughout, crossing vast distances of almost completely flat, dry terrain. I made it a point to stop in a little town called Clifton where we found a motel to spend the night.

I thought of a former Southerner I knew decades earlier, growing up in Penang, by the name of Robert Clifton. I knew him not by his secular name, but as Ven. Sumangalo, an American monk, who ran a Buddhist Center in Penang. It was from him that I first had the opportunity to formally learn Buddhism, beginning in 1960, the time when I was in a teachers' college. He was long gone, I knew nothing about his Southern roots, but I felt good honoring him this way, briefly stopping in the Texas town bearing his name.

As we headed north, into the panhandle, the sun began to set over the isolated landscape. I woke up early the next morning with the window light brightening. Looking out, I could see the road stretching into the desert. It would take us northwest to Colorado.

I caught sight of some desert cactus flowers glistening with dewdrops. The thought came that I had gone past the darkness, and perhaps I would soon catch sight of rare, transforming dewdrops, the kind that blossoms 'spiritual life-seeds' previously planted.

As we continued down the road, it started to loop and wind and finally shrank to two lanes. I knew we had crossed into the northeastern corner of New Mexico. It was a quick journey, riding through valleys and crests spanned by vermillion cliffs, and sweeping vistas of distant plateaus. As the interstate highway gained altitude rapidly, I knew that Colorado was close ahead. Once on Interstate 25, one by one, familiar cities beginning with Trinidad, whisked by on the way north to Boulder. The highway, unlike the way it had been in my salad days, was jam-packed with frenetic traffic and noise. As sundown darkened the red skies, I could see ahead the dark purple slopes of the Flatirons and the city's skyline.

Return to Boulder, Colorado

It was exactly half a lifetime ago that I first arrived in Boulder after I had made the pivotal decision to commence the journey to America to be a student. In Malaysia, when this ambitious purpose was first proposed to me by my Peace Corps friends from Boulder, it sounded ludicrous. There was no way, since I had no money saved from the meager teacher's salary, nor assets to draw on, and besides I had a dependent family. But, my American friend, Bob, was undaunted by reason, and said that the only obstacle was a lack of hardiness to accomplish my dreams.

Bob was right. One evening, walking past some stalls toward the town's cinema hall, I saw a fresh sign in one storefront. Apparently, a palm reader had arrived in town and had put up a shingle. The cost was ten Malaysian dollars for a half-hour reading. I walked in and nodded at a small man with twinkling eyes, seated behind a small, red table.

I said, "I have three dollars."

The man smiled back saying gruffly, "You have my time for three questions."

Not wanting to reveal my true purpose, I asked the usual question of some lotto numbers to bet on. Gazing past me, he quickly rattled off seven digits.

Casually, he said, "Check those numbers out. If you had paid attention to the last four digits in your I.D. card, and placed a bet last week, you would have won a small fortune."

He had never seen me or any identification of me before, but to humor him I took my card out, showed it to Pat who was with me, and looked at the number. He was right. They were the correct digits in my I.D.! I had never seen this guy before, and I simply could not rationally explain how he could have guessed it correctly.

I came up with my second and real question, "Should I go abroad to study?"

He asked for my birth date, and slowly scanned my face.

"I'll put it this way. Your situation is like the dough-mix on the baker's table. The fresh, yeasted dough is rising fast, ready to be placed into the oven. If the baker delays a moment longer, the dough will collapse, and the outcome will be a lump of hard rock, instead of a loaf of fresh bread."

"Act now, or you will not have another opportune time come your way any time soon," he urged.

Impatiently, he told me to ask my final question.

"If I go, will I be successful in my studies?"

Yawning, he replied, "You will succeed beyond anything you can imagine at this time."

In due course, I opted to go west for the first time. I took the long train ride from Penang to Bangkok in late December 1968 and a ship out to Hong Kong. From L.A., on the first day of January, I finally landed in Denver and from there took a bus to the small university town of Boulder.

I had discovered America, called 'Mei Kuo' in Chinese, signifying beautiful kingdom. From the perspective of the Chinese Lunar Calendar, this is the land of the 'Fire-Monkey', the zodiac sign for the year 1776. In 2637 B.C., the 'Ten-Thousand Year' calendar was initiated, by the great Yellow Emperor, Huang Ti, the legendary founder of Taoism and the medical science of longevity. In the lunar calendar, a complete cycle takes 60 years, made up of five simple cycles of 12 years.

In each 60-year cycle, each of the 12 animal zodiac signs is combined with the five elements–wood ruled by Jupiter; fire by Mars, earth by Saturn; gold by Venus; and water by Mercury. Each element is further split into two magnetic poles, positive (or yang) and negative (yin) energy.

So America is born with the energy of the celestial Fire-Monkey and a yang energy sign. This energy is endowed with great drive, fertile imagination, creativity, and resourcefulness. These attributes are conducive to fulfilling a destiny to become the dream machine of the earth. True to form, it was in the realm of the Fire-Monkey that Mankind's dream of landing the first man to walk on the moon became reality. It happened in 1969 during the first year I was living in Boulder, some seven years prior to the American bicentennial anniversary. This technological marvel tells us that creative minds working in unison can achieve any feat.

But it did nothing to solve the greatest mystery–how our minds work in order to understand how to purge the inherent violence..

The first few weeks of my arrival in Boulder were far from my initial rosy expectations. It was close to being unbearably depressing. I had never felt so alone, missing family that I had left far behind. I desperately needed them in Boulder but it seemed it would be years before I could afford to see them. I soon had a plan to bring them over, however. I could save half the cost in five months and borrow the rest from friends.

It was lunch-break in the broom factory where I worked. That was a needed relief from the din and the muscle strain of bending steel wires and stuffing them in a base of molded plastic. When reinforced and strapped together, they were mounted on the back of vehicles, used by the city's sanitary department to clean the streets of Boulder. The broom aptly was symbolic of my life then–sweeping out the old, and preparing for the new.

I sat outside, leaning against the wall, talking to my bearded friend Jim, a lanky Texan and self-professed 'hippie.' I told him my worries about my family back home in Malaysia. They were expected to arrive in Boulder within a month. Pat, my wife, had to get from Penang to the U.S. Embassy in Kuala Lumpur, the capital city, to obtain entry visas. The problem was that a pogrom had broken out against ethnic Chinese and Indians in the country, and martial law had been declared in the country, making it extremely perilous to set foot on the streets, let alone travel to the capital city.

Jim told me to wait a minute, strode over to his tie-die-painted covered truck, and sat down next to me. He untied a red bandanna to reveal a book.

"That's the *I Ching*," he smiled with a wink, and said, "Not to worry," when he noticed my puzzled look.

With a quiet drawl, Jim explained that this was a 5,000-year-old book of divination, and he would show me how to identify the hexagram that would answer whatever question I had. Somehow, my energy field would tune into and attract the correct hexagram and message. He asked me to frame my question silently, and as I watched, he threw three old Chinese coins six times, noting the configuration after each throw.

Finally, he said, "Ah, it's hexagram number 37!"

Jim turned the pages of his *I Ching* book, and showed me the page for interpreting the hexagram 37. As soon as I read the oracle, I knew that this was an auspicious hexagram, that I could trust that the family would be safe, everything would work out, and that good fortune would smile on the reunited family.

Six months after arriving in Boulder, I knew that I was in the one place where it was possible to fulfill whatever I wanted to accomplish. Basic needs were quickly met. I was offered accommodation on campus in 'Vetsville,' with pre-fab quonset huts built after WWII for veterans and their families. I found adequate work to support a young family of five with three children, all under age six. The Malaysian fortune teller's analogy of why I should come to the U.S. was true in another way. I got a job as a baker. I clearly was no baker, but after a few days, my hands knew what to do. I turned out dozens of doughnuts, pies, turn-overs, long-johns, squares, and whatever.

For the first time, I owned a car. It was no Jaguar but a slightly dented 1963, sky-blue Chrysler Newport. Bought for $150, it lasted until we left Boulder. Back when I first arrived in the city, I remembered a convenience store on Arapahoe Street, that had a store-sign, 'Cornucopia', hung over the door. Beside the letters was a picture of a huge horn overflowing with an abundance of fruits, flowers, and grain. When I think of Boulder in those days, I felt like I was in a lotus-like land of Cornucopia, walking around some Oriental bazaar, filled with endless choices of exotica.

Canyons and mountains to climb or ski were within sight of the campus, as well as woods, snow-clad peaks, and unearthly, sun-drenched deserts to lose oneself, far from the madding crowd. Out of curiosity, I mingled with the clusters of euphoric youths and flower children frolicking sensually, or stoned out of their minds on some chemical high. Or I joined the smorgasbord of mystics, yogis, and self-proclaimed divinities, who had come down from their far away holy mountains to encamp in Boulder.

But, I was like someone knowledgeable about bazaars. I knew it was easy to be talked and tempted into buying something, that on returning home, would turn out to be a cheap imitation. Or be attracted by the glitter of fool's gold. I remained a wary observer, and kept out of trouble.

In Boulder, heady changes occurred at giddy speeds on all fronts, and were transforming in nature. At the University of Colorado, my dream seemed imminently reachable. What was impossible in Malaysia, took only four years as I finished three degrees and was set on a new course leading to a new life. More importantly, my family thrived in Boulder, I had matured, and in the process found self-worth, trust, and faith in others.

Returning to Boulder is always a homecoming and celebration. There is our friend Henry, the Boulder mailman born in Singapore, who moved to Texas as an adolescent. He went to high school in Galveston, and served in the Marines during the Vietnam War. Henry, now middle-aged, has a new job in a city department. He asked for a book on energy and Buddhist philosophy. I immediately thought of the "Heart Sutra", that I had once studied in Malaysia, and agreed I would locate a copy for him sometime.

Bob, my Peace Corps friend, who had become wealthy years ago, owned a Lear jet, and was retired as his last business venture ended in near disaster. In a state of despair, he found a flyer about meditation, and has become a practitioner. At fiftyish, he also became a father for the first time. Bob mentioned some retreat place in central Massachusetts where one could train in Vipassana meditation. Henry and Bob's new-found interest in mysticism somehow did not surprise me, even though neither had expressed any such attraction in all the years that I had known them.

There were also friends who were former graduate students working in the area to meet and talk with. However, it was too late to get to know Fred, a neurologist and researcher from Boulder, whom I met the previous year during the conference in Virginia. That was the first and last time that I saw him.

Fred's presentation of research work on the neurophysiology of transcendent states was illuminating and inspiring. He talked about how he first conducted studies on gifted healers in Boulder. One subject, an Australian, had a reputation for transmitting healing energy to others. When he held his hands over someone, the latter would feel warmth, vibration, and energy moving. For patients with consonant belief systems, the tears would also flow. Then the measuring instruments that Fred used, such as a magnetometer held two feet above the healer's head, would also change.

In the healing mode, deep spikes of beautiful ascending frequencies and power were radiated by the healer. So did the frequencies of the patient change as well. The healer emitted high frequency gamma brain waves soaring up to 128 cycles per second, with powerful amplitudes that were totally off the normal range. At the same time, lower frequencies in the alpha, beta or theta ranges had shifted to other brain areas or disappeared.

Fred's research has suggested to me some physiological clues of Sifu's radiant meditation technique. First, when the healer begins to focus on healing, the characteristic high alpha activity becomes frozen. Alpha seems to be an inhibitor of shifts to transcendent states. In normal consciousness, during cognitive learning, one makes a great amount of alpha. The more well-educated the person, apparently, the greater the amount of alpha indicated in the brain.

"When one lets go of alpha, the individual is also letting go of externally imposed knowledge, memories of the past, and expectations of the future," I surmised.

There comes fuller awareness of what is in the moment. This change allows the healer to essentially split away from the normal ego-self, to bring full exclusive attention, and awareness to merge with the energy of the patient. That means a shift away from a time-consciousness to a space-opening consciousness. As the alpha is replaced, at first, there seems to be a shift to a slower or low frequency, and high amplitude emissions localized at the center of the head. Then the electrical activity moves out to the temporal lobes, lighting up in higher gamma frequencies.

From the energy perspective, high frequencies at high voltage signify the introduction of a purified, incoming energy. In the purified consciousness of a healer, this universal energy can be radiated for self-healing, and transmitted to heal others.

I was saddened to hear of Fred's sudden death from leukemia, in the prime of his life, a few months after meeting him. I saw a video made of his last few months. He spoke movingly of five light beings who came to comfort him in addition to family and friends. He was at peace drawing from the love that radiated to uplift his spirit.

"Wonderful, transcendent experiences, however, are apparently insufficient to remove the causal agents of disease," I thought. I again wondered what this state of golden, perfect health would be like.

My brief nostalgic visit to Boulder was coming to an end. Intuitively, it became clear that the excursion to Boulder would lead to the next step of the journey upon which I had embarked. There was one more thing to do before leaving Colorado, however. I was to meet again with Kathina who was visiting in Denver, to talk about a trip to Mexico for an unusual conference.

In Chicago, I had felt no interest when she first mentioned a conference in Mexico. I re-read the conference flyer that she left me. It was to be held in Palenque, a Mayan archeological site, and something about 'Ascended Masters of Light' caught my eye. I suddenly felt that I wanted to go. Somehow, I felt that this was part of the next giant step in my journey of self-discovery.

13

Down Mayan Way

I met a traveler from an antique land;
Who said: Two vast and trunkless legs of stone
Stand in the desert...
Near them, on the sand
Half sunk, a shattered visage lies...

Shelley

The airport taxi had taken me within Villahermosa city limits, before the driver told me that, Palenque, my final destination was 90 miles away. The conference brochure had said to take a taxi into town, and then find the bus to Palenque. Too weary to take a bus, I agreed to let the taxi driver continue on to Palenque. But I told him to stop at the Villahermosa Museum first. I wanted to look at the giant Olmec heads, a great source of mystery from the earliest civilization in Meso-America, displayed in the museum's outdoor garden. I was told that their mysterious civilization suddenly sprang up around 1200 B.C., and lasted for 800 years. All that is known about the Olmecs came from their surviving art.

I saw three giant volcanic heads, each weighing 25 tons, with faces that have distinct undulating lips, broad noses, and oriental eyes, features that experts have dubbed as 'Polynesian.' The faces have an uncanny likeness to the gargantuan faces of '*devarajas*' or god-kings in the ancient cities of the Khmer Empire, in present-day Cambodia.

There is growing evidence to confirm that the Mayans are direct descendants of the little known Olmecs. At the time of the decline of the Roman Empire in 250 A.D., the Mayans began to build exquisite temples and palaces, in the form of terraced pyramids, hewn from limestone and covered with artistic, sculptured reliefs.

The Mayans developed the first written language in the Americas, a complex system that resembles Chinese writing in principle. The golden age of their feats of architecture, astronomy, and art span nearly seven centuries. Yet the Mayans, a Stone-Age culture, did without metal tools and had no use for gold, but instead revered jade as the most precious commodity above all else.

It appears unfathomable how they worked out a system of numbers and mathematics that surpassed anything in ancient Europe and Asia. They invented the idea of '0' which aided greatly in computing multi-digit numbers with ease. Mayan priest-astronomers were able to calculate that the planet Venus took 584 days to complete its stellar circuit, while astronomers today measured it as 583.92 days. The Mayas' calculation of the lunar month was 29.53020 days compared to our 29.53059 days.

The long ride to the town of Palenque, formerly Santo Domingo, located in the Chiapas Highlands, was uneventful, even though an Indian uprising had just erupted. It is in the Yucatan, part of the Mayan heartland. Finally, as we crossed an intersection, the driver held up five fingers, presumably meaning five minutes more. Soon, as we moved downhill, I saw a flock of small birds lifting, and soaring up in front of the road. I smiled to myself, recognizing the doves often mentioned in this area, as the town of Palenque suddenly became visible ahead.

Early the next morning, the conference's participants gathered at the Agua Azul Falls. There were over a hundred people, including the small contingent from Colorado. The Mexicans belonged to various groups from the Yucatan, but were mostly from Cozumel Island, Cancun, and

Mexico City. I moved close to Kathina and her friends from Denver. We all stood in a large clearing beside the Agua Azul rapids.

The roar of the rushing water mingled with the drizzle of rain, as the conference host, Rosa, welcomed everyone and explained that we were all to do a 'Heart opening meditation.' We could invoke a spiritual teacher or 'Ascended Master' of our choice. After a few minutes of silence, people began to fan out and explore the jungle area in reverence. The Agua Azul cascade lay amidst a section of the wide river flowing through a tropical rain forest, and was indeed a perfect place to commune with the elements. The water was a dazzling blue as it cataracted down a series of falls. Each of the fifty levels was covered with swirling pools of water which could be approached from flat rock surfaces on the embankment.

Standing from a rope-bridge slung across the river, one could take in the whole spectacular scene, lit by rays of sunlight shining through the green forest canopy above. The blue water ran past protruding rocks, forming into rapids as it drew closer to the bridge. A few minutes after closing my eyes, as all sounds ceased, a feeling of elation enveloped, and everything seemed to merge. I was glad to be there.

In the afternoon, the sun broke through the clouds and I joined a Denver group on a visit to the archaeological site, the most beautiful, and evocative of all Mayan ruins. Palenque, among all the Mayan sites excavated, is the most sacred ceremonial center with the finest 1,300-year-old temple pyramids, and unparalleled architecture that surrounds an imposing old palace.

This was also the period when another great ruler, the Tibetan King *Sron-btsan-sgampo* (born 617 A.D.) was converted to Buddhism when he married two devout Buddhist princesses, one from Nepal and the other from China. This marked the beginning of Buddhism as the national religion of Tibet, the last Mahayana country to accept Buddhism.

We headed toward the tallest building, a graceful terraced pyramid called the Temple of Inscriptions, because of its many exquisite and deciphered glyphs. It is the most famous of Mayan structures because of a secret that remained hidden until 1952. On the floor of the temple chamber, at the top of the pyramid, a secret stairway was discovered that led to the first ever, archeological discovery of the sarcophagus, and mortal remains of a great priest-king. It was covered with splendorous jade jewelry and precious ornaments of Mayan royalty.

The red color of the inner crypt signified homage to the Lord of the East, the direction of the daily symbolic rebirth of the sun. A jade-green mosaic mask that covered his face, matched the face on the stucco head found below his tomb. Beside his left foot, stood an exquisite, jade sun-god statuette. The glyph beside it named this ruler Pacal.

Amused, I wondered, "Is this symbolic of the jade-green Jaguar that I had longed for all these years?"

Pacal meant 'Sun-shield,' indeed a fitting name for a radiant sun-king. I noted that the unearthing of this sun-god had coincided with the discovery of the exquisitely radiant, larger than life-size, solid-gold Buddha in Thailand. In Mayan cosmology, god-kings had a dark side as well since their gods have both good and evil, heavenly and hellish qualities, as well as masculine and feminine attributes. In the case of the Sun-god, sure enough, as the sun sets, the benevolent sun turns into a nefarious, Jaguar-god to stalk the Underworld darkness. Perhaps Pacal of Palenque was my jade-green Jaguar.

We were indeed peering at the sacred mausoleum of the mystical 7th Century Mayan monarch. We walked single-file down a steep stairway through a damp, narrow, and arched passageway to the tomb below ground. The sarcophagus lay under a five-ton slab of stone, carved on bas relief, showing the monarch descending into the underworld on a 'foliated cross', the symbol of the Tree of Life in Mayan religion. Past the royal mausoleum, is the largest building complex, simply called the 'Palace'. Stucco friezes, throughout the Palace, indicated that this was the abode of Lord Pacal, and his clan. Behind the large ceremonial chambers, are narrow side rooms, each with walls that arch into an apex. As we entered the vault-like cloister, there was a distinct sense of coolness, and feeling of ease.

"I suspect," turning to Kathina, "these were meant for priests to prepare themselves to conduct their ceremonial activities."

From the imposing five-storied tower, as well as several pagoda-like roofs, the king's temple was visible. Mayan architects could well have designed it with an eye to locating the ideal spot to observe the sun rays filtering into the tomb below.

Along a path eastward away from the Palace is a triad of smaller buildings. The temple sculptures showed some baffling connections to contemporary religions. There are intriguing friezes found in the 7th century Temple of the Foliated Cross. The sculptured bas reliefs have an extraordinary resemblance to some found only in the wondrous temples of Angkor, also built by 7th century Khmer kings. The flower motifs in the Mayan temple, mirror the lotus flower, symbolic of Buddhism, but supposedly unknown in ancient Maya.

"Yes, it is the energy connection and exchanges that would make sense of all these inexplicable mysterious similarities," I confided to Kathina, looking into her sky-blue eyes.

I knew that Kathina had some Plains Indian ancestry. "Let me, first, give some plausible possibilities of the Mayan origins."

Archaeologists suggested that Asian peoples entered the Americas probably before the Ice Age when a land bridge between Siberia and Alaska existed.

"Clearly," I continued, "even if Meso-American Indians, such as Olmecs and Mayans, are descended from a common Asian ancestry, this in no way accounts for the apparent similarities in their stone pyramids, temples, religious symbols, and practices that we have seen in the last millennium here and in the East. Unless they all come from the same earlier civilization that once existed but is now lost in time."

It was getting dark, and I could see the shadows lengthen, as the sun descended behind the canopy of hillside trees above the site. I turned around to look at the silhouette of the Temple of the Cross one last time. If one were to gaze at a newly built temple, the whole pyramid would be covered by a light, cream-colored stucco. In the moonlight, the temple would be a dazzling bright gold. I remembered the moon-lighted coach ride in the Pagan Kingdom of Burma with Pat, filled with the glow of the Ananda Temple in all its pristine beauty.

"There is no physical explanation for all the similarities here except for the energy connection," I surmised.

As we left the site, I had the strong feeling that, across time and space, despite their uniqueness, there is an energy connection between Palenque and Pagan, and between mighty empires in the old and new worlds. I looked again at the remarkable site, at Kathina standing there (her eyes had turned jade green), and finally connecting with the joyous faces of the 'spiritual light buffs' from Colorado.

Elated, I thought, "Just like what the Mantra promises, it's all simply beautiful, wonderful, and perfect."

At the moment, the charged energy and enchantment of the environment sustained the original overflowing feeling of timeless perfection. It hung on for the rest of the evening walk with my companions back to the Palenque Inn.

The Light of Palenque

The next morning was to be spent at the Misol-Ha Falls, and as the name implied, perhaps the abode of the Sun-god. Rosa informed me that she wanted me to lead a meditation for the entire group. My job, I felt, was to somehow bring through the healing Gold-body energy, and transmit it to the audience at the Mayan site, where we were to convene at 8 a.m. the next day.

We arrived late at the Misol-Ha area. Rosa introduced me to the group of well over 100 people seated in a thatch-covered clearing. The air was cold and misty, and the clear roar of the waterfall resounded.

I said everyone seemed to have an optimistic view that there are celestial as well as living spiritual masters that can show the way to an enlightened path. I spoke briefly of meeting Master Yap, and the benefits of Golden Light energy to cleanse the body and mind of impurities. I suggested that in the meditation, they invoke whichever Master they connected with. Finally, I guided them through the sitting meditation. They were to relax their bodies and release the impure energies. I told them that as the energy moved out, they could experience strong physical movements, and various types of sensations. After a while, they might experience more subtle and lighter energy to expand their consciousness.

About twenty-five minutes later, the whole group stood up in unison and walked outdoors, toward the waterfall. Standing still in front of the towering waterfall, everyone was singing and chanting, and the collective sounds seemed to soar skyward, reverberating in the drenched rain forest. As the standing meditation went on, soft sunlight filtered through the tall emerald forest trees onto the congregation, and the space seemed to become charged. The sound of the cool waterfall was energizing. My body was warm and my clothes dry, even though a misty rain was falling.

The space within expanded, and my body sensations seemed to disappear. In front of me, the waterfall was strangely muted. Yet it poured straight down, from a cliff about 100 feet high, forming three white cords of water streaming into the deep emerald-jade pool below. Perhaps, that had something to do with the ecstatic feeling that vibrated from my head and chest, as three streams of white light seemed to pulsate through me. The vibrations carried me along ever outward. My awareness shifted to the enormous tree trunks covered with vines, and foliage encircling the banks of the blue water, cascading gently downhill.

But I continued to be in a state of transparency and lightness. The light seemed to change color, and I felt a serene vibrance that was familiar, and totally safe. I picked out a vivid image of a moss-covered trail crossing a precipitous ravine. From there, looking from behind the roaring waterfall, the whole forest stretched out while past the wet rock trail going uphill, a cave lay ahead.

At the entrance floor, from the interior, a stream could be seen in the dim light, gliding around pebbles and large rocks resting in midstream. All of a sudden, the dimness behind me brightened, warming my heart, that throbbed with waves of joyous pulsation, seemingly resonating with the energy present.

But when I felt shadows flickering on the cave wall, I knew that I should leave the cave. Suddenly, I opened my eyes, startled by voices announcing that we were finished, and should break for lunch. I was still standing exactly where I had been all along throughout the meditation.

My body felt light and easy as I walked to join the group. I was surprised by the reactions to the morning's meditation. Rosa beamed and smiled at me saying that she liked the energy.

"I want to dance with you as soon as possible," she said because I needed it.

A woman came rushing over to me excitedly. She quickly introduced herself to me as Alma, from Cozumel. She had a chronic debilitating back pain that seemed to disappear as she ended the meditation. There were endless hugs from the people returning to the buses. Kathina thanked me, and said it was wonderful. She looked at me with her glowing eyes, and said she had never felt so safe and loved. I felt good that I had contributed something worthwhile to the group.

That evening, I turned over in my mind the day's events and ethereal experiences. There was the meditation facing the Misol-Ha waterfall where I seemed to have shifted to an entranced state that transported me into the dim cave. There I had felt both passion and trepidation encountering the light shining from behind me.

It was five a.m. the next morning, and everyone was already awake at the Inn. All were dressed in white, as we had been instructed. Rosa called me over, and to my surprise, said that she wanted me to join her group waiting in her van. Her group was the advance party scheduled to enter the Palenque ruins to perform a cleansing ceremony, and to invoke the energy of the Masters as the morning sun ascended the skies.

I was invited to join the ceremonies. She introduced me to the passengers which included her mother, aunt, and an uncle. I knew her charismatic uncle Daniel, who shared a room with me at the Inn. I knew also that Rosa's mother, who lives in Brownsville, Texas, was a well-known spiritual healer. Each day of the conference, she performed several outdoor cleansing ceremonies wherever the group went. She articulated the mantras used to awaken the 'internal master' within the spiritual explorer. Altogether including myself, there were seven people as we drove off to the Palace.

We were the first group to arrive at the deserted site in pitch darkness. The sleeping security guard was aroused, and he lifted the gate to allow us to enter. With some oil lamps, we made our way across the buildings, passing the Temple of Inscriptions, to Lord Pacal's Palace. We walked single-file through the galleries, and finally down the steps into the courtyard.

Nobody spoke except the group's elder aunt Cecilia, who whispered instructions to the rest. Candles and incense were lit, and I followed them as they circumvented the courtyard along the walls. I understood that this was the initiation of the cleansing ceremony. Each person was repeating some sort of prayer as he/she paused to face a section of the Palace courtyard's walled enclosure.

I began to softly intone my Mantra. Soon, I had turned inward, and stopped watching what the others were doing. Thoughts about purification welled up as I connected with Sifu.

"Open the heart, and transmit the pure energy. Keep this up until the air feels thick and sticky with the fine vibration. Move to every corner of the space that needs to be purified. Transmit the vibrations in all directions. Empty the mind, and be totally aware of the Mantra," Sifu would instruct.

He claimed that invoking psychic energy had the potency of karmic cleansing. In the present context, all the negative energy patterns that have lingered in this spot over the centuries can be dispersed, so that the pure light from this sacred site can radiate the vibrations to unify the earth.

The open sky above began to brighten, heralding the sky god's arrival. I noticed a tinge of red from sunbeams that lit up the tower and roofs. What a sight the fascinating Palace must have been in the time of Lord Pacal! As the sun lifted from the treetops, it would illuminate the haunting sides of the massive Palace and its red painted walls, symbolic of the eastern direction from which the sun rose.

"Today, the Spring equinox begins marking the first day that light and darkness are of equal length. Surely a propitious time to celebrate with the Sun-faced Lord, as it journeys through the entire sky to determine the Mayan concept of the Universe," I figured.

As I opened out, the energy spontaneously manifested as movements that became a totally relaxed and effortlessly balanced energy dance. From deep within, the free flow of energy was brought to light, like divine doves soaring, swooping, and looping in fluid motion over the boundless sky. At other times, I was motionless, as my posture mirrored the entrancing Mayan figures etched on seven-foot high slabs of limestone on the palace walls. Their rapturous faces, with enigmatic smiles, were tilted upward, right hand clasped over the heart area, and left hand on the belly. I felt my fingers tap a rhythmic beat like a shaman's drumming.

The thought echoed, "Bring the energy down, and touch the Heart center to open up the heavens."

Later, Daniel, a Rosicrucian, confided that he had seen, as I danced beneath the sun-trekked skies, wondrous streams of purple and golden light shooting out of me.

At some point, I felt a movement of white shapes at the top of the steps. The rest of our 100-strong group, who had waited patiently in the wings all this time, had arrived. As the assembly took positions around the entire perimeter, the cleansing group became the hub to lead the entire group in meditation without pausing. Locking fingers and rocking sideways, wave upon wave of voices reverberated in the courtyard as they chanted the litanies, enriched by the dampened echoes that resonated from the towering, mist-shrouded foliage.

As the sun moved higher up the sky, my body felt as soft as a puffed cotton ball, and nothing could hold back the Light now. I discerned a surge of energy concentrated into a column from around me, going skyward with explosive force, before descending like scintillating rays of sunshine, to warm the green forest canopy and assembly below.

"Ah, the Golden Light is alive and well!"

It dawned on me that the energy vortex was the source of life and the essence of all forms. As the sun rises, symbolically, death is transcended, and transformed to rebirth, just as the sun's passage through the heavens duplicates immortality. I had experienced the radiant energy breaking through that seemed to reverberate to the ends of boundless space.

14

Lady of Guadalupe

The conference had ended. Everyone said farewell and prepared to depart for home. I would have to catch a plane and wait overnight in Mexico City before finally getting back to Canada. I shared a taxi with two others departing for Villahermosa airport, fellow passengers who lived in Mexico City. We sat in the taxi conversing for the first time.

Alma, a corporate accountant in her late thirties, was taking a two-year hiatus from her job to explore her spiritual beliefs. She was studying an occasional university course, had joined a study group, and came to the conference with a couple of her friends. By the time we landed in Mexico City, she became insistent that I should see a little of Mexico with her family. She was obviously a warm-hearted person, sophisticated, yet unpretentious and sensitive.

The following afternoon, a luxurious car came to fetch me from the Hotel Canada. Alma introduced her husband, a wealthy executive, and her sixteen-year-old son, who had just spent the morning horseback riding. We headed to the southern district of the city center to Polanco, one of Mexico City's trendiest neighborhoods. This was to be a slow tour through the city. Alma's husband thought we should go to one of their favorite restaurants, Hacienda de los Morales, instead of Chez Wok, a fashionable Chinese restaurant. It turned out to be an excellent choice.

The Hacienda is a huge, 17th century Spanish colonial mansion. We stepped on the cobbled floor through the plant-filled inner courtyard, graced with fountains, and garden statues. Following my host's example, I ordered tequila to drink and a special delicate soup. The seafood was delicious, the dessert exquisite and the service polished. After dinner, we had coffee in the courtyard. We wandered around the mansion, a wonderful place of Spanish colonial nostalgia.

Alma asked where else I wanted to go.

"Perhaps a tour of the Zocalo or Zona Rosa?"

"No, thanks," I said. I thanked them profusely for their wonderful hospitality. As we drove off, I asked Alma about churches, and sacred paintings of the Madonna in Mexico. I mentioned that in Palenque, during the closing dinner, I had bought a small, leather etching of the 'Lady of Guadalupe'.

Alma asked suddenly, "Would you like to go to the Basilica to see the original image of the blue-mantled Mother Mary of Guadalupe?"

She brightened up when I said yes, obviously happy to do one last thing for me in Mexico. I had no foreknowledge of the significance of the Basilica, nor that this Lady is the patron saint of Mexico.

It was only much later that I read that the old Basilica was the location of a 16th century sighting of the Virgin Mary by a peasant, and that a bishop found a dark-faced Madonna imprinted on the shroud-like cloak of the peasant. A church had been built on that spot and became a religious center, filled with an endless flow of pilgrims.

In recent years, the fragile old Basilica had to be closed and a new one built next to it. I was oblivious to all that, and only felt the inexplicable urgency to go there.

When we arrived, I could see an old cathedral spotlighted on the hill. The new Basilica we entered was a modern, audacious, subterranean chamber. There was a large congregation seated in sloping tiers, perhaps engaged in the evening mass conducted from the stage. Alma quietly pointed out that we would go straight to the back wall, which was well behind the raised stage.

Something peculiar seemed to hit me within seconds of entering the Basilica. I had no expectations to begin with, other than to admire some image of antiquity. I was totally unprepared for what happened next. Something, that felt like a vibration, was occurring in my chest, and simultaneously I felt light-headed.

Strangely, my heart rate and breathing started to pick up, but I could not figure out what was going on. Even though we kept on walking, my limbs felt wooden, sounds became muffled, and the air seemed to thicken. Getting closer to our destination, my eyes began to be fixated on the face of the blue Madonna, her palms and fingertips touching in reverence. I swallowed hard to breathe easier with mouth opened.

As I stepped on the moving electric walkway, I could not hold back the tears welling up. The heart surged and expanded, breathing became labored, and the fluid began to stream down copiously as I tilted my head to look up at the dazzling Madonna. A Golden Light seemed to emanate from her head.

The remarkable shrouded image was framed in streaks of gold emanating from the entire Madonna. My heart felt swollen in incredible softness, overwhelmed by the countenance of compassionate love. There was only the unimaginable feeling, but its wordless meaning was direct, even to me, a non-Christian.

In amazement, the thought came that, "The pangs of separation are illusory, and the only intention is to be churned into a passion for eternal, unconditional love."

With the emotional outpouring, the chaotic feeling and yoke of weariness was lifted, to be replaced by a super lightness. The entire experience came by itself, without forethought or effort on my part. I shook my head in awe, as I almost broke out in laughter at the irony of what had occurred to me.

"Is this the spontaneous eruption of the Gold-Body state, found in a Catholic church, in front of a sacred icon of love?"

At that moment, explanations were distractions, as I wanted only to taste the adoration and grace, for a little while longer.

I attempted to explain to Alma the aftermath of the Madonna experience that seemingly permeated to the core of my being.

I heard my voice telling Alma, "It is knowing and rejoicing that at long last, fulfillment is at hand. The voyage of ascension, promised as human destiny, has arrived home."

As the unexpected visit came to an end, I profusely thanked and embraced my hosts for taking me to the Lady of Guadalupe.

"I couldn't imagine a finer gift of true perfection than this," as I bade farewell to my friends.

The Mayan experience had ended as well. At the airport, I again saw Kathina who was waiting for her flight. I told her what had happened at the Basilica.

"I seem to have broken new ground in Palenque that made the Basilica experience possible. In both cases, the cave is symbolic of a perplexing, human dilemma pondered by many, including early philosophers such as Plato."

The Platonic division of the cosmos splits it into two worlds–the ordinary world of change, mortality, evil, and suffering, and the criterion world of perfect and eternal Forms. Of the latter, the world of sense experiences is only a distant, and illusory reflection. One can choose to stand on the side of a shadowy world, or trust in the unseen, but true reality.

Relating to Plato, I said to Kathina my companion seeker, "He too used shadows on a cave as a metaphor."

But armed with faith, one steps outside the cave and its shadows to meet and know the Light that we are. My journey had led to ancient civilizations from Pagan to Palenque, across contemporary cultures to amazing connections between Eastern images of sublime love and mantras and Christian icons and chants whether they be from the Old or the New world. Both experiences are but the two sides of a single reality, like coinage from the same cosmic mint.

I confided, "Paradoxically, Kathina, while the Mayan '0" was created to calculate nothingness, in truth, it does not imply canceling out the finite, emotional frailness, and identities of mortal life. In Zen, zero also manifests as a wondrous, unbroken, circle of Heart vibrations, a merging into an ocean of fullness, to be co-creators in conceiving the infinite energy possibilities of the Cosmos.

Our eyes and hands bade farewell but our hearts knew that we would soon meet again.

A Quantum Pure Energy

In the light of the Pagan, Palenque, and Guadalupe experiences, I felt an inkling of what this magnificent, Golden Emptiness must be like. I recalled a more concrete question that Kathina had posed during our conversation waiting at the Mexico City airport. It warranted an answer requiring a more intellectual frame of reference.

"Is cosmic energy, or the Void, as you call it, is that God?"

"Eastern philosophy, posits an Absolute Purity or Heart, preferable to an absolute, nihilistic void," I replied. "This Heart is hinted to be made up of pure energy at the core, that is homogenous, ultra-fine vibrations from which all things are evolved. To fit human needs, some may find it helpful to call it God.

"Quantum physics has radically changed the scientific view of reality that verifies and closely parallels the concept of existence in Buddhist traditions."

At the human level, there is literally, an endless round of birth and death, with two-and-a-half million red blood cells born every second, to replace the same number that die. The typical cell lives 110 days, and our entire complement of body cells is replaced every seven years. At the molecular level, atoms with clouds of electrons whirl and dance around tiny nuclei, within an enormous space of nothingness. Yet within them, there are numerous subatomic particles shifting states, and facilitating the shifting of states of other particles.

However, most of an atom's volume is occupied by empty space and orbiting electrons, the latter being responsible for the atom's chemical properties such as color, stiffness, strength, and chemical reactivity. The extraordinarily stable and dense nucleus, which has no influence on its chemical nature, contains more than 99.9 per cent of the atom's mass, and most of its energy.

Kathina noted, "In modern Science, matter continues to be differentiated into ever smaller and refined wondrous particles in search of some ultimate identifiable intrinsic unit."

"But should we get closer to them, they too," I ventured to forecast, "will give up all pretense of solidity, with greater uncertainty, and patterns of higher vibration.

Smiling, she added, "And so, just as the mystic uses inner, intuitive wisdom to experience the world in terms of some underlying reality, the modern physicist uses science and mathematics to predict and confirm what is most basic to reality."

Scientists say that all phenomena appear and become manifested, only because of the presence of some underlying core energy. Energy is not a quality which a form gains in the course of its momentary existence, but is infused with it from the very beginning.

"This," I reflected, "is analogous to ancient eastern mystical traditions of universal energy where Emptiness does not mean nothingness or the universe is nihilistically empty, since it is experienced as full of 'serene, vibrant energy.'"

Ultimately, as physicists and mystics suggest, the body is made of the emptiness of space, filled with energy and vibrations. From stars to electrons there is no solidity, only a continuous, dynamic dance of energy.

Kathina agreed warmly, "In this light, it is possible to see all forms emerging out of this silent pulsation, as waves or particles at the cellular level."

Alex, a hard nose Canadian inventor friend, had engaged me on the issue of quantum energy that seems to converge into one energy field from an Eastern perspective. First, Alex described to me the reality of the physical world in conventional terms that he understood.

"There has been a quantum leap from the three elementary particles of the 1920's—positively charged protons, negatively charged electrons, and electrically neutral and massless photons, i.e., the particle of light. The neutron was added in 1937, as was the positron.

Alex continued, "Similarly, assumptions of a predictable world, governed by a few forces in nature are crumbling. Until recently, scientists thought that there were only four forces in nature."

The force of gravity holds planets, stars, galaxies, and globule clusters together. Electromagnetic and nuclear forces exist that are partly responsible for energy release in stars and radioactivity. Lastly, strong nuclear forces hold the nuclei of atoms together. These four forces interact according to fixed and unchangeable laws.

I replied, "None of the laws of quantum physics has yet contradicted the essence of Buddhist tenets."

Alex explained that the forces can be transferred between particles by yet another set of newly discovered particles called gauge bosuns.

"Bosuns is the current notion of the 'smallest' or most elementary, indivisible particle in subatomic matter. Some physicists now propose a fifth non-gravitational force to explain the existence of bosuns," Alex said.

"Clearly," I responded, "the building blocks of matter are transient and lack permanence. All of this gets us, in a circuitous route, to the new science, whose 'new' ideas approached Buddhist philosophy when it is postulated that many particles could decay into others."

Alex said, "I have been toying around with the origin of the universe that involves bosuns. It seems to parallel what you have been telling me about cosmic energy."

I sighed, but without him catching on that I really did not want to listen to more theoretical physics, even about the origins of the cosmos or its creator, the one topic that all Buddhist traditions wisely avoid.

But I encouraged him to go on, knowing that he always had an interesting spin on things.

"I started with the assumption that all matter, even inert and supposedly stable matter, such as gold and iron has a half-life, and will eventually resolve itself into pure energy. I assume that the conversion of matter to pure energy is a finite cycle. I assume that it has a finite end, at which time, all matter penultimately turns into bosuns, when gravity overcomes the outward forces of energy."

"Can you explain your analogy?" I asked, with eyebrows raised.

"Bosuns are metaphorically compared to the mortar in a brick wall, where the bricks are different types of matter. Once matter has decayed to bosuns, it temporarily remains stable in that state. When this happens the implication is enormous. The entire mass with some sort of connectivity, like super saturation, converts the entire volume into a pure energy," Alex said.

"We are talking about incredibly long times, but when the last bit of matter converts itself to bosuns, the entire mass changes into pure energy."

"And how is this tied to the creation of the universe?" I asked.

Warming to the possibility, Alex gesticulated excitedly.

"This enormous implosion and explosion, where the universe becomes as big as it is small, is a big bang. There is not one big bang, but many."

In millionths of a second, this energy is on its way to creating new globule clusters of galaxies and all the life and matter in them, he explained. "New complex molecules will be created that we have never seen. With the expanding big bang, we have the collapse of galaxies and solar systems in ongoing cycles of birth and rebirth."

"Great theory and nicely put," I replied, unable to match his enthusiasm.

I had already spent half of this life-time pursuing the Pure Heart, and I was way past my own 'half-life' in terms of the normal human lifespan.

I said to Alex, "I am hopeful that matter with consciousness can convert to pure energy a whole lot faster.

"Especially," I added, "for humans seeking enlightenment."

He toasted my glass in affirmation.

Reflecting back, I knew I was absorbed in the search for experience of the state of Golden Light. That experience could only come from the wisdom of the Pure Heart.

Pure Transparence

The optimism I felt was based on solid ground cultivated since I began the journey. I recalled a conversation with Sifu about creation and cosmic energy. He theorized that different vibrations give rise to different forms of existence. All matter, including physical bodies, are confined to certain kinds of vibrations that are quite static by nature, while consciousness comprises dynamic energy vibrations that can respond to external stimulation by the five senses. Our original nature is perfection in terms of health, intelligence, functioning, and so on. But the law of impermanence rules, and eventually the process is overwhelming, as there is a build-up of dense energy forces, that produce disease, aging, decay, and finally death.

"Energy meditation is a purification process," Sifu had said.

"By successfully converting and reducing the process of tension accumulation and reversing it, eventually, the mind-body goes back to pure cosmic forces. That is cosmic consciousness itself."

"That sounded," I remarked, "like saying that in the process of purifying and cleansing, we are doing more than simply preserving the health of the body, to a spiritual enlightenment as well."

He nodded replying, "The underlying assumption is that if the present life is not emancipated, life will continue even after the death of the physical body. There will be rebirth, a transference of energy and certain residual pattern of functioning acquired in this life process, which is carried forward to the next life process.

"There is then an infinite process of transformation that never ends. Emancipation means that we begin doing something; we start purifying now, and we get truly enlightened, truly purified."

"Then one converts into Pure Energy in an instant," I thought.

But the concern, Sifu had added, looking directly at me, was for me to get the direction and just follow the path to emancipation.

I pointed out that scientists agree that all matter is comprised of energy, but remain baffled by what consciousness and its origins are. Indeed science had been unable to understand phenomena beyond the physical realm.

Sifu agreed that even electrical and nuclear energy was physical by nature.

"When we get into spiritual energy, it goes beyond the scientific paradigm. The ability of scientific methods to measure energy is limited to certain vibrational frequencies and velocities. Beyond these limits, pure or super-fine spiritual energy is neither measurable nor dealt with by available technology."

"So," I added, "at some point physical energy that is measurable, becomes spiritual energy, or becomes living, conscious energy?"

"Correct," he replied.

I liked Sifu's conscious energy theory that unified matter and spirit. But I was still dissatisfied.

I said, "I agree that science traditionally laid no claims for understanding spiritual life, since spiritual beliefs have been accepted on the basis of faith. But modern humans still want objective explanations to understand the basis of spiritual beliefs."

He laughed, "But the mental activity of the rational mind is precisely not conducive to understanding the spirit. One can use one's conscious, analytical mind or one can use one's spiritual mind. These two, in extreme, are polarized, and cannot be compromised."

"But what is the purpose of cosmic creation, that begins with pure energy without identity, changing into myriad, impure forms?" I persisted.

He responded that probably we might never understand that. There was no absolute purpose. All that can be said here was that it just happened. There was a change in vibration, or differentiation in vibration and the changes took effect.

"But, more usefully, let us talk about the purpose of purification," said Sifu changing direction.

"One is happy to get closer to and return to the pure cosmic energy, or God if you will, in the process. That's what a spiritual person will say.

"A 'material' person will not accept this idea. Yet in times of crisis, they often ask help from some higher intelligence, being, or source. Such spiritual beliefs become acceptable under these circumstances."

For a spiritual person, such beliefs would provide benefits such as peace that is much needed today, because one of the negative aspects of material beliefs and existence is the feeling of insecurity. Materialistic people then become afraid of the infinite uncertainties of existence, about life, the future, and death itself.

"Most of the time, skeptics and critics avoid or deny such fears, but deep inside, it's there. In times of sickness, or overwhelmed by life's problems, they will feel so fearful that they plea for help. Meantime, they may denounce spiritual beliefs, and they are entitled to do so," Sifu said.

15

Pioneer Heart Meditation

I needed to reflect more fully all that I had experienced since I began cultivation of the Gold-Body energy state and integrate it into my world view. I sensed energy changes brewing that I knew would eventually become explicated as external events. I was content to let events unfold and become the next step of the journey. Within a couple of weeks after returning home to Fredericton, an opportunity to connect with Sifu soon presented itself when I was invited to Thailand to conduct a series of university seminars. I was to depart from Canada in July, so that there was a three-month period of gentle consolidation after the epiphanies in Palenque and in the Basilica of Guadalupe.

Several weeks before leaving for South-East Asia, I received a letter from Kathy, whom I had not seen since first meeting her in Germany a couple of years earlier. We had been drawn to a destination where Mother Meera lives–reputedly a most amazing being who bestows divine light and blessings. Kathy worked at the Insight Meditation Center in Barre, Massachusetts, and was writing a book about her travels. Pat and I accepted her standing invitation to have a little vacation at her home in Barre.

I had no idea then that I would be going into a region that was once the center of colonial New England with the same sort of architecture and atmosphere that have been preserved in the St. John River Valley. It was a leisurely, pleasant seven-hour drive, crossing the New England border from Maine, driving south to Massachusetts to over-night on the outskirts of Boston. It was there in Concord in 1775, that the first official battle of the revolution took place at North Bridge. A year later, in Philadelphia, on July 4, independence and freedom were declared. And that began the birth of the American Fire-Monkey.

American Fire-Monkey

It was noon by the time we arrived in the village of Barre, where we were warmly welcomed by Kathy. We stayed at the Center for Buddhist Studies, a renovated, 200-year-old farmhouse on 90 acres of rural farmland. Kathy introduced us to the Center's director, Mu Soeng. The Center's mission is to help establish the ancient traditions and lineage of Buddhism traceable from the Golden Peninsula in an American context. The goal is to provide a bridge between study, scholarly understanding, meditative insight, and dialogue between different schools of Buddhism, as well as other religious and scientific traditions.

In the converted farmhouse, there is a library and study room, housing a complete collection of the Buddhist canon. Outside, there is a new, single-storey building built as a seminar and meditation hall. We walked barefoot on the tamarack wood floor of the empty meditation hall, which had, on the right, a plain, seated Buddha of Thai origin.

Kathy took us for a tour of the great outdoors of central Massachusetts heading out to Pioneer Valley, a region embracing the course of the Connecticut River. During the 18th century, this was once the American frontier, where settlers forged westward into the interior from colonial America. Here, in the Valley, enterprising capitalists, emancipated from Imperial British control, constructed factories, lucrative textile and paper mills along the river, bringing wealth to the whole region. The accumulated wealth has had a lasting legacy of historic and prestigious colleges and universities, now the pride of the region.

As we returned to Barre, Kathy pointed out that the Buddhist Center, founded in 1989, is located next to the parent organization, the well-known Vipassana or Insight Meditation Society. Kathy took us there the next day walking a half-mile to the grounds of the Society. This was a special time since the center was celebrating its 20th anniversary established in a place that I associate with the innovative spirit of the Pioneer Valley. I knew something about how the institution originated and about its founders who were a different genre of pioneers.

In the late 1960's, young Americans had become attracted to South-East Asia not only to make war by enlisting in the armed forces, but some for peace. A few found Vipassana meditation and became monks in the Thai Forest tradition as well as in Burma. On their return from Asia, these spiritual pioneers founded the Vipassana Center to plant the roots of the strict Theravada meditation, a tradition of Heart liberation, on American soil.

As we approached the Center, I saw an imposing and huge Georgian mansion, apparently previously owned by a Catholic noviciary. Above the white pillars supporting the portico, were five bold letters to form the word, 'Metta'. It is a fitting description of a meditative mind seeking purified energy, that also relates to Barre's motto: 'Tranquil and alert'.

The large meditation hall, and the meditators, who were standing and walking in mindful meditation, reminded me of similar scenes in the famed Mahasi Meditation Center at Rangoon. I recollected an early period in Malaysia in 1960, when I first began the study of Buddhism. This experience led to an attempt to learn meditation by spending two weeks with a famous monk and meditation teacher, Acharn Buddhadasa, in the forest monastery in southern Thailand.

Each morning, after breakfast, the Venerable Acharn would talk to the large group, who had come from many parts of the world. He taught mindfulness with breathing (or *Anapanasati*), the meditation technique that the Buddha himself most often taught, and practiced. Following the breath clears the mind, and helps the practitioner to be more sensitive to the consequences of feelings, emotions, thoughts, memories, and to become grounded to cope wisely and calmly with all changes.

In addition, the practice of examining the mind, soothed and balanced by contemplation of each physical inhalation and exhalation, helps us to learn to live more in the present moment. With each breath, by letting go, releasing, and severing past and future apprehensions, the practitioner lives in the boundless present, free from karmic attachment, ready to grow into whatever comes next. The mindfulness of Anapanasati, also helps to let go of the destructive, self-centered thinking that plagues people's lives, that probably prevents the possibility of world peace.

Vipassana, or true insight meditation, literally means 'clear seeing into the true nature of things', that is characterized by impermanence, unsatisfactoriness, and non-self. But true realization of Vipassana cannot be taught, only experienced by the meditator.

Acharn Chah, the renowned Vipassana teacher in Thailand, whose influence had personally brought Theravada Buddhism to American soil, emphasized the point repeatedly, that it is necessary to be constantly aware or mindful of what is happening within the body and mind at the present moment, and to learn how to simply watch and let go.

When asked about peace, wisdom, and wonderful states that can be attained, the Acharn would instead speak of the confusion that one should first get rid of.

Or as he put it, "Peace is the end of confusion."

But ultimately one has to even let go of attainment.

"There's really nothing to develop, and nothing to give up," the Acharn would say.

"Of course, there are numerous meditation techniques, but just let it be. Step over here where it is cool, out of the battle. Why not give it a try?"

The Heart Sutra

Back in Barre, we had been introduced earlier to Kathy's friend and colleague, Mu Soeng. He had been a Zen monk, and former abbot of a Korean Zen monastery in Rhode Island. He stirred in me thoughts of another Indian monk, Bodhidharma, one of the most charismatic of Mahayana monks, who in 526 A.D. went to China. There he founded the Ch'an sect of meditative Buddhism, which spread throughout China and Korea. About six centuries later, the sage's unique enlightenment approach became established in Japan as Zen.

I told Mu Soeng of my interest in energy, and in locating a copy of the Heart Sutra for a friend, who lived in Boulder. On the morning that we headed for home, he handed me a slim book he had written.

The book cover had a brush stroke of a circle or zero, and below it, the title, '*Heart Sutra: Ancient Buddhist Wisdom in the Light of Quantum Reality*'. I instantly recognized that, besides seeing Kathy, the serendipitous reason for coming to Barre must be to become reacquainted with this most widely revered, ancient *Prajna-paramita* text on the topic of enlightenment.

This is no ordinary ancient text but one that upheld a truth that is more precious than anything material I had ever set eyes upon—neither the once lost, pure Golden Buddha I saw residing in Wat Trimitr temple, in Thailand, nor the countless solid gold bars that shaped the Golden Dagon in Burma.

The Heart Sutra is a major doctrinal text of Zen and Mahayana Buddhism that teaches intuitive wisdom, revealing the insight of '*sunyata*' or Emptiness as the essential nature of all phenomena. In the Buddhist traditions, the ultimate nature of reality is Emptiness, seen as a dynamic pattern of relationship that one form has to other forms. Each is dependent on the other for its existence. It is thus a tension that holds the momentary appearance of forms together. This tension is purely relational in nature and does not exist independently as a form.

This cosmic tension, according to ancient Taoist beliefs is an energy configuration which is positively and negatively charged, as symbolized by the tai-chi symbol. The positive and negative charges create constant changes symbolized by the *I Ching* hexagram and thus it gives birth to all forms in the phenomenal world. Every form is impermanent and react to karmic forces as it passes through the transitional states of formation, stability, destruction, and emptiness. But all forms evolved from an Emptiness that has a core quality of a vibrant energy purified of karmic forces.

The essential teaching of the Heart Sutra is to experience the wisdom teaching concerning letting go of one's attachment to forms. The path to the Awakened Mind is neither faith, will power, nor scholastic knowledge, but 'Prajna' or wisdom. The mind is strengthened not by exercising it, but by bringing it to rest, and gradually letting its thinking unwind. One simply lets the *Dharma* flow into the Heart as it reveals itself. One keeps continuously open to its flow in the present moment, letting that happen on its own accord, without struggle or effort.

The key practice is learning to let go fully, not to increase holding on, or attachment.

"If you let go a little, you have a little peace. If you let go a lot, you will have a lot of peace. If you let go completely, you will have complete peace," Acharn Chah said.

Enlightenment appears when one stops wanting anything, as Nirvana has no desire, only tranquillity. So letting go includes even the desire for enlightenment, and only then is one truly free. Intuitively, I felt the Heart Sutra was essential to the Gold-Body State of perfection.

"The Heart Sutra," according to Zen teacher Mu Soeng, "by positing a simple faith in the thought of enlightenment and diligent practice, sought to make the Buddha's enlightenment available to any and all, lay-persons, and monastics alike."

The Sutra's teaching of the timeless truth of *Sunyata*, is expounded by *Avalokitesvara* or present day *Kwan Yin*, the celestial Bodhisattva, who is the embodiment of compassion *(karuna* in Sanskrit). The 'Bodhisattva' is an awakened being progressing toward enlightenment who exhorts believers to invoke and recite the Prajna-paramita Mantra of Perfect Wisdom.

In the experience of *Sunyata* there is no separation between self and other. And so the Bodhisattva is inseparable from those who are saved or have faith in Him/Her. The aspiring, human bodhisattva, realizing the truth through the cultivation of intuitive wisdom of perfection, finds a sense of completion, and an end to all suffering. Then there is a peace and completeness where nothing is lacking, and a clear consciousness of reality and being.

This wisdom opens up a totally relaxed, supreme and unequaled transcendent state, *'the transparent state of Pure Energy and wondrous light that shines into the Eternal.'*

Even the attainment of Nirvana is transcended, as this would be striving to overcome the fear of the world of desires and becoming (*Samsara* in Sanskrit).

"Here," I thought, "there is only the 'Unmoved Heart', and detachment of everything in the phenomenal world."

Mu Soeng explained that having 'attained' perfect, unexcelled Awakening, there is access to the 'ten powers' including the possession of intuitive knowledge, and paranormal abilities. The compassionate Bodhisattva can heal distressed individuals, teach suffering humanity to cleanse, and transform their karma toward perfection.

I realized what that 'Ultimate' goal meant.

"It is the pure experience of our nature as *Sunyata,* an inseparable Oneness connecting everyone who draws forth the free choice of compassion for all beings," Mu Soeng said.

Then compassion becomes a social responsibility.

"We are doing no more than giving expression to our own Buddha nature. It is only in compassionate Metta that wisdom finds its fullest expression."

I looked up at the night sky the evening before leaving Pioneer Valley, the illustrious seat of a diversity of institutions of higher and spiritual learning. I realized that in cultivating the Gold-Body State over the past two years, I had been reconnecting again with both Vipassana meditation and the Heart Sutra.

"That's it!" Everything leads to it," I exclaimed.

My entire body stirred strangely as whispered words came, "It will only take just a little while longer."

Part Six

Return to the Gold

16

Hearts Wide Still

When the Wisdom of the Heart Sutra is realized,
the person becomes liberated from the unreality of all ills,
and the unreality of the one experiencing ills,
thus becoming freed from the clutches of
the world of related things.

Sumangalo

On the return to New Brunswick driving home along the St. John River, I felt that my journey to the Gold-Body State was reaching an imminent end. There was something else about the Heart Sutra that I had long forgotten. As I packed the books and materials I needed for my trip to Silpakorn University in Thailand, I soon re-discovered what that was. I vaguely recalled that during student days long ago in Malaysia, I had put away some pages of mantras written by the Ven. Sumangalo. He was the respected monk and former native Texan whom I knew, and who remained and lived in Malaysia until his death. I could never find those lost pages among my books, but my search located something even more significant.

I was overjoyed to find the single issue of a well-thumbed, quarterly periodical, that for some reason I had filed away long ago. The American monk, decades ago, had founded and edited this publication in Penang for a number of years. The Venerable had written a paper entitled, 'Mantras and Dharanis.' However, the middle pages were missing, presumably the pages I could not find.

On the last paragraph of the paper, Sumangalo summarized several, single-versed mantras that included a final commentary of the Heart Sutra, often referred to as 'The medicine that cures all ills'. He translated the Sanskrit *Prajna Paramita* Mantra as, '*Gone, gone, utterly gone, gone beyond all describing, O Enlightenment, Hail*'!

I had long forgotten another feature of the periodical, and felt astonished as soon as I saw it, realizing its significance. On the front cover of the periodical, dated July 1960 (or 2504 B.E., Buddhist Era), there was a drawing of an exquisite hand, with a flashing white, blue and red background, and the logo above that read, '*The Golden Light*'.

I suddenly realized that the journey of rediscovery had started a lot earlier than I had previously thought. Everything that had happened since then was events and experiences to help in emptying in preparation to replenish the spirit. Intuitively, I felt acutely that the Gold-Body State must be the experience of awakening to *Sunyata* referred to in the Heart Sutra. Sifu was the marathon runner who had just about gone through the whole distance. I yearned to somehow meet up with him at the finish. It was time to return to the East where it all first began.

Three days later and after a night's rest, I sat in the elegant dining room of the exclusive Selangor Club, with friends who had invited me for lunch. Even with eyes closed, just from the rich fragrant aroma that filled the restaurant, I knew that I was back in Malaysia. The hot, spicy Malaysian food ordered was a gorgeous array of exquisite tastes, reflecting the best of a blend of Indian, Chinese, and Malay cuisine. I had arrived in Kuala Lumpur, the premier metropolis of Malaysia, the previous evening. Early Greeks searched for a fabled land of gold and riches and imagined that it was located in the Malay Peninsula. The skyline is a fusion of golden domes, soaring minarets, spires, clock towers lacquered with copper domes, and multiple Moorish archways of remarkable elegance. Together, the dozen or so buildings in central Kuala Lumpur give her a distinct, Islamic architectural design, that is instantly recognizable as the capital city of modern Malaysia.

At long last, after jetting the globe from east to west and back again repeatedly, the journey had reached a pivotal moment. The following day I headed for Penang from where I first left for North America, half a life-time earlier.

That afternoon back in Sifu's Healing Center, I was musing to myself that perhaps in the old days, enlightenment and wisdom came easier, in places that were remote, tranquil, far from the hustle and bustle of living. Living among people, one discovers the best approach to a liberation that can deal effectively with daily problems. This itself is enlightenment. The peace that comes, despite dealing with problems in harsh reality, is better.

I felt that I had come a long way in my quest. I wanted to understand more clearly how Buddhist and energy meditation had led to Sifu's own liberation.

"On the one hand," I began, "you have said that CFQ attempts to attain the traditional goals of the Tao, in terms of transforming the body and mind toward perfect health. But then you also say that the meditation does not follow the acquisition techniques of contemporary Qigong. Please clarify."

"O.K.," he explained, "our strong argument is that CFQ adheres to four Taoist principles universally accepted in Qigong practice.

"Nourish the essence to convert to qi; Refine the qi to convert into Spirit (*sern*, in Chinese); Refine the Spirit to return to Emptiness; and Cultivate Emptiness to return to *Tao*."

Traditional Taoism interpreted these principles as the four processes in the practice of Qigong, treating them as four different stages of attainment.

"First, one must learn how to nourish one's essence to turn it into qi energy, and then gradually proceed step by step, to each of the other stages in turn. In CFQ practice, all four processes are adhered to, but they are not considered as separate steps, or stages of progressive cultivation."

"Instead," he emphasized, "all four practices are incorporated and done simultaneously in meditation."

"So it is not a gradual approach?" I queried.

He nodded.

"Consider the notion of 'nourishing essence to turn into qi'. In CFQ, the body is not permitted to move too much or become over-excited. Spontaneous movement in meditation is not wasted energy, but a release of what is stored in the body and causing problems. This is in line with not wasting our essence. One's essence is naturally converted into the essential body energy," Sifu said.

"CFQ practice also pays particular attention to our spirit (sern). The energy Mantra is used for this purpose, so that at all times we are reminded of our spiritual existence by virtue of the Mantra. We make sure that the Mantra is continuous. That means the sern is quite alert, and that it exists all the time. We do not doze off during practice. That's converting the qi into sern."

"How does meditation cultivate the sern or spirit to convert into Emptiness and return to the Tao?" I asked further.

"At all times our consciousness is fully alert. The sern is purified by means of what we do with relaxation energy. This energy generated during meditation dissolves the karmic forces from the body, accumulated in the form of tension forces. The Gold-Body energy of relaxation is radiant by nature, that is, it radiates or opens out, and goes back to the cosmos or the Tao. In other words, we empty ourselves of impurities and defilements, to eventually become part of the cosmic consciousness. If successful, we return to and become one with the Tao."

Most types of Qigong, however, are based on the belief that one had to go step by step, or stage by stage, as a gradual process.

But Sifu asserted, "This is not the right way."

"Why not?" I asked.

"It creates confusion and contradiction when practiced separately to master each step before proceeding to the next. In the first two processes, there is a kind of gap between qi and *sern* and confusion of where *sern* or Spirit is to be found.

"Normally, for example, Qigong held that one must bring the qi up from the lower abdomen to the heart, then from heart to brain, and that is then called *sern*. That assumes spirit accumulates in the head. Then one is supposed to return *sern* to Emptiness. But CFQ questions whether this is the correct process of the return to Emptiness."

Sifu asserted further, "It must involve a downward releasing. The big problem is that if one already has absorbed and accumulated so much, can one actually want to, or be able to, release anything at all?"

Continuing, he elaborated, "Then from Emptiness, one is supposed to merge with the path or Tao. My experience is that one step does not lead to another. But, if we practice all four together, they simply merge together beautifully."

"And also from the letting go aspect of CFQ," I added, "following complicated processes in a system, defeats and contradicts the process of letting go?"

"Yes, that is creating something, not letting go. That's acquisition, and when one acquires so much, I doubt if one can ever return to Emptiness."

I asked another question, "Is the conception of Tao the same as the Buddhist understanding of Enlightenment?"

"Yes," Sifu agreed.

I protested that I had not heard him refer directly to Buddhist sources of CFQ meditation, and how that was linked to Taoism. I pressed him to elaborate.

"I can begin with qi energy. Traditional definitions of qi refer to it as a very basic force that enables life to function. But qi is defined with different words depending on the type and location in the body. Universal external energy is called *wai qi*, and what is in the body is called *nei qi*.

Taoists also believe that qi can be absorbed to strengthen the body. This notion, CFQ rejects–one gets healthy by not absorbing, but by releasing.

"Here, we really do not talk of, or refer to such ordinary qi energy at all," Sifu said.

"So, CFQ energy meditation is more in line with Buddhist meditation than Qigong?" I asked.

"Yes, indeed."

Sifu explained Buddhist epistemology, based on eight types of senses, or consciousness. The first six senses comprised the body's five senses and the mind or thoughts. The seventh sense, touching one's spiritual essence, called *mano* consciousness registered all stimulations from the first six senses, and memories of all past experiences, including those from past lives. They are stored in the form of dense energy or karma that accumulates as forces attaching to he body.

"They can only be erased in three ways: 'Ripening of karma by suffering their full effects; Neutralized by actions of the opposite karmic effect, e.g., a good deed done can reduce the effect of bad karma; and last, unwinding through cultivation of the Way."

Sifu elaborated, "The Way of CFQ, in unwinding energy from the 7th or *mano* sense stimulates the tension forces created by the first six senses. Hence, all kinds of reactions are possible. The release of these karmic forces increases its activity level to heighten one's consciousness and sensitivity to their effects. One effect on the six senses gives rise to out-of-ordinary functions, commonly referred to as psychic powers and phenomenon."

Brightening, I said, "That can be seen in the radiant *darshan* with the Holy Mother Meera as her divine eyes gaze right into my spirit!"

Concluding, Sifu added, "The ultimate goal is to cleanse these karmic forces out and then go beyond the 7th consciousness. Then the 8th sense or *alaya* consciousness appears, and this is generally referred to as cosmic consciousness. And that is also the Gold-Body state."

I knew that each of us, in our conscious hearts, already has the spark of '*alaya seeds*,' our heritage to the Divine. The essence of CFQ is more related to Buddhism than Taoism as a very basic principle in Buddhist cultivation, such as in Vipassana and Zen meditation, is also letting go.

"In our meditation," Sifu declared, "when one lets go, the hindrances and defilements are removed in an optimal way, so that whatever needs to happen in the body will be created. Whatever qi required is already available and present in the body. We just make sure that in practice, we do not create a hindrance to its flow."

"This is also consistent with the belief in traditional Chinese medicine that when something unhealthy happens, the qi in the body is blocked," I recalled.

"Does the Buddha talk about energy?" I asked.

"Indeed, Buddhism refers to energy all the time. The sacred texts and the Buddha when referring to mind, spirit, and karma, really talked about energy. Pure energy is called Emptiness or the Void."

I said that his constant highlighting of letting go and Emptiness reminded me very much of the core of Buddhist philosophy.

He replied, "Yes, the essence of CFQ meditation is the Heart Sutra."

I let what he had just said sink in slowly. This was the first time Sifu ever mentioned the Heart Sutra to me. I explained that I had been studying it, just before leaving home. In fact I had been fascinated with it since early youth. I suddenly understood why I had been so much taken with CFQ meditation, when Sifu first introduced it to me more than three years earlier.

Wanting to hear what he thought of the Heart Sutra, I said, "Please explain."

"The Heart Sutra is the core philosophy of CFQ. It describes a state of meditation that prevents and does not allow interference by any or all the five senses. Interpretation by one's five senses forms a relationship with the impure energy, creating tension whose products are all illusory.

Through meditation, one experiences going beyond, deeper into the pure energy state, which is called Emptiness in the Heart Sutra.

"When a person is purified, to that extent, that individual will see the truth of all events happening, and will not be deluded by any physical event. It will also help to dissipate and clear out all the undesirable future physical events from happening."

I nodded, "Then the Heart's needs simply and instantly unfold into external reality."

He went on to explain that the Heart Sutra was often recommended for people to clear off undesirable problems and to create better health and good karma for themselves. Through the attainment of pure energy, one understood and saw that all impurities were only illusions.

"That is why the Gold-Body energy state is in line with this," he ended.

For the first time, everything I had done cultivating the way became crystal clear. Pure Heart means cosmic consciousness. Perfect purity is cosmic energy.

"Also, does the development of intuitive wisdom leads to instinctive knowledge?"

"Absolutely! When you move into the *Prajna* of the Heart Sutra, pure energy illuminates, and one just see things for what they are."

I knew one aspect of what that meant. In all my observations of his healing abilities, in many hours of intense interactions and dialoguing with Sifu, I had never seen him consulting, worrying over, or 'research-ing' other sources of information. All his actions and words were direct, immediate, and 'just so', like a clear, spontaneous sparkling flow from the fountain of truth.

Sifu amplified on instinctive knowledge.

"At this stage, you no longer distinguish between pure and impure. One then can see all–the physical, as well as the non-physical impurities. The unrealized person sees only the physical impurities. Such a person will dis-tinguish between impurity and purity. But once enlightened, things are seen just as they are. One is so unmoved that nothing changes; there is only timelessness."

Smiling, he ended, "The moment a person gets perfected, that's Buddhahood."

Compassionate Metta Light

I felt it was time to ask Sifu about his personal experience of the Gold-Body State. The opportunity came the day before my departure to return to the Golden Triangle. That evening we were alone together.

"After I began my professional life as a healer there were two earlier initiations into the Golden Light, and each initiation was two-and-a-half years apart. The third one occurred just three months ago, in the spring," he said.

I said that the timing was fascinating as coincidentally, during the Spring Equinox, I was in Palenque and Mexico City, where some transcending experiences had also occurred then.

Sifu congratulated me and explained, "This last initiation was a further unfolding of not only more knowledge, but a clearer vision of the further development of CFQ and its final purpose.

"The most recent experience is different from the Golden Light revelation. In the earlier initiation, at that time, I was part of the information. I was in it and of it," Sifu explained.

"In the present initiation, 'I' was away from my body. My body was covered with a cloud-like energy, in a vibration that was still not entirely pure. I looked back, and I could see myself. 'Oh, what am I doing out here, I thought?'

"Then something not quite vocal told me: 'Look, this is your body!'

"As I looked at the form," Sifu continued, "there appeared a central channel of light all the way from the crown to the waist. It was radiating and changing into different colors. Then the energy centers or chakras started to rotate and shine. There were five of them, from the base, the navel, the heart (the heart and the plexus chakra had no distinction), the throat, and the forehead. The thought came, 'Oh, this is what you are going to get!'"

As he described his latest initiation of the Gold-Body state to me, my body rhythm seemed to resonant with his words. Each of us, in our own way, had glimpsed some core element of the Golden Light.

"So as you experience the Gold-Body energy State," I asked, "have you essentially reached as close as humanly possible the pure energy state?"

"Gradually, the body does not seem to exist. During meditation, you cannot find your body. Physically you know you are alive, but the body is simply not there. Part of the body is now so loose and so free."

He explained, "Fully alert, one feels that the radiation is everywhere. In this state, you can't even find the body. In normal times, when out of meditation, you feel that the body is very light, and very loose. You feel you are so boundless."

He added, "There is no 'as if' quality about it. You experience it physically and there is no doubt of its reality."

Urging him to continue, I asked him to describe further the purified, bodiless state.

"The vital vibration or one's spirit is so free that it is one and part of the cosmic. As I experience this cosmic state in subsequent meditation, it becomes very clear that the body itself becomes physically transparent, clearer, brighter, and it just shines."

He reiterated, "You feel that it is transparent. You are the cosmic itself, unhindered by the heavy, bulky physical body. Since you are the cosmic, everything comes from the pure cosmic energy."

Sifu expanded on another facet of the Gold-Body state.

"In the transparent state, a couple of times, I have managed to touch timelessness, that is beyond cosmic consciousness. In timelessness, you touch your higher self, your original nature. Words in physical reality fail to truly describe the experience.

"But I can tell you that it's a transcendent experience filled with joy and free of anything troubling. There is consciousness, but no distinctions or any categorization of all perceptions. The body is so loose, and light, it seems that you have melted yourself out. You are like thin air. It feels even more vivid than physical awareness and sensations."

Sifu provided another insight, "Once you are not interested in seeing anything, the past, present, and future are all there. But it's all illusion, and there is no concern with them. Impure energy is not the reality anymore. Pure energy is a straight line–it's a thought. The Heart is so still, so relaxed, it does not matter whether one exists. You are at-one-ness. This is ultimate reality."

"Is there more to come?" I pressed Sifu.

"Yes, if I have a longer time in timelessness. I had only a split second of touching and knowing just that. With more purified energy, there will be more repetitions, and longer ones of the transparent, Gold-Body state, so that one can move into it more easily, and stay for a longer time. That's probably the ultimate."

Reading my thoughts, he continued, "There's still much work to be done. But to go further, you have to actually detach from the body, to separate, before you can see that."

Sifu pointed out, "Recall another thing I said, that came during the last initiation regarding the crown opening. I thought then–All the body's chakras or energy centers must open, but how about the other inactive ones?

"No answer came–it's as if to say, 'Just these will be sufficient.'

"As for the crown chakra, the intuition was, 'Never open it unless you wish to die. You are no longer attached to the body if you do," he added.

"There may be other higher states, he concluded, "but what has been attained is enough to do the work needed now. In the Gold-Body state, the impression I have is to just move along, whatever it is."

Sifu was insistent about the reality of all he had described to me.

"The revelation," he said emphatically, "was real as I knew I was part of the information. I have a vivid memory of all that happened, and what to do thereafter. I am more certain of that than what normally comes in through the five senses.

"Yes, I saw it and I felt it," he impressed upon me.

"I felt the vibrations and sensations as they were very clear. But I didn't seem to be totally in the body. I was away from the body. I was shielded from the body by all the impure energy, by the cloud-like sensation. It was almost like looking through milky water. It's purer to be outside the body and you see more easily. This is the Gold-Body State."

Sifu added, "If all personal karma has left, and of course the karma has not totally left me yet, as shown by the cloud around my body, then one becomes free of karma. That means whatever action one does will not carry further karma."

I became aware that what he had to say next was a revelation of great import. Sifu then described, for the first time, the Gold-Body state purpose that went beyond one's own self-enlightenment.

"This is precisely the Gold-Body Bodhisattva state in the lay healer. When practicing and cultivating meditation you are a bodhisattva, but a lay energy healer, following a vow of spiritual evolution and trying to help out. This is what came to me," he said.

I understood then another dimension of my emotional yet cleansing experience in the old Basilica in Mexico. I had somehow tuned into, and become moved by the compassionate energy associated with the loving Heart or Madonna Light of Guadalupe. Now Sifu was articulating a compelling and ultimate purposive meaning to that experience.

"Why were the experiences filled with golden light?" I queried.

"In the purified state, energy vibration is more or less colorless. But it's slightly tinged with gold. The gold is a light golden hue. Gold also signifies love. So there is a golden glow here of Metta just like the bodhisattva vow to help people."

"I wonder what that vow means for me," I said, thinking of the compassionate Mother Mary.

Sifu replied, "Let me elaborate on what this path is about. According to ancient Eastern texts, that's a person who makes a vow to help others. But it is not an ordinary vow. It is very special–unique."

I asked how the radiant energy healer differed from the traditional concept of the Celestial Bodhisattva.

"Traditionally, if a person is to make a vow to become a bodhisattva, there are so-called moralistic precepts that you need to follow to live a virtuous life. There are over 200 rules, which are extremely difficult to adhere to. One becomes a monk, and retreats from society. This worked in the past when society was not so complicated.

"Today, a bodhisattva, in order to help solve the world's problems must live right in the community to understand the kinds of problems faced by others. And one has to learn how to purify in the midst of society."

"That describes a present-day energy light-worker," I mused.

"In the Gold-Body energy path, one feature of the practice is, you don't have to let anyone know your purpose. In the process of helping yourself, as a cultivator, you are helping others already. That's because you can't stop the energy or merits generated influencing and benefitting others.

He expanded, "The practice is the way whereby you keep creating merit, and this radiates and affects the surroundings, and helps people at the same time.

"Gold-body practice, of course, is not only physically helping others, but also means invisible or absent healing."

"When I radiate out energy to the environment, is it non-specific?" I probed.

"People embark on meditation, for whatever reason, perhaps to take care of their health problems, or out of curiosity. It doesn't matter. It will help dissolve the karmic tension forces within yourself. But as it also goes out, in the process of melting to return to pure energy, you are also influencing or purifying the surroundings.

"This itself is the path of the bodhisattva."

Attempting to understand clearly what was implied, I said, "So the light-worker, in relation to the Gold-Body state, lives a life fulfilling the role of social responsibility, or the way to deal effectively with contemporary problems in modern living?"

Sifu nodded, "Yes, in order to help yourself, you also have to change the conditions around you–that's very important."

"But not by changing the conditions directly to change society?" I questioned.

"No, that's too physical, too direct. Energy change is subtle but real. Energy interventions can make changes without others knowing it."

I asked him what could cut off whatever shielded the pure energy cycle.

"In meditation, you can catch brief glimpses of the 'free of karma' state, in between the cleansing of one layer of karma and another new layer surfacing. What is then experienced is cosmic consciousness, i.e., reunification with the cosmos."

"So ultimately, the Gold-Body path leads to a complete transformation?" I asked.

"Eventually, a person's energy system is further purified. At the point they become fully purified, they won't be attached to their bodies. Then the truth comes that living life itself is just a physical illusion. There is a transformation of physical life.

"Those who transit into this state know that there is still an obligation. 'I'm still here, and I want to help others as well, for their benefit.' The vow helps the cultivator to maintain such physical existence."

"In other words," I surmised, "to become more alive, the old identity, the ego or ordinary self has to die first, and when that happens one becomes even more alive as purer energy?"

"You are more alive as you see your extended self as one with the cosmic energy," Sifu replied. "When death is transcended this way, you can also fulfill any other purpose."

He looked at me and asked, "You see how that relates to the Gold-Body-State?"

"Yes, I feel it, see it, and it's totally boundless with no hindrance. It's like knowing and clearly seeing myself shine, radiating from within without any hindrance. So whatever healing action the light worker undertakes will purify even further."

17

Path of Gold

Round the Cape of a sudden came the sea
And the sun looked over the mountain's rim:
And straight was a path of gold for him
And the need of a world for me.

Browning

On the last evening of my visit, Sifu summoned me to his modest house. It is a small, compact, three-bedroom unit within a long, terraced building. He had recently moved his family from his busy Center, and renovated the house as their new home. He could now devote his energies to his main goal in life–energy meditation healing and its perfection. After a simple meal with his family and two young children, we strode over to a small patio overlooking some hanging orchid plants in bloom. While I was pouring the steaming tea, he turned to the one thought that was uppermost in my mind–my journey and quest.

Sifu was born in 1956. This is also the zodiac sign of the Year of the Fire-Monkey that signifies remarkable energy, willpower, inventiveness, and natural leadership. Sifu had chosen to use that energy for cultivating spiritual leadership. All the ingenuous fire-power of his birth-sign had been tempered into a cool, beneficial healing Light.

"Sifu, over the past seven years, you have been moving ever closer into the Gold-Body energy state. The first initiation was the Night of the 64 Hexagram forces. But its profound significance was not revealed to you until the subsequent initiation at the age of 37. At that time, the knowledge came in a flash with the Golden Light that shone out from the Heart."

I knew that in the *I Ching*, the hexagram for '37' denotes the power and love of the family spirit. I felt confident that the Sifu's Golden Light initiation came through from having connected with his spiritual family and lineage which was the same energy as the golden hue I experienced in the lands of the Golden Peninsula.

"You too have been initiated with many more to come," he said. Expect more transforming changes on the path that you have already begun to experience. The transitional process can be painful when the bodhisattva experiences the physical transformation. As you go on, you understand more about energy. You can see and feel energy forces that cling to you. Soon you learn how to prevent anything from attaching to the body."

I felt that he comes from a spiritual lineage with a karmic link pointing to the Golden Sage, the foremost spiritual energy teacher of all time. The Buddha's birth-date, according to modern scholars, was probably 563 B.C. (crossing over to Nirvana in 483 B.C.) That, in all likelihood falls on the Year of the Fire-Monkey.

I queried, "In the process of reaching the Gold-Body state, are there intermediate states that ultimately lead to the end-state?"

"Thinking of a self striving to attain desirable states is not good enough. You are part of a whole. As you come to it, you seem to understand it. You just know–that's what is meant by *Prajna paramita*, in the ancient texts. The process of consciously acquiring knowledge is not necessary."

"Yes," I nodded, "The famous Zen Patriarch, Hui Neng was illiterate."

"As you come to wisdom," Sifu reiterated, "you know it, it happens that way, and to you it is undisputable. You get a full, complete explanation."

"Participation in observing photons changes particles to waves and waves into particles," I responded.

"Yes, you can put it that way," he replied. "Any attempt to describe it further deviates from the truth of what it is, and is no longer pure. It's adding impurity to the ultimately indescribable experience."

I paused reminding myself, "There are no likes or dislikes, sadness or happiness, fear or tranquillity, no aging, no death, no birth, no Buddha. The Bodhisattva light itself is golden because it is a Compassionate Light. Its true essence, of course, is without any hue or light. Pure energy vibrations are so fine that they do not register in the human brain and are beyond communication through language."

It was almost time to bid Sifu farewell. I asked my final question. "Is this possible to do–finding enlightenment in one lifetime?"

"With the right approach, it's not impossible. Just do it, and forget about doing it. If you have to continue into the next life, that doesn't really matter to you anyway, does it? So let it be. And that itself is letting go.

He continued, "Still, someday, at some point, you could turn around, to ask what you're doing now. After healing many, you suddenly become aware what has happened. Actually, you have become what you want, reaching the enlightenment of a Bodhisattva. At that point, you have let go sufficiently so that your individual self is gone, and you are not attached, and essentially become identified with the universal self.

"So there's Nothing at all!" he concluded smiling.

"Absolutely no Gold-Body state! No matter, no mind, and no ego consciousness whatsoever," I concurred.

Rolling my eyes up, I continued, "It's like Bodhisattva baloney! As for the Golden Light–what a great hue and cry over Nothing!"

As our eyes met, the tension burst as laughter exploded in the air.

"There is only magnificent, boundless *Sunyata* that shines perfectly on All," Sifu noted.

I felt a sense of completion having experienced what I needed to know, and that I had pretty much finished a journey started long ago.

"Ah, thanks for a most perfect landing into the Gold-Body path," I said to him.

I lifted my teacup toasting him and said, "I expect, in 2016 A.D., to be there when you celebrate your sixtieth birthday. That's the next cycle of the Year of the Fire-Monkey, when the Gold-Body State surely comes of age!"

He returned my toast, saying, "I'm counting on that."

"And I bet, with the longevity of the Gold-Body energy, after sixty years more, you may well be dancing the Tao for another Fire-Monkey cycle at 120 years young!

"Coincidentally," I enthused, "the year 2076 A.D. also marks the sixth Golden Jubilee commemorating the Land of the Fire-Monkey. Imagine the biggest star-spangled tea party on July 4, heralding the tricentennial celebrations of the realm's Golden New Age!"

Sifu's smile was a sheer delight.

Pathom: Light of the Golden Sage

When I arrived at Bangkok's Don Maung airport, the next day, a van from Silpakorn University, was waiting for me. We drove to the campus in Nakhon Pathom, some 30 miles away. From the seventh floor of the hotel room, looking over the darkness above the town, I could make out the colossal landmark of an unusually tall pagoda that soared above the surrounding rooftops. As the sun rose the next morning, I could detect details of the Great Pagoda or *Chedi* shrouded in the mist.

The Chedi resembled the inverted bell-shaped, and spired pagodas common to Burma of northern Indian origin. The whole massive structure was covered with a glistening orange-yellow, ceramic glaze. As the dome caught the filtered rays of the dawn, it shimmered with a golden hue. I was gazing at the Pathom Chedi, at 127 meters high the tallest Buddhist pagoda or stupa in the world.

I soon learned that the quiet, little town of Nakhon Pathom had a long, distinguished history. Pathom City (derived from Sanskrit which means First City), is considered to be the oldest city in the region that predates old Siam. Records also suggest that it was here, in the 3rd century B.C., that Emperor Asoka's missionaries from India had stopped to establish a base, commemorated by a great stupa, to propagate Buddhism eastwards in the Golden Peninsula.

It was in 1860, that construction of the new Chedi on the ancient site began during the reign of the first modern Thai King Mongkut. The King's fame in the West comes from the glamorized story of 'Anna and The King' best portrayed by actor Yul Brynner. Before ascending the throne, the King was a monk for 27 years. Upon seeing the ancient pagoda in Pathom overgrown by jungle, he resolved to restore the badly damaged and long-neglected pagoda.

Acharn (the customary title for all teachers) Tiplada arrived and extended the traditional 'wai' greeting, hands with palms together, held close to the face. It was a heart-warming greeting that I quickly returned. Seeing Tiplada, with her incredible air of gentle lightness, was indeed inspiring. She took me for a visit to the Chedi where I was beginning to sense that something of special importance was taking place. We wound through the open market, bought some incense and jasmine flowers, and walked barefoot into the temple grounds.

I realized that once again. my journeys crisscrossing the ancient golden land of *Suvannabhumi* were an enigmatic call to discover the same Pure Energy of Heart Perfection.

Of all the Buddha images in the Chedi, I was most drawn to two White Buddhas, each 3.7 meters high. One is in the main oratory, and the other located outdoors in front of the pagoda's main entrance. Here the Buddha, unlike those in more traditional form, is depicted sitting in a natural and comfortable position, with feet resting on a foot-base of blooming lotus.

There is also an interesting connection between ancient Pathom, formerly the land of the Mons, and Pagan, capital city of the first Burmese Kingdom, far to the Northwest that was intriguing for me. For in 1057

A.D., in the Year of the Fire-Monkey, King Anawratha of Pagan extended Burmese territory by assimilating ancient Pathom. The ruins of many ancient pagodas and temples there suggest that the ancient city was also destroyed and looted by the Burmese king. Silver coins of antiquity, with identical distinct marks, dug up in Pathom today, are found only in ancient Pagan.

Tiplada, her slender figure dressed in exquisite golden Thai silk, adorned me with a garland of fragrant flower buds and escorted me to a traditional northern Thai restaurant. She stopped to show me the ancient ruins in Pathom including an exceptionally attractive old temple. As I gazed at its ancient remnants, I was attracted by its elegance, but felt something more. The ruins turned out to be the Temple of Meru. I soon realized that even in its decayed state, it had a design with a striking similarity to the incomparable Ananda Temple I had seen in Pagan.

For me, the quest from my Canadian home base had drawn me to all these historical, yet living reminders of the immediacy of the liberating experience of the Golden Sage that had thrived through the ages. Wherever I was, whether in Penang, Pagan or Palenque, from the Pioneer valley to the desert Plains, and now in Pathom, I felt the presence of the *Prajna* Perfected Master as the same Pure Light.

Throughout, the Light of Asia, paradoxically, the only world-religious figure of white Proto European stock, continues to stir the human spirit. Humanity comes in various colors but differences are merely skin deep. Looking within, everyone is the color of blood red. The Buddha demonstrated that when external form is blended with shades of brown, black, and yellow, the core Heart energy becomes golden. The mind's discriminations vanishes and superficial matter is spiritually transformed along the path of Golden Light to the Sublime.

In the succeeding days in Silpakorn University, we conducted the series of seminars as planned. I demonstrated how relaxation energy could also be extended to healing others through the transmission of radiant healing energy. There is a connection between changes in thought, brain chemistry, and cell vibration that leads to a renew healing capacity. Everything, then, starts from consciousness, and the state of consciousness determines the vibrance of one's energy pattern. However from the infinite space between thoughts comes a relaxation energy that is our inherent healing capacity. Energy meditation, as I know it, can raise the inner vibrations to enhance healing and emancipation.

When it ended in the afternoon, it was evident that the workshop had stimulated a great desire to learn more. Half the participants stayed until the end of the night. Tiplada, who had earlier shown me the ancient temples, was elated. She had been feverish with some infection and during the workshop felt the powerful yet gentle beneficial healing energy. Letters I later received indicated that many had put the consciousness de-stressing energy tools into practice, with some pretty amazing health outcomes.

Tiplada, who acted as translator during the workshop, introduced me to a participant, Dr. Petsri, who is a health department director up north. The immediate outcome was the scheduling of another seminar at *Payao*, close to the Golden Triangle. That meant extending my stay in Thailand for several more days.

That night, Tiplada wanted to drive me around Bangkok, especially the city center, for a special event. The megapolis of ten million people was exploding into a wonderfully special celebration. All the streets were lined with brightly lighted and decorated arches over the major roadways. Every national monument, and all the statues, Bangkok temples, royal palaces, and buildings lining the bustling Chao Praya River were flooded with dazzling colored lights and decorations.

Tiplada said that the whole nation was celebrating the Golden Jubilee of Thailand's most respected and beloved Chakri dynasty king. I knew that this most extraordinary monarch, descended from King Mongkut, was born in Cambridge, Massachusetts, in 1927, when his father was studying medicine at Harvard University. The King is no aloof, figurehead of royalty but he is indeed the most loved earthly 'son of heaven' living in yesterday's golden Suvannabhumi land.

The night before departing Pathom City, I was wondering about the journey to Payao, the seventh and last location ahead. We returned to the iridescent Chedi for the last time, where we lighted incense, and placed our flower offerings on the altar. Tiplada knelt in homage before the entrance hall Buddha with hands clasped to forehead. When she stood up, she smiled and inquired whether I wished to ask for a message as was the custom. This is done by rattling the numbered fortune sticks in a bamboo container. I could not think of any wish, but went through the ritual.

Shaking the container, the stick that dropped out had number '7' on it. I returned the stick back to its container, and rattled it again. The new stick that fell out raised my eyebrows, as astonishingly the number was again a '7'. To find out what the number meant, Tiplada went over to a wall cupboard with numbered, pigeon-holed compartments. She fished out the message for number '7'.

"It means, Chok," reading the Thai writing and laughing, "your unfinished business will end."

When she saw my puzzled look, she added, "It's all right, it will turn out wonderfully well."

18

Beyond the Golden Triangle

I arrived in Chiengmai City and was met by two former students who were faculty at the local university. We drove past a huge welcoming billboard, announcing the 700th anniversary of the founding of the capital of the Lanna Kingdom that emerged when the Northern rulers of Payao, Chiengrai, and Chiengmai united. Her golden age blossomed in the mid-15th century during the reign of the warrior-King Tilokaraja. The king then hosted the Eighth Great Council inviting all of the Buddhist world to the dawning of the Third Buddhist Millennium celebrating the anniversary of the Buddha's crossing into Nirvana.

On the way to Payao city, I had a night to rest at the graceful *Rincome* Hotel, an older but the first luxurious western-styled hotel built in pristine Chiengmai. I began doing a energy channel exercise of seven steps to stimulate meridian flow that Sifu had taught me. The movements balanced the energy body to exchange with cosmic energy. Soon the energy blockages that feed emotional disturbances–the product of disharmonious living–had disappeared. I felt a qi and blood flow that was wonderfully smooth and experienced a state of consciousness that was calm, relaxed and at peace with Nature.

Continuing to stand in moving meditation, with my entire body slowly and effortlessly extending and opening, I noted changes and physical sensations as the energy stirred and flowed smoothly. Whatever happened was permitted to occur, without any restraint or control. Sometimes, the energy swelled up, and felt as if it were bursting like a bubble from the muscles, before shaking itself off. At other times, I could feel my muscles stretching, and pulling so strongly that they felt like they were tearing apart. As the dance went on, I became more sensitive to the energy forces, as the energies felt gluey and rubbery. My body felt more solid, as if coated with glue that was drying fast. I observed my body literally pulling itself out from the dense energies that I knew were clinging to me.

Healing movements again helped in the process. It was a natural totally relaxed, effortless and complete letting-go process, as the 'spirit' struggled to be freed from the gluing forces. Someday, the body will become still, and then the core spirit's consciousness is completely freed. But this process toward Stillness must come naturally; otherwise one was not sufficiently purified.

All at once, my perception of my body changed, as it lost its normal contours and features. I could 'see' my body taking on a new shape, or geometric pattern. Perhaps, Picasso, in his creative state, experienced this. My eyes remained shut, but I perceived different colors and shades of light. All that I experienced felt absolutely real. At the end of the meditation, I felt as if I were completely cleansed, weightless, and wondrously connected with purified energy.

I knew then that such Heart energy could be transmitted to others for healing during energy movements that effectively remove pain, trauma and illness. When I led participants in sitting meditation, they shifted into conducive states that released the flow of relaxation energy. In Chicago, for example, when each participant radiated energy, the energy flow induced had produced remarkable effects. In Palenque, conducting the group meditation, I had no time to plan what to say, or do. I just helped the person to move spontaneously, and soon everyone joined in. The healing worked very well. Some months later, Kathina, the energy practitioner, had written to say that her trauma had cleared up–the migraine, the whiplash, and fear of driving that resulted from an auto accident.

Sifu would say that when one does healing, by not being overly concerned about the consequences, one is more powerful.

"It's like playing a game. To perform optimally, you should not be too serious, just go with it. The more relaxed one is, the more conducive it is for the energy to flow through."

Recalling this, I thought, "Yes, that explains why people in Pathom responded so well."

One person was Tiplada's friend, Khun Wan, who was troubled by an allergy problem. Unable to breathe, she often had to be rushed regularly to the hospital emergency unit in the middle of the night. When she wrote to me after our session, she had been free of her problem for over a month.

As she put it, "I sleep very well and feel very fresh, and full of life in the morning. I have stopped taking all medication. I feel happy and healthy."

Her doctors, who had prescribed pills, medicated sprays, etc., could not believe it. More than that, Wan's husband, also changed.

"He had a routine checkup. We were both surprised to see that his troubling blood pressure, blood sugar, and lipids had come down to normal levels," she reported.

One Night in Payao

I returned to the eastern corner of the Golden Triangle to conduct the final seminar in the misty Payao mountain at *Wat Analayo*. I thought of a singular problem that seems to breach our faith in human nature striking at the very core of civilized society today–the horrifying violence in all its forms done to exploit women and children. It was here on this ethereal mountain top, grappling with the harsh and brutal realities of terror, disease, and gruesome death, that remembrance of the innocence and carefree days of childhood brought solace and peace to the heart.

Healing takes up where science cannot lead because of its limitations. Wisdom, compassion, seeing reality as it is, and universal benevolence, constitute not only an ideal for the individual, but the same message holds true in resolving the global problems of today. Doing healing work provides the path. It exemplifies the manifestation of the '*Four Sublime States*' in action as one treads the Path of Perfection espoused by the Golden Sage.

The cosmic healer's expanded consciousness upholds these collective sublime states to transmit purified, relaxing Heart energy. While working on the recipient, the cosmic energy-state radiated is defined as '*Metta*' loving kindness, '*Karuna*' compassion, sympathetic joy *(Mudita)*, and equanimity *(Upekkha)*. These qualities may well be the new ethical code for today's therapists to uphold when healing others near and far. It begins with self-transformation and a new ethic of personal responsibility to actively nurture and heal the vulnerable and to promote their resilience.

It was the last night in Payao. Resting in the hillside villa nestled on the side of the evergreen hills adjacent to serene *Wat Analayo*, I gazed at the reflective waters of Payao Lake below. Sitting in peaceful meditation, I soon forgot about my surroundings on the summit of the mountain as I reached into the remembrance of a completed sojourn in pursuit of the keys to health and cosmic consciousness.

I looked up at the twinkling lights and glittering celestial bodies without end in the night sky. The focus of the journey, with each repeated cycle of traveling, became clearer and sharper taking on a noetic quality to turn inward to look at what the Heart knows. The Heart of Perfection is indestructible, beyond the ravages of history and time, as well as boundless, beyond the confinement of place, space, and form.

I awaited the arrival of my healer partners, Kathina and Tiplada, to join me in planning a workshop on the emerging energy field connecting meditation and healing. Many of our hosts are seekers of healing and *Prajna*. Over the next few days, in and out of meditation, I seemed to have connected with a flow of information regarding the mysteries of human existence and destiny. The seven-faceted Tao of Energy Healing, the way to perfected health, ageless longevity, cosmic identification and consciousness is synthesized and expressed as the '*RADIANT*' process of self-discovery and healing energy illumination.

Seven Facets of Radiant Energy Healing

RADIANT Heart energy dissolves the
Antecedents of disease and aging of
Dense noxious energies the culprit.
Inoculate against disease by letting go of
Antecedent disease carriers vaporized by
Nature's Golden Light of
Transparence that illuminates ALL.

One: Radiant Heart
To discover the host's true self, look inward
Which is simply the purity of
Heart Energy relaxation

Shift from the mind-body and its host of identities, to the One host at the center of the Heart energy as your locus of consciousness. The uncommon core that fills mind and living matter can only be found by searching deep into the Heart. Liberated from a self-limiting consciousness, one can know the fundamental resilient spirit that balances vast energy. This Spirit is the innate source of perfect healing, rejuvenation, and wholeness. Unfettered of impure energies, the golden-hued Wisdom Heart treasures breeze through. Radiate this pure energy!

Two: Antecedent cause of Disease and Aging
Neither mind, microbe, or malfunctioning body parts is the culprit.
The cause is noxious stale energy forces that attach
to the body Seizing up energy flow and gumming the human machinery
to a dead stall

Understand how the fundamental noxious energy antecedent victimizes the host-body causing it to deteriorate into the frailness and darkness of a diseased, aging state. The dense noxious energy, like layers in an onion gone stale, decays and rots the body, preventing its self-healing core from sustaining normal healthy functioning. Cast these energy blockages out from the host to begin the healing process.

Three: Dense Noxious Energy Accumulation
Disharmony in living draws in noxious energies that
Traumatize the Heart and
Precipitate disease

Here more is less. Environmental arousal drawn into the body and mind is disturbing, clouding, and overloads the host's soma and psyche. The more demands and pressures you load on, the more noxious energies you host and the denser one's consciousness becomes. Then the urgency to eliminate such blockages becomes acute. The noxious energies arising from a 'brains-and-brawn lifestyle' are of highest risk, creating a traumatized consciousness and stagnating at the heart. It is this factor that spins our conscious mind out of control and plugs up the energy flow. In turn the disharmony creates an energy imbalance throwing the entire human apparatus 'out of sync'.

Four: Inoculate against Disease.
To strengthen the host remove its weaknesses.
Trust that the human Spirit is Perfection,
fully capable of healing and rejuvenation

Inoculate against the noxious energy with an effortless cultivation of true relaxation energy. Learn to move out what weakens you. Dance to unwind physically to home in, flush out, and meltdown the noxious energy. Born of spontaneity, extemporaneous movements dissolve the boundaries of spent identities providing an unparalleled vehicle for true self-expression. Here, the spirit takes control of the body moving and cleansing it in ways that are unique to each individual. Eject not inject and observe as the noxious energy self-destructs through spontaneous motion. Resilience is yours.

Five: Antecedent Disease Carriers
To vanquish the twin-carrier of disease/aging
Let go of the acquisition needs of the mind
that produces endless karmic effects decaying the body

To be free from these defilements, shift from acquisition to letting go to undo the past. Restore harmony and balance by releasing noxious energies out-of-body. Shift from an over-stimulated brain and a top-heavy awareness and find your body's center with a grounded mindfulness. From there, the host opens the fire-door expelling the noxious agent. Then roll out the golden carpet to welcome an energetically balanced consciousness and body-mass that feels 'weightless, transparent, and light as air'. You are host to a new guest–a radiantly beautiful, healthy body that is self-regenerative and ageless.

Six: Nature's Way
The host with glowing health radiates
beneficial energies of giving and receiving.
Radiate Mother Nature's cosmic Metta energy

These actions connect and raise the host's consciousness to a higher vibration. This is the way to a state of Ultimate Relaxation. The energy of a higher consciousness purifies and remodels the host's energy as well as radiates benefits to the environment. Invoke and draw on the Metta energy of golden Compassion of the host family–your spiritual family or lineage–and allow its blessings to flow through the host. The body and its environment's limitations are transformed.

Seven: Transparent State of Enlightenment
The final step is an unending line into Heart Energy.
Unmoved by the host's physical or mind states
Shift to your unbounded Spirit.
Awaken golden, transparent consciousness
Be fully liberated.

Ancient writings talk about experiencing an aspect of pure energy as a radiating Light shining into the Eternal, a code to describe the indescribable Transparent State. Approach Enlightenment as experiencing transcendent energy and varying forms of wondrous, pure consciousness that is the energy of Oneness. What visionary wisdom can bind together ageless concepts of time, space, mass, and motion to free us from the world? In absolute terms, it is a timeless, motionless, and massless pure Space–becoming an ultra-light Pure Energy vibration that is as small and as big as an isolated quanta of energy freed into boundless conscious supernova brilliance.

As the Heart's perfection has been found, the creations of intellect, mind, energy, and consciousness are all left behind as they point to what the Heart already knows. To transcend and experience cosmic love, do the letting-go dance to the rhythm of the smoothest, most perfect energy flow. As you purge what must be undone, the pure seeds planted blooms in the season of enlightenment So it is with renewed enfolded radiant energy that the journey is resumed, this time joined by a host of dancing Gold-Body energy buffs riding on the golden winds of destiny as it unfolds.

Epilogue

In the New World

Fully purified the person is physically perfected
Completely purified the Human Spirit drops all identities
Forever connected to the Cosmic spirit
You are One with it -Infinite radiance.

In previous centuries, people led simple lives that were more physical, predictable, with much less stimulation and limited material enjoyment, facing fewer problems than today. So an Enlightened One who came along had only to point them to a simple path: 'Practice this way, cultivate the Heart. Search for your Heart; Purify your energy, and eventually that will lead you to Enlightenment'.

The 21st century predictably seems to be heading toward another 'Age of Insecurities'. Humanity is bracing against fearful uncertainties and unsettling changes ahead, whether it be of random violence, personal safety, global conflicts, and a world melting down in free-fall. Paradoxically, people have become accustomed to needing stress to boost themselves, to stay awake, and to remain vigilant. Or they are desperately trying to overcome numbing depression. The World Health Organization predicts this disease, together with heart problems, to be the leading malady of the 21st century.

Suffering is meant to allow the individual to cleanse off whatever wrong has been done. Instead, the person reacts to life's inevitable uncertainties with depression, discontent, and hatred creating further suffering or new problems. Calmness, peace and harmony go out of sight. So the negative karma cycle and the trauma are repeated to perpetual end.

However, the only time one can change one's karma is when the spirit itself is in human form. Human birth and consciousness provide us with the free-will, thought, and freedom to be purposeful and to wisely select our response to life's exigencies. Human consciousness is connected to a pure energy vibration within which is perfect health. Regardless of the impending doom evident, each person needs to have a field of security. What matters is peace within. Karma acts like something that clings to and always cloud consciousness and dampens the human spirit. To optimize health, only a karmic-energy cleansing therapy that reaches into the human spirit can totally free the host from the fears of deprivation, depression, disease, and dying.

According to ancient Eastern philosophy based on the yin-yang principle, when things are already so bad, as in today's world, something that is good or constructive, inevitably will turn up as well. Cultivating the Gold-Body state can be the new hope. The tension-free path leads the person to self-rejuvenation, optimal consciousness, and health. Practitioners become convinced because it is an energy practice that is so tangible. As one moves into more advanced states, our consciousness and vital energies become purified for the body to undergo a physical transformation process.

Tension is the most damaging and artificial thing there is. When all tension is ended, what remains is our true self, spirit, or our essential nature. *"True relaxation that's left is permanent that comes from a pure consciousness that survives death itself."* What is left is the Pure Energy state. It is the transparent state of illuminated timelessness. It is eternal. Nothing more needs to be done.

Our awareness of ourselves, in terms of sensitivity to energy, and our sense of relationship with Nature itself, is very poor. Choosing cultivation of radiant Metta energy, we have Nature's grace of pure Compassion to change and purify what we need to. As we purify our energy in harmony with Nature, this energy goes through us, and radiates outward. All the energies that are drawn within, whether good or bad, become part of our consciousness, extending to the space around us.

The human spirit is indeed resilient and the body is a vessel for healing. Spirit means the vital vibrations. With our energy cleansed, our purified consciousness becomes vibrant and radiant. With the spirit freed, the cause of disease as well as aging of the physical body, is also eliminated. Birth or death is no longer an unknown mystery.

The Enlightened Master of cosmic consciousness and prophet of human destiny said, "*Ehi passako.*" Or come and see for yourself. Our actions, right at this moment and in this existence, can purify and cleanse all to verify the transcendent truth of Enlightenment!

Bibliography

Hiew, C. (2000). *Cosmic Freedom Qigong Healing Exercises: For trauma and organ cleansing.* Presented at the Toronto Meeting of the Association of Comprehensive Energy Psychology. Instructional videotape available from author: Email: hiew@unb.ca

Hiew, C. (2000). Trauma, resilience building, and energy healing. *Trauma Course in Trauma Psychology* at the International Center on Psychosocial Trauma. University of Missouri-Columbia.

Hiew, C. (1999). *Energy meditation: Healing the body, freeing the spirit.* New York: toExcel iUniverse Publishing. Book available from Amazon.com

Hiew, C. C. (1999). Stress and health: The letting go response. In Roth, R. & Neil, S. (Eds.), *A Matter of Life: Psychological theory, research and practice.* Lengerich, Austria: Pabst Science Publishers.

Hiew, C. (1998). Longevity and healthy aging: The self-repair response. *Japanese Health Psychology, Vol. 6*, pgs 1-16.

Hiew, C. (1997). *Goldbody energy healing.* Workshop presented at the International Society for the Study of Subtle Energies & Energy Medicine , Boulder, CO.

Yap, S. Y. (2001). *Revealing the secrets of healing: CFQ Energy Manual.* In Press.

9 780595 157532